Craig N. Murphy (*editor*)
EGALITARIAN POLITICS IN THE AGE OF GLOBALIZATION

Michael Niemann
A SPATIAL APPROACH TO REGIONALISM IN THE GLOBAL ECONOMY

Markus Perkmann and Ngai-Ling Sum (*editors*)
GLOBALIZATION, REGIONALIZATION AND CROSS-BORDER REGIONS

Ted Schrecker (*editor*)
SURVIVING GLOBALISM
The Social and Environmental Challenges

Leonard Seabrooke
US POWER IN INTERNATIONAL FINANCE
The Victory of Dividends

Timothy J. Sinclair and Kenneth P. Thomas (*editors*)
STRUCTURE AND AGENCY IN INTERNATIONAL CAPITAL MOBILITY

Kendall Stiles (*editor*)
GLOBAL INSTITUTIONS AND LOCAL EMPOWERMENT
Competing Theoretical Perspectives

Caroline Thomas and Peter Wilkin (*editors*)
GLOBALIZATION AND THE SOUTH

Geoffrey R. D. Underhill (*editor*)
THE NEW WORLD ORDER IN INTERNATIONAL FINANCE

Amy Verdun
EUROPEAN RESPONSES TO GLOBALIZATION AND FINANCIAL MARKET
INTEGRATION
Perceptions of Economic and Monetary Union in Britain, France and Germany

Robert Wolfe
FARM WARS
The Political Economy of Agriculture and the International Trade Regime

---

**International Political Economy Series**
**Series Standing Order ISBN 0–333–71708–2 hardback**
**Series Standing Order ISBN 0–333–71110–6 paperback**
(*outside North America only*)

You can receive future titles in this series as they are published by placing a standing order. Please contact your bookseller or, in case of difficulty, write to us at the address below with your name and address, the title of the series and one of the ISBNs quoted above.

Customer Services Department, Macmillan Distribution Ltd, Houndmills, Basingstoke, Hampshire RG21 6XS, England

---

# Understanding World Order and Structural Change

## Poverty, Conflict and the Global Arena

Hans Abrahamsson
*Department of Peace and Development Studies*
*Göteborg University*
*Sweden*

First published 2003 by
PALGRAVE MACMILLAN
Houndmills, Basingstoke, Hampshire RG21 6XS and
175 Fifth Avenue, New York, N.Y. 10010
Companies and representatives throughout the world

PALGRAVE MACMILLAN is the global academic imprint of the Palgrave
Macmillan division of St. Martin's Press, LLC and of Palgrave Macmillan Ltd.
Macmillan® is a registered trademark in the United States, United Kingdom
and other countries. Palgrave is a registered trademark in the European
Union and other countries

ISBN 0–333–77385–3

This book is printed on paper suitable for recycling and made from fully
managed and sustained forest sources.

A catalogue record for this book is available from the British Library.

Library of Congress Cataloging-in-Publication Data
Abrahamsson, Hans, 1949–
    Understanding world order and structural change: poverty, conflict,
    and the global arena/Hans Abrahamsson.
        p. cm. – (International political economy series)
    Includes bibliographical references and index.
    ISBN 0–333–77385–3 (cloth)
        1. International economic relations. 2. Globalization. 3. Poverty. 4. Social
conflict. I. Title. II. International political economy series (Palgrave Macmillan
(Firm))
HF1359.A24 2003
337–dc21                                                          2003040546

10   9   8   7   6   5   4   3   2
12   11   10   09   08   07   06   05   04

Printed and bound in Great Britain by
Antony Rowe Ltd, Chippenham and Eastbourne

*To the memory of **Carlos Cardoso***
*while actively contributing to the structural opportunity for peace –*
*brutally assassinated by his opponents – before it could be seized.*

*Through his journal located in a small Maputo garage, he challenged various national and global structures impeding development in Mozambique.*

*Through his death the world runs the risk of becoming more subdued and the achievement of global citizenship even more distant.*

# Contents

# List of Figures

# Foreword

Understanding global structural change is no simple undertaking. In an era of disbelief in the value of 'grand theory' many would even doubt the usefulness of such an undertaking. Others persist in believing that some form of 'revised modernity', that is improving human conditions in a spirit of rationalism and humanism, is still possible.

Hans Abrahamsson has been grappling with this challenge for many years. His main concern is how to seize the opportunity, when structural conditions on various levels of the world system combine, to create an opening to improve matters.

This is not done in the kind of determinist way marking many of the now discredited 'grand theories' of the past. The difficult task is not to find the critical factor in promoting change, but to make the analytical framework complex enough without losing consistency and conceptual clarity.

A key problem is the understanding of how a multilevel world order operates. For this it is important not to be carried away by abstractions, but to get to know some contexts and structures very well and in depth. Hans has studied the conditions of underdevelopment in one of the poorest and most war-torn countries of Africa over a long period. He has learnt how the international institutions operate by interviewing numerous key figures about their work. His knowledge of Mozambique, later extended to Angola, is of the calibre to make its government ask for advice on precisely the main issue dealt with in this book. How much room for manoeuvre exists for particular actors in our globalised condition ruled by one hegemonic economic philosophy? How can globalisation be made more global, i.e. more inclusive?

This is a question asked by rich as well as by poor governments – by transnational elites as well as by poor peasants trying to survive to the next day. Not least, the question is asked by the growing movement for social justice as it is faced by the unprecedented task of reforming a global order where no democratic institutions exist. By at least starting to look for an answer to this question Hans has done us all a great service.

I thus warmly recommend this book, but above all I recommend political decision-makers as well as global activists to think carefully and explore further the issues raised.

BJÖRN HETTNE
*Professor, Department of Peace and Development Studies*
*University of Göteborg, Sweden*

# Acknowledgements

I have a quite remarkable story to tell. It is seldom told, as its narration requires a rare combination of circumstances. You need a case, access to documents and access to people wanting to share with you their understanding of what happened. You need a sympathetic research milieu, colleagues who encourage you to persist, allies who will helpfully discuss your doubts and, most important, friends who do not abandon you despite the many good reasons to do so. Finally, you need someone to check that you have said what you wanted to say. I had them all.

The Mozambican and Angolan hospitality allowed me to take as my cases the immensely painful experience of those countries. I am heavily indebted to many committed individuals within these communities and governments for unfailingly providing me with the support needed to carry out the project. Equally important was the open-minded and cooperative attitude of a number of US officials and colleagues without whose extraordinary assistance the fieldwork in the USA would have been impossible. In a similar manner various Swedish officials at the Ministry of Foreign Affairs and Sida, provided essential encouragement. They are all referred to in the list of interviews (pp. 224–9).

Since its inception in the mid-1970s, the Department of Peace and Development Studies at Göteborg University has shared my research agenda, a fact that is well reflected by this study. The founding father of the Department and my friend, Björn Hettne, was, together with Anders Nilsson, the main source of inspiration during my voyage. Björn has read through several drafts over the years, always encouraging me to continue what sometimes seemed an impossible mission. Anders is not only a colleague and a friend but, above all, an ally. We have worked together for some fifteen years, day and night, summer and winter. During recent years Helena Tagesson has joined in. She scrutinised my logic and did her best to make it all comprehensible. Thus, science, whatever that is, is not based on individualism and competition. It is created through reflection and intimate dialogue with others with common concerns.

Thank you all very much.

*Göteborg*                                                           Hans Abrahamsson

# List of Abbreviations

| | |
|---|---|
| AGRICOM | Empresa Nacional de Comercialação Agricola |
| AIM | Agencia de Informação de Moçambique |
| ANC | African National Congress |
| ATTAC | Association for the Taxation of Financial Transactions for the Aid of Citizens |
| BM | Banco de Moçambique |
| BPD | Banco Popular de Desenvolvimento |
| CARE | Concerned Americans for the Reconstruction of Europe |
| CEA | Centro de Estudos Africanos |
| CENE | Comissão Executiva Nacional de Emergência |
| CIA | US Central Intelligence Agency |
| CFM | Caminho de Ferro de Moçambique |
| CMEA | Council for Mutual Economic Assistance |
| CODESA | Congress for a Democratic South Africa |
| COMECON | Council for Mutual Economic Assistance (CMEA) |
| CONSAS | Constellation of Southern African States |
| COSATU | Congress of South African Trade Unions |
| CNP | Comissão Nacional do Plano |
| DAC | Development Assistance Committee (of the OECD) |
| DANIDA | Danish International Development Agency |
| DIA | US Defense Intelligence Agency |
| DPCCN | Departamento de Prevenção e Combate das Calamidades Naturais |
| EADI | European Association of Development Research and Training Institutes |
| ECA | UN Economic Commission for Africa |
| EU | European Union |
| EEC | European Economic Community |
| ERP | Economic Rehabilitation Programme |
| ESCOM | Electricity Supply Commission |
| ESRP | Economic and Social Rehabilitation Programme |
| FAO | UN Food and Agriculture Organisation |
| FAPLA | People's Armed Forces for the Liberation of Angola |
| FNLA | National Front for the Liberation of Angola |
| FONDAD | Forum on Debt and Development |
| FPLM | People's Forces for the Liberation of Moçambique |
| FRELIMO | Frente de Libertação de Moçambique |
| GATT | General Agreement on Tariffs and Trade |
| GDP | Gross Domestic Product |

| | |
|---|---|
| GRREC | Groupe de Recherche sur la Régulation de l'Economie Capitaliste |
| IAEA | International Atomic Energy Agency |
| IBRD | International Bank for Reconstruction and Development |
| IDA | International Development Association |
| IFI | International Financial Institution |
| IMF | International Monetary Fund |
| INGO | International Non-Governmental Organisation |
| IPE | International Political Economy |
| ISRI | Instituto Superior de Relações Internacionais |
| ITO | International Trade Organisation |
| LDC | Least Developed Countries |
| MAI | Multilateral Agreement on Investment |
| MDB | Multilateral Development Bank |
| MIGA | Multilateral Investment Guarantee Agency |
| MIT | Massachussetts Institute of Technology |
| MNR | Mozambique National Resistance |
| MONUA | United Nations Observer Mission in Angola |
| MPLA | Movimento Popular de Libertação de Angola |
| MTR | Massive Transfer of Resources |
| NATO | North Atlantic Treaty Organisation |
| NEPAD | New Partnership for Africa's Development |
| NGO | Non-Governmental Organisation |
| NIC | Newly Industrialised Countries |
| NIEO | New International Economic Order |
| NP | National Party (SA) |
| NSAM | National Security Action Memorandum (US) |
| NSC | National Security Council (US) |
| NSD | National Security Directive (US) |
| NSDD | National Security Decision Directives (US) |
| NSDM | National Security Decision Memoranda (US) |
| NSSM | National Security Decision Study Memoranda (US) |
| OAU | Organisation for African Unity |
| ODA | Overseas Development Assistance (UK) |
| ODC | Overseas Development Council |
| OECD | Organisation for Economic Development and Cooperation |
| OMA | Angolan Women's Organisation |
| OPEC | Organisation of Petroleum Exporting Countries |
| PAC | Pan-Africanist Congress (South Africa) |
| Padrigu | Department of Peace and Development Research, Göteborg University |
| PAIGC | Partido Africano da Independencia da Guiné e Cabo Verde |
| PFP | Policy Framework Paper |
| PPI | Plano Perspectivo Indicativo |
| PRE | Programa de Rebilitação Económica |

| | |
|---|---|
| PRES | Programa de Rebilitação Económica e Social |
| PRN | Programa de Reconstrução Nacional |
| RENAMO | Resistência Nacional de Moçambique |
| RSA | Republic of South Africa |
| SA | South Africa |
| SADC | Southern Africa Development Community |
| SADCC | Southern Africa Development Coordination Conference |
| SADF | South African Defence Force |
| SAL | Structural Adjustment Loan |
| SAP | Structural Adjustment Programme |
| SAPRIN | Structural Adjustment Participatory Review Network |
| SAREC | Swedish Agency for Research Cooperation with Developing Countries |
| SATS | South African Transport Service |
| SDR | Special Drawing Right |
| Sida | Swedish International Development Cooperation Agency |
| SWAPO | South West Africa People's Organisation |
| TINA | There Is No Alternative |
| TNC | Transnational Corporation |
| UDF | United Democratic Front |
| UDI | Unilateral Declaration of Independence |
| UK | United Kingdom of Great Britain and Northern Ireland |
| UN | United Nations |
| UNAVEM | United Nations Angola Verification Mission |
| UNCTAD | United Nations Conference on Trade and Development |
| UNDP | United Nations Development Programme |
| UNDRO | UN Disaster Relief Organisation |
| UNEP | United Nations Environmental Programme |
| UNESCO | United Nations Educational, Scientific and Cultural Organisation |
| UNICEF | UN Children's Fund |
| UNITA | União Nacional para Independência Total de Angola |
| USAID | US Agency for International Development |
| USD | US Dollar |
| WFP | World Food Programme |
| WIDER | World Institute for Development Economics Research |
| WTO | World Trade Organisation |
| ZANLA | Zimbabwe African National Liberation Army |
| ZANU | Zimbabwe African National Union |
| ZAPU | Zimbabwe African People's Union |
| ZIPRA | Zimbabwe People's Revolutionary Army |

# Introduction

This book deals with world order and structural change. Its main concern is how the process of globalisation could become more inclusive and be guided by humane principles, of which equity, sustainability and democracy constitute vital parts. Hence, the issues to be addressed are (a) the room for manoeuvre and (b) the social forces capable of achieving such a change in the international political economy. Abstract notions such as world order, globalisation and structural change have to be anchored in a concrete social context. In this study, lessons learned from Angola and Mozambique provide the required localisation.

Globalisation is a contested concept. How you understand the world order, depends on where you are sitting and whether you consider yourself a winner or a loser (or both), according to which time-perspective you use. Consequently, it is possible to view globalisation variously as a process bringing prosperity, as an unavoidable threat, or as an imagined construction – a myth. The existence of these different perspectives recalls Robert Cox's remark (Cox 1995) that theory is always 'for someone' and 'for some purpose'. According to the first view, globalisation should be understood as an immanent, mainly economic process immune to political influence. Despite temporary imperfections and disequilibrium this process provides the assured route to prosperity (Fukuyama 1992). The second, also widely held, view takes as its point of departure globalisation's exclusive character. The failure to eradicate global inequalities and poverty is taken to show that Western values, contrary to what used to be thought, are not universal. In order to defend its own strategic interests and life-style the western hemisphere needs, according to this view, to strengthen prevailing parochialism and strengthen itself albeit at a regional or transregional level. Such understanding of a future in which the West must repudiate the Rest was first, somewhat hastily and less elegantly, elaborated by Huntington (1996a) in *The Clash of Civilizations and the Remarking of World Order*. While strongly contested in the West, the argument attracted much attention in the south. The third approach, rooted in the traditional European Left, considers globalisation to be a myth (Hirst and Thompson 1995). This view understands it to be a neo-liberal fabrication aimed at promoting the idea of the end of politics. Instead of denying political agency, its proponents point to the need to reintroduce political process believing that the nation-state project and its welfare based social contract should be revitalised through reregulation.

This book contends that the process of globalisation should not be understood in any of these ways as globalisation is a reality – we live in a state of globality whether we like it or not. The complex processes that together constitute its driving force, and whose impact we still do not fully understand, have created a new transnational arena for economic, social, political and cultural interaction, in which the nation-state is no longer in a controlling position. Despite qualitative changes in the post-Cold War era as regards speed and space, globalisation must be seen as a historical and irreversible process. However, it is a process amenable to influence. Its pace and structure are still in the making. Political actors and their decisions create the structure behind its dynamic and orientation. Provided that political processes are reactivated, the structure, dynamic and orientation of globalisation can also be changed by actors.

The urgency of the challenge ahead – how to make globalisation global – is motivated by the fact that global governance by corporate capital reinforces the unevenness that has characterised development since the inception of industrialisation. In the global village, as presently emerging, people live closer together, more interdependent but on very unequal terms and with very uneven access to opportunities. Such unequal distribution is seen to be unfair. Deprivation and frustration reinforce conflicts that unless they can be resolved through dialogue, are likely to result in violence and socio-political instability. Empirical evidence points to the fact that market forces do not provide, despite the claims of the neo-liberal fundamentalists, a self-regulating mechanism. Neither will the fortress mentality provide a viable route. National/cultural borders are irrelevant to the inequities created by globalisation. Its unfairness consists of an exclusion which is independent of geographical location or colour of skin. Consequently, the negative and inherently conflictual aspects of globalisation can only be dealt with through making the process more inclusive and more humane – this is what is understood by the expression the 'globalisation of globalisation'.

## Framing the problem

Such an understanding of globalisation, as a historical – irreversible – but also a process amenable to political influence, raises two fundamental issues. The first relates to the political decisions that created the international regimes and structures in the first place, thus activating the process of globalisation. The second relates to the conditions and circumstances under which structural opportunities for global structural change occur, and under what circumstances politicians could seize such opportunities.

These were, in essence, the research questions that the Mozambican government included in their terms of reference in the early 1990s when they invited Padrigu, the Department of Peace and Development Studies at the University of Göteborg, to contribute to an ongoing internal Mozambican discussion on these issues. Their main concern was the international room for manoeuvre for national governance in the post-apartheid and post-Cold War era. At Padrigu research related to peace and development is characteristically problem-oriented, interdisciplinary and multilevel. National development strategies are not socially neutral: attempts to implement them challenge the power structures within society. This is why development should be understood as a process of social change driven by conflict. The strength of the civil society determines whether such conflict can be dealt with through dialogue or whether it will provoke violence. A national development strategy is also subject to global constraints and international influences. It is therefore based upon how society perceives the internal and external environment and consequently the contents and interaction of the crucial concepts of identity, security and development. Accordingly, the approach to development and subsequent social change is a politically driven process.

The research task that the Mozambican government entrusted to Padrigu required a reappraisal of the Bretton Woods Conference, at which, in the early 1940s, the present economic world order structures were created. The project involved extensive archival research and some 150 interviews and conversations with concerned decision-makers in the USA and southern Africa. The research questions focused on the circumstances that created the structures, their impact at local level, and the circumstances which could bring about change. The methodological approach was a mixture of interpretative and critical focusing on contradictions and change. More important, it was based on interactive conversations which included feedback and follow-up contacts. This research method, which I call 'confrontative triangulation', has turned out to be most valuable when conducting research related to contemporary developments where the risk of misperception is great.

The initiation of the project coincided conveniently with the White House Conference on Africa (Washington DC, summer 1994), which tried to redefine the Western national strategic interests towards the continent, and the debate on the African Conflict Resolution Act that followed in the US Congress. The invitation Padrigu received from the US Senate to cooperate on these issues facilitated the creation of the network needed.

Some years later we were asked by the Angolan authorities to apply our framework to Angola. After some initial hesitation, including some 70 interactive conversations with Angolan governmental, non-governmental, military and civilian actors, we somewhat surprisingly found that the framework was applicable. These two countries have apparent similarities as regards colonial heritage and their liberation struggle. Yet, the international community has seen their development ambitions, political orientation and devastating destabilisation as being very different – Mozambique representing a success story and Angola a complex emergency. Our investigation suggested that these characterisations fitted neither country as both faced the same challenges and opportunities for peace and development.

Contrary to what could be expected, the findings of the research project refuted the notion, that there is no political room for manoeuvre on the global political arena. On the contrary, the combination of unsustainable contradictions and coinciding enlightened self-interest on the part of different elite groups in tackling the problems created a historical opportunity for structural change. However, whether such an historic opportunity could be seized or not depends on the interaction and involvement of civil society. Here, the project presented a less optimistic view. Although by intention not researched by the project, the required involvement from a strong civil society on the national level creating political pressure for structural change from below seemed to be lacking.

The perception of a passive, inward-looking civil society was soon to be taken over by events. It all started with the postponement of the signing of the Multilateral Agreement on Investment (MAI) and the transnational Jubilee 2000 campaign in the late 1990s striving for cancellation of poor countries' debts.

Motivated by their success the fast-growing global justice movement went to Seattle, striving to stop the delegates from getting into the WTO conference centre, and then on to Washington and Prague, with the aim of stopping the delegates from getting out from the joint meetings of World Bank and the IMF known as the Bretton Woods institutions. Although the impact of these movements has to be assessed they have created important links with civil society on the national level, be it in Mozambique or Angola, where various conferences demanding peace, reconciliation and development have taken place.

It is also still too early to evaluate the possible impact of the devastating terrorist attacks on the World Trade Center and the Pentagon. Some say that the global justice movement has lost political momentum and that the world is moving in a more xenophobic direction. The historic opportunity for structural change has been lost and we are fast moving away from a more inclusive world. However, my reading of the situation is different. Some of the elite groups advocating debt relief and poverty reduction, for reasons of enlightened self-interest seem to have increased their leverage after September 11. During the UN conference on finance in Monterrey, Mexico in spring 2002, the prevention of terrorism was used by the US administration as a motivation for increased and strengthened international development cooperation. Increased awareness of the link between poverty and conflict is inspiring more focused attempts to deal with questions of injustice and relative deprivation. Nevertheless, the outcome of the Monterrey meeting seemed much the same as that of other meetings of this kind over the past decades, same business as usual, i.e. too little too late. Little was achieved as regards the crucial issues for poverty reduction – debt forgiveness and trade. Thus, it should not taken for granted that the long-term self-enlightened interest of some elite groups will guide policy formulation. In fact, civil society, provided sufficiently strong involvement and political pressure from below can be mobilised, still constitutes the main subject of history.

## The objective and its justification

Indisputably, it is not the lack of knowledge or bright ideas about what should be done that explains the present state of affairs of the global political economy. If anything, there is an abundance of information. Obviously, politics is not a tea-party, it is about transformation of power. More recent power theories underline the importance of discursive power, i.e. the power over our thoughts, the formation of prevailing opinion and our actions. As will be elaborated upon, however, present discourses within international political economy frequently underlines the need to come to grips with the shortcomings of the market-led globalisation. Despite UN General Secretary Kofi Annan constantly pointing out that 'if globalisation is not good for many it will soon not be good for anyone', agreed reforms are not implemented. One argument of the present study is that the reason behind this is not only a question of political will. The problem seems also to be rooted in lack of normative strength. This is a concept coined by Anders Nilsson (1999) in his effort to combine paradigmatic coherency and theoretical congruency with the politically possible. Indisputably there is a need to elaborate analytical tools and models that enable a better understanding of the driving forces behind ongoing processes of change, identifying room for manoeuvre and potential entry points so that the political process can be entered into in due time and with proper actions.

Accordingly, one important objective of this book is to discuss *how* to study world order and structural change in the present state of globality as well as to develop the conceptual and analytical framework to be used.

Two events, analysed in the research projects accounted for, will provide fruitful guidance in this regard, namely the underlying motives and driving forces behind the Bretton Woods Conference in 1944 and the abolition of apartheid in southern Africa some forty to fifty years later. By providing a framework capable of identifying the room for manoeuvre for political action at various levels, the book aims to contribute to a better understanding of the importance for structural change of the various elite groups motivated by enlightened self-interest as well as of the role of the civil society and the interaction between them.

The approach needs to be holistic, historicist and empirical. The need for a holistic approach is indicated by the state of interdependence within a given system. One part or structure cannot be separated from the other. Yet I do not mean to suggest the vertical multi-level approach often implied by the holistic approach of international relations theory for this can cannote hierarchical structures and vertically subordinated levels. This is not the case for the cobweb of a world society that is in focus for our study. To employ a holistic approach is to recognise that not only vertical but also horizontal relations are relevant, especially so when dealing with crucial issues like social trust and social cohesion where the question of legitimacy becomes fundamental.

The need for a historicist approach is explained by the need to contextualise the structures under consideration. A contemporaneous (synchronic) analysis will be static, only cover the actual events and miss contradictions and conflicts inherent in the structure that can provoke transformation of the structure over time. Hence it is by a combination of a synchronic with a diachronic approach that social processes of change can be observed and understood. The need for empiricism is explained by the fact that the envisaged model can only be derived empirically and based upon how the interaction between the global structures and local development manifests itself in reality.

## Theoretical guidance

While International Relations Theory deals fairly well with how the world-order structures came about (cf. Marxist thinking on power) and more obviously how they are maintained (cf. liberal thinking on interdependence), the research area related to structural change is less well charted. Global development tends, even for such a normative discipline as peace and development, to be understood as an immanent process, almost impossible to influence, let alone to change.

Thus, when discussing the agent–structure relationship, positivist rational choice theory conceives national governance's room for manoeuvre as constrained by the surrounding world-order structures. Though limiting itself to problem-solving within given structures, it none the less made an important contribution to our understanding of social change through its focus on elite interests. The more historical materialist-oriented (and world system theory-inspired) approaches increased our understanding further, through pointing to contradictions in the sphere of production and the role of social movements in the processes of change. However, the constraining structures were still analysed in terms of 'longue durée', and therefore taken for granted.

Guided by critical theory, the research area within International Political Economy has recently developed to include the conditions for change of the world order structures themselves. How the structures came about and what could bring them to change have become important research questions. The work of the Hungarian anthropologist Karl Polanyi, the French historian Fernand Braudel and the Italian Marxist-inspired philosopher Antonio Gramsci has provided important guidance for such an undertaking. The Canadian scholar Robert Cox, one of their interpreters and a founding father of the new approach, has skilfully adapted and integrated the thinking into the discipline of International Relations Theory.

Polanyi discussed transformation processes of prevailing structures similar to those analysed by Braudel in terms of slow-moving historical processes, in the form of double movements (Polanyi 1957). For him, the expansion of the market and the dismantling of social safety nets constituted the first movement. The reaction and self-defence of society constituted the second. It is this dialectic area of tension that creates history. Polanyi labelled such cycle of market expansion and societal response the great transformation. Björn Hettne has added the hypothesis that such dialectic change is followed by a great compromise valid for a limited period (Abrahamsson *et al.* 2001). One of Polanyi's important points was that it was not only the completely impoverished in society who exert pressure for change. They were accompanied by sections of the elite perceiving themselves as losers in any given development. Nilsson contributed to such logic by an adaptation and elaboration of Gurr's theories of frustration and relative deprivation to include different elite strata (Nilsson 1999).

Lately, the importance of the Italian philosopher Antonio Gramsci and his analysis of the inter-world war political development in Italy has received renewed interest. Gramsci developed the notion of elite interest by introducing a discussion on legitimacy and hegemonic wielding of power (Gramsci 1971). He pointed to the role of the state and the network of complex political alliances that constituted and gave political strength to different phases in the development of society. Gramsci analysed such alliances in term of 'historic blocs' based upon prevailing modes of production. Structural change emerged as a consequence of the changed political configuration of a historic bloc or as a consequence of a rival and challenging historic bloc. Hence, relatively slow-moving 'wars of position', fighting for hegemonic power in society, are constantly going on between different actors. Following the notions of Hettne, therefore, structural change should be conceived as a process in which the counterpoint gradually substitutes, or at least modifies, the mainstream (Hettne 1995).

## The structure of the book

For pedagogical reasons the book will be divided into two parts, according to focus. Part I deals with how the world-order structures came about and impacted upon local development with reference to the experience of Angola and Mozambique.

Chapter 1 introduces the conceptual framework. What do we actually mean by world order structures? Which forces and circumstances bring them about, and on whose premises?

Chapter 2 applies the conceptual framework in order to analyse the origins of the present world-order.

Chapter 3 discusses US structural power and how it influenced political development in southern Africa.

Chapter 4 deals with the political impact of world order structures on the development of two of the most poor and conflict-ridden countries in the world, Angola and Mozambique.

Part II deals with how structural change could be brought about. In Chapter 5 our conceptual framework will be complemented by some theoretical ideas from the research area of International Political Economy, in order to better understand opportunities for structural change and the forces behind it.

Chapter 6 suggests an analytical model for understanding world order and structural change based upon three core concepts, each one representating an important force of change.

In the chapters that follow, the suggested analytical framework will be applied to different levels of the world system in order to assess the room for manoeuvre for political action. Chapter 7 discusses contradictory circumstances and emerging coinciding elite interests on the global level.

As the conditions for structural change vary, the model suggests different outcomes depending on which part of the world is in focus. Applying the model with a regional prism Chapter 8 accesses the room for political manoeuvre in southern Africa.

Chapter 9 addresses the questions of what ought to be done and how the African elite could use the existing room for manoeuvre to implement an alternative development strategy in order to escape from low-level security equilibrium.

Chapter 10 analyses the role of aid and discusses how international development cooperation should be designed in order to become an important catalyst in this regard.

In concluding, the book points to the importance of paradigmatic coherency and theoretical congruency in order to identify the political possible and to skilfully use such a room for manoeuvre.

International Relations Theory could give an important contribution for such an undertaking provided a more fully integration with development studies could be achieved.

# Part I

# Understanding World Order Structures and their Local Impact

# 1
# Conceptual Framework

There is no value-free theory. Hence, there is no value-free research. Peace and development studies focus on the inequalities between and within rich and poor countries that challenge international peace and human prosperity. Research in this field seeks to explain how these inequalities came about, how they are maintained and what can be done to lessen them. This study, informed by such research, challenges the predominant conviction that there is no alternative to mainstream development thinking. Through its normative and critical approach it calls into question the present world order and its structures that constrain the room for manoeuvre for such an alternative development.

In this chapter I discuss the conceptual framework we need for making such a challenge. By conceptual framework I mean a set of concepts through which to view and understand the present world order, its rules and power structures. The concepts can only be precise when they are related to a specific historical context and to an actual situation they intend to clarify. The context and circumstances change over time and, accordingly, so does the proper meaning of the concepts. Consequently, this chapter provides neither conceptual deconstruction nor reconstruction. It indicates the conceptual understanding that underlies the study and constitutes its points of departure.

By 'world order' I mean a system of structures sustained by various rules and norms regulating international economic and political cooperation and transactions. The rules and norms in force reflect the underlying values and security interests of the principal actors of the system as well as their prevailing power relations. The actors' values and belief systems are in turn shaped by the political configuration of the society they represent and its social relations of production. We will start our conceptual review at this level.

## State, market and civil society

The notions of market, state and civil society vary very much for different kinds of societies; hence it is important to contextualise the concepts.

Market, refers here to the economic system as such, although at the aggregate level one could at times look upon this very system also as an actor. State refers not only to its role as a political and bureaucratic organisation in the development process where the question of legitimacy is linked to the social contract, the concept also refers to its role as a political territorial organisation, usually called nation-state and central to discussion of identity, security and sovereignty. The concept of civil society is more problematic. In what follows, 'civil society' refers to the 'civilness' of a given society. By civilness we understand its informal and formal institutions that can bring together and thereby articulate the different demands and interests of various groups of people in society in order to facilitate dialogue and avoid violent conflicts.

There is no inherent contradiction between state and civil society. However, the functional development strategy, characterised by economic growth and state-led redistribution, has lately been challenged by the forces that the process of globalisation has put in motion.

Consequently, declining economic growth has been accompanied by a diminished state redistributive capacity, thereby aggravating the state's problems of legitimacy. The process has meant that former national developmental 'corporatism' oriented towards internal sources of accumulation, has gradually been complemented, and in some cases substituted, by new informal international and externally oriented corporative structures.[1] Indisputably, this has fundamentally changed the role of the state. One of the most important aspects of this change is the *internationalisation of the state*, a process that gradually transforms the state from a 'filter', absorbing external shocks, to a 'transmission belt' exposing most of its economic activities to international economic requirements and conditionalities (Cox 1996, p. 107).[2]

Recent developments have increased doubts as to whether the neo-liberal concept of the minimalist state, originally introduced by the Bretton Woods institutions, is compatible with requirements for a sustainable market economy. The World Bank is intensifying its state capacity-building efforts. The important role of the state as a development agent, providing security and social capital required for the reconstruction of social trust has been reconfirmed. The shift is partly due to increased pressure from the international business community which 'needs stronger states in Africa, not weaker'.[3]

The role and functioning of the market is fundamental for social change and development. As Hettne reminds us, Polanyi gave the concept of market two meanings (Hettne 1995b). Market can be understood as a market place where commodities are exchanged; also in more abstract terms as a 'system'. In the market place the exchange of commodities takes place according to the laws of the market. Commodities are priced according to the rules of supply and demand. The fact that there are market places and trade, however, does not mean that a market in the form of a market system has developed. A market place can coexist with other principles for exchange, among others household economy, reciprocity or redistribution. The former implies exchange in local communities based upon mutuality and social obligations, while the latter implies some kind of administered distribution according to needs or hierarchical position in society. Polanyi distinguishes between three different kinds of markets (Polanyi 1957). Externally linked markets for distant trade and local markets for the surrounding neighbourhood are characterised by complementary trade, national domestic markets and characterised by competition. The emergence of the latter implied a division of labour where the market for merchandise was complemented with a market for labour and land. Neither the externally nor the locally-oriented market implied destruction of the economic system in force, be it the household, reciprocity, or some kind of redistribution. These markets could be classified as market places. People approached the market mainly as consumers. The destruction came as a consequence of the expansion and penetration of the national (domestic) market, whereby the market was increasingly approached by producers. According to Polanyi, the state played a preponderant role in dismantling the regulations restricting internal trade, not least through the restrictions imposed by the bourgeoisie of the cities, something that made the expansion of the national market possible.

In fact, the market system starts to be dominant as a mechanism for exchange when producers and consumers give priority to market laws over traditional social relations and social networks. The process of commodification came to include land and labour. Hence, the social relations and beliefs of the community no longer determine how and when production activities take place. These decisions are instead taken by the laws of the market, and social relations thus start to become embedded in the market system (Polanyi 1957). This will gradually lead to the formation of the market as a market system. Here, Polanyi referred to the self-regulating market where people strove to maximise their income, where the relation between demand and supply determined the price, and where prices determine the profits and thereby what to produce and how to distribute (Polanyi 1957). Such expansion of the market forces constituted what Polanyi called 'the first movement'. However, as underlined by Polanyi, there is no such a thing as a self-regulating market. Sooner or later alternative forms of social protection against the imperfections of the markets are sought and a civil society starts to develop. Such societal response constituted what Polanyi called 'the second movement'. Polanyi draw our attention to the interventionist state facilitating the emergence of the market in the first place – the 'first movement'. As the market needed freedom from state intervention for its existence and expansion, the state had to withdraw from interfering. Later, the state had to in protect civil society from the social consequences of the market imperfections, through some kind of regulation, thereby starting to facilitate the 'second movement'. In modern economies, non-regulated markets have not been predominant until recently. Instead '… modern industrial societies were typically distinguished by a market-redistribution mix. Depending on the nature of this mix we called some "capitalist" and others "socialist" ' (Hettne 1995b, p. 5).

Polanyi stressed the importance of social forces within civil society. Through his illuminating account of the development in Speenhamland in the late eighteenth century, he drew attention to the distinctive role of the elite and its interest in the shaping of the reaction of civil society. The by-law stipulating minimum wages paid to the peasant labour force to enable them to survive without having to move to urban centres was the result of the elite – the landlords in power – wanting to maintain a certain labour force in the countryside. The law was abandoned only when the emerging industrial elite took power as a result of this elite's need to use the same labour force for its accumulation purposes.

Gramsci conceived civil society as a kind of a 'superstructure' articulating the 'spontaneous' consent given to the dominant group 'by the great masses of the population to the general direction imposed on social life by the dominant fundamental group; this consent is "historically" caused by the prestige (and consequent confidence) which the dominant group enjoys because of its position and function in the world of production' (Gramsci 1971, p. 12). For Gramsci, civil society was a complex constituted by the totality of social relations in society and capable of organising and formulating the needs and visions of the different social groups and movements.

The more these needs and visions could be satisfied, the greater the legitimacy of the state and the government. Accordingly, Gramsci conceived a strong civil society as the necessary base for the legitimacy of the state, i.e. a strong and legitimate state presupposes a strong civil society. Hereby Gramsci distinguished between a hegemonic state (the ideal expression of democracy) and various kinds of authoritarian, coercive and repressive states. If a strong civil society does not exist there is no base for hegemonic relations of the state. Gramsci labelled this kind of situation as an 'organic crisis' and understood it to be extremely unstable, developing either into a highly repressive state or an anarchical stalemate with widespread social chaos.[4]

According to Cox (1997, p. xx):

[We can] use the term 'civil society' to represent the way societies are articulated apart from the state, that is the various interests and identity groups that self-consciously coexist. These interests and groups may be thought of as existing among a more amorphous agglomeration of people who do not seem to be articulated into specific interests or groups, sometimes referred to as 'the people' or 'the masses'. The balance between articulated civil society and the amorphous mass is a key criterion of the quality of a society. There is a kind of populist or Caesarist authority that can be based on a direct relationship between a charismatic leader and an unarticulated mass, but such a formation is not conducive to durable authority in the state, let alone in the world system.

According to this definition, increased numbers of people excluded from economic, political and social life will reduce the strength of civil society and bring about the 'organic crisis' and subsequent risk of more authoritarian coercive and repressive states taking over.

Hegemony at national level is based upon what Gramsci calls the 'historic bloc', on the social foundation on which hegemony can rest and may include different social classes, groups and movements that, together, are ambitious to obtain hegemony and to guide the structure and functioning of the state in a specific situation. A historic bloc is not a simple class alliance, but the complex totality of the relations of production in society. A historic bloc cannot exist if there is no social movement, social force or class that has confidence in other group formations and the capacity to take the leadership in actions designed to create hegemony in civil society. Gramsci thus underlined not only the role of civil society but furthermore the importance of the formation of new historic blocs on which hegemony could be based and the role played by the working class and by their 'deputies' in the form of 'organic intellectuals' (Gramsci 1971, p. 12). The intellectuals are vital for creating and maintaining hegemony, in the sense of defending the common objectives and ideologies that are the basis for the cohesion of the historic bloc. However, intellectuals are not a distinct and relatively classless social stratum. Gramsci saw them as organically connected with a social movement. For Gramsci, 'everyone is in some part an intellectual, although only some perform full-time the social function of an intellectual' (Cox and Sinclair 1996, p. 132).

According to Polanyi, the dialectic between markets and civil society 'the double movement' characterises the development of society as a whole (Polanyi 1957). Gramsci integrated this dialectic into a society/state complex by emphasising the interdynamics between the social relations of production and state formation, as well as the state's importance for a strong civil society (Gramsci 1971). Both Polanyi and Gramsci considered the development of the market, as well as the constraining reactions from the society, as historic necessities. In that sense they accepted, to a certain degree the functional principle of the economic system and its hierarchical networks based upon exclusivity.[5]

As discussed by Hettne (1995b), historically civil society is in need of the legal framework and protection of the state, whereas a legitimate state is in need of a strong civil society. The fact that the process of globalisation with its internationalisation of the state has constrained the state's redistributive capacity and thereby decreased its legitimacy, and has subsequently reduced the capacity of civil society to bring together and articulate demands and interests from various social groupings. The pertinent question in a global era with a decreased role of the nation-state is to what degree a civil society could be revitalised through another security regime than that provided by the state to facilitate dialogue. This is a question of extreme importance for Africa where low 'stateness' and 'civilness' maintain the primary groups (tribes) as predominant social units.

While both the state and the market in Africa are most frequently consequences of externally (European) driven processes, civil society should in an African context rather be described in terms of material life (following the terminology of Braudel) or some kind of a substantive economy built upon reciprocity and redistribution (following the terminology of Polanyi). In both cases reference is made to a 'traditional' society where economic processes are embedded in social relations: something that guarantees the society its capacity of reproduction. One important post-independence preoccupation has been how to transform these traditional societies into market economies with a higher degree of civilness. However, the low stateness and subsequent civilness did not imply that one could not find islands of civility or local capacity in these traditional societies capable of bringing together the demands and different interests of various tribes and to articulate these vis-à-vis, for example, the colonial state. In fact, the system of indirect rule used by the colonial state gave a certain protective framework for this. These islands of civility however, were frequently dismantled after political independence by the new rulers, opting for a more radical modernisation and transformation of traditional society to achieve a higher degree of civilness and to avoid the inefficiency of the small-scale activities of such primary groups.

The power relations between state, market and civil society, constituting the political configuration of a society, vary over time. During the 1960s and the 1970s, the first and the second development decades of the United Nations, the state had the upper hand. At the start of the 1980s, entering into the third development decade, the development discourse drastically tilted in favour of the market economic system. Today, it seems that civil society is more and more considered to constitute the genuine force for envisaged social change. The variation of these power relations over time can easily be observed in Africa. As will be discussed, the African elite has since independence allied itself for convenience with the state and only after the introduction of the structural adjustment programme with the market. However, the increasing marginalisation of the African elite in the world economy has not only led to the emerging new political economy with its very much analysed global and local criminal networks, but also to an increasing number of the African elite shifting its accumulation of social power base into non-governmental organisations constituting what frequently (but wrongly) is understood by civil society.

## The Western values and development paradigm

The consensual relationship permitting a hegemonic leadership on the international level is based on a sufficient number of subordinated states acquiescing in the belief system of the hegemony and accepting it as a universalised principle. According to the thinking of Cox, 'hegemony derives from the ways of doing and thinking of the dominant social strata of the dominant state or states insofar as these ways of doing and thinking have inspired emulation or acquired the acquiescence of the dominant social strata of other states. These social practices and the ideologies that explain and legitimise them constitute the foundation of the hegemonic order. Hegemony frames thought and thereby circumscribes action' (Cox 1992 in Cox and Sinclair 1996, p. 517).

Accordingly, the world order since World War II (Pax Americana), as well as the preceding order (Pax Britannica), reflects 'ways of doing and thinking' inherent in Western civilisation and are based upon claims of universality for these Western values, i.e. the Western development paradigm.[6] In this set of values, rooted in the Age of Enlightenment and consolidated by the Industrial Revolution in England and the political revolution in France, some main features of importance for this study can be identified: expansionism (growth and modernisation) and individualism (man has an individual accountability to God). These notions have subsequently, and at least rhetorically, been complemented by the ideals of the French revolution articulated in the demands for freedom, equality and fraternity.

From these values a number of imperatives were derived, among which nation-state building, private ownership and market economy principles were predominant and constituting what I would call the first 'generation' of values. They were followed by second 'generation', namely the promulgation of multiparty democracy and human rights and so on. Whereas the first generation values has seldom been questioned, the second generation is more open to negotiation. During the Cold War they were, for instance, frequently downplayed for geo-political and strategic reasons. Even if the first 'generation' values were used primarily as a means (not as goals) to maintain the Western supremacy they were not mere rhetoric. US decision-makers believed (cf. NSC 68 1950/04/14–00176), and many of them still believe, in these principles. Hence, this first generation of values came to constitute an important base for the US long-term interest, inspiring vital parts of its foreign policy. However, in my opinion, such principles for accumulation can never be universal. Neither can the second generation and the relationship of social being to social consciousness claim to be universal if the content is not adapted to its socio-cultural and historical context. The Western powers, however, diffuse these values instrumentally and in an institutionalised form. They might see the values as goals but are not concerned with their content in relation to the social context where they are to be applied. Hence, it is the lack of normative strength that renders the values rhetorical. As will be discussed in the next chapter, the Bretton Woods institutions became important US tools for the diffusion of these values, especially during the Reagan administration. The values were imposed, implying a process of homogenisation of the global political space.

According to Burton, values constitute 'those ideas, habits and beliefs that are characteristic of particular social communities. They are the linguistic, religious, class, ethnic or other features that lead to separate cultures and identity groups' (Burton 1990, p. 37). With these values mankind was supposed to satisfy its human needs. The welfare state could be created with sufficient growth and redistributive capacity to release society from the traditional struggle between the haves and the have-nots. By human needs I understand both material and non-material, with the former frequently considered a prerequisite for the latter. These human needs can be considered universal. However, different cultures and civilisations have different belief systems and values concerning how best to satisfy these needs. These ways of fulfilling the universal needs are culturally specific, and thus by definition are not universal. The expanding capitalist mode of production characterises the way in which Western civilisation has organised its reproduction in modern times.[7] Scholars as dissimilar as Galtung and Huntington point out that expansionism and claims of universality were embedded in Western civilisation from its very inception (Galtung 1996; Huntington 1996a and b).

Throughout history, different elites have used these values to mobilise popular support for different kinds of international activities that are in the interest of the leadership. By interest we understand 'the occupational, social, political and economic aspirations of the individual, and of identity groups of individuals within a social system ... They typically relate to material goods or role occupancy' (Burton 1990, p. 38). According to Burton, interests, as distinct from needs and values, are negotiable. The inherent expansionism of capitalism has been reinforced by the claims of universality for the Westernised belief system. Huntington phrases this in the following manner:

> The West – and especially the United States, which has always been a missionary nation – believes that the non-Western peoples should commit themselves to the Western values of democracy, free markets, limited government, separation of church and state, human rights, individualism, and the rule of law, and should embody these values in their institutions. Minorities in other civilisations embrace and promote these values, but the dominant attitudes toward them in non-Western culture range from scepticism to intense opposition. What is universalism to the West is imperialism to the rest ... Culture follows power. If non-Western societies are once again shaped by Western culture, it will happen only as

a result of the expansion and deployment of Western power. Imperialism is the necessary, logical consequence of universalism, yet few proponents of universalism support the militarisation and brutal coercion that would be necessary to achieve their goal. (Huntington 1996a, pp. 40–1)

Over time, elites from other civilisations have declared their faith in important components of the same belief system. Through adherence to similar values they strive for the fruits of modernisation. For these elites, the widening income gap between the rich and the poor countries – a major concern of this study – is viewed as a cultural problem. Development in the westernised sense of the word occurs and the inequality gap is narrowed when a broad set of Western values and institutions is present. As a consequence, a common concept of mobilisation and allocation of resources has developed within the emerging transnational managerial class (Cox and Sinclair 1996) or business civilisation (Strange 1990).[8]

## National security interest

The striving to catch up with the Western world is also a question of perceived security; to develop and modernise in order not to be absorbed, or further marginalised. The same rationale can be found behind the concept of national security interest. The strength of the economy and security are working in interaction. A strong state (even though small in reach) is considered vital for both. Thus, providing its citizens with security has been and remains the main traditional function of the state. The concept of national security interest is fluid. Different governments have different perspectives on what is in their country's national interest, especially as regards more than short-term immediate interest. These short-term interests may over time become subordinated to a more long-term or so-called 'enlightened national interest' of a more permanent and constant nature. Such gradual subordination explains why a certain continuity in foreign policy-making can be observed albeit the short-term approaches can cause temporary diversion, in the light of the prevailing geopolitical context. The concept 'national security interest' is of importance for this study in that it contributes to the making of the world order's structures. In a globalised world, the question of security does not only arise between states but also between sub-national and transnational actors. Buzan provides a concretisation of the ambiguous concept of human needs earlier referred to, through the expansion of the security concept to encompass individuals' physical security, economic security (material needs), as well as the security of rights, position and status (non-material needs (Buzan 1991)). However, such an expansion should in no way be understood as if national and international security could be reduced to individual security (Buzan 1991, p. 54). Following Galtung and his concepts of negative and positive peace, the security concept can be further expanded through a similar distinction between negative and positive security, where negative security is the absence of threat while positive security concerns possibilities for the individual to use his or her potential for increased quality of life (Galtung 1996). The reason this study focuses on state security is that the state, with its monopoly on violence, is still the principal actor for providing protection. As Buzan observes: 'governments stand at the interface between the internal dynamics of the state, and the external ones of the system. It is the job of government, indeed almost the definition of its function, to find ways of reconciling these two sets of forces. The fact that no other agency exists for this task is what justifies the primacy of national security' (Buzan 1991, p. 329).

In the same way as individuals needed protection by the nation-state, and accepted limits on their individual freedom in exchange (cf. the social contract), the elites of the nation-state need protection and rules for their international relationships. Economic needs (in the form of a liberal international order) together with political necessities (i.e. the post-World War II policy of containment) constitute the dominant national security interests, which, in interaction with the dominant belief system, frame the rules and structures of the post-World War II world order. For a long time the security of states was considered an outcome of power and dependent on peace. Lately, it has been observed that the logic of security involves high levels of interdependence among actors striving to make themselves secure (mutual security). Though the standard unit of security is the sovereign territorial state, the concept of security concerns first and foremost the defence of a society's cultural values and belief system, reflecting the prevailing political configuration and social relations of production. Hence, national security policy is a product of national reaction to the perceived threat from the internal or external environment. Absolute national security, however, can never be achieved. Hence, the crucial question is to identify those means which can contribute most efficiently to a satisfactory security in terms of reduced vulnerability. These vary over time, depending on the sources of different perceived threats faced by a given society, which makes the concept of security fluid and extremely dynamic.

National security interest is as important for small countries as it is for large ones. This applies both to sub-national causes of threat and to international sources. While big powers can strive to achieve their national security uni- or bilaterally, small states are in need of cooperation and multinational channels on both regional and international levels to pursue their national security interests. National security interest is also often used to mobilise reluctant domestic political forces to support certain foreign policies or international commitments that the national leadership wants to pursue. Prevailing interests or awareness of long-term international threats which justify maintaining international involvement are legitimised by the identification of short-term threats. In the post-Cold War era and with a reduced communist threat, intensive efforts are made by internationally oriented interests in the United States to create a new national security interest that can be supported by domestic opinion.[9]

## World order structures

The term 'world order'[10] is interchangeable, in my conception, with the system of international political economy (or international economic order), provided we are referring to the Westphalian system in which states are important actors.[11] A system consists of structures and interacting units. The structure is constituted by the pattern of interaction between the structure and the actors in the system. Structures do not exist by themselves. They are analytical constructions (Waltz 1986, p. 72) made visible by the actions of the actors (or their impact on the objects) at the same time that the structures constrain these same actions. Robert Cox expresses this concisely:

> A structure, as I have suggested, is a picture of reality, of the world, or of that aspect of the world that impresses itself upon us at any particular time – the power relations among nations, or those of the workplace, or of the family or local community. This picture, shared among many people, defines reality for them; and because they think of reality in the same way, their actions and words tend to reproduce this reality. (Cox and Sinclair 1996, p. 32)

Hence structure is a concept I use to describe the pattern of thoughts and actions earlier referred to, which constitute the framework within which people, states, companies, organisations or institutions etc. are acting. In his book *Production, Power, and World Order*, Cox gives the following definition: 'Some authors have used "structure" to mean ideas or patterns of relationship that exist independently of people: they think of people merely as bearers of structures. No such meaning is intended here. ...Historical structures, as the term is used in this book, mean persistent social practices, made by collective human activity and transformed through collective human activity' (Cox 1987, p. 4). He develops the idea further in an article in *Approaches to World Order*:

> Structures exist in language, in the ways we think, in the practices of social and economic and political life. Any particular way of life in time and place, when analysed, will reveal a certain structure. Any particular sphere of life will have its structure. Structures are then the larger context within which institutions are to be located. ... Institutions are the broadly understood and accepted ways of organising particular spheres of social action – in our own era, for instance, from marriage and the nuclear family, through the state, diplomacy and the rules of international

law, to formal organisations like the United Nations and the International Monetary Fund. (Cox and Sinclair 1996, p. 149)

These patterns of thoughts and actions reflect the power relations among the interacting units, they are 'a picture of a particular configuration of forces …that does not determine action in any direct, mechanical way but imposes pressures and constraints' (Cox 1981, in Cox and Sinclair 1996, p. 97). When the framework, created by the pattern of thoughts and actions, has been established it becomes part of the structures restraining the actions. The pattern of thought might prevail long after the conditions that gave rise to them have ceased to exist. In the same way the created frameworks might last after the political configuration that put them into practice has changed and as their transformation may be delayed by their own rigidities. In my opinion, these patterns of thought reflect both what Cox calls 'intersubjective, or collective, meanings' (i.e. shared notions of the nature of social relations and expectations of behaviour), and competing 'collective images' of social order held by different groups of people (Cox and Sinclair 1996, p. 99). The intersubjective meanings are predominant and give the structure in question a consensual character (the so-called hegemonic structure). However, the frequently conflicting perspectives (collective images) provide evidence of the striving for alternative patterns of development. According to Cox, 'these intersubjective ideas hold so long as they appear to make sense of the material realities people confront collectively' (Cox 1997, p. xxii). Significant efforts are made at different levels to encourage the development of collective images consistent with prevailing power relations.[12]

Thus, by 'world order structures' I mean a system of rules and norms regulating international economic and political cooperation. This system is based upon long-term hegemonic values and short-term security interests of the dominating state and its national elite, which reflect the predominant social relations of production, the political configuration as well as the prevailing power relations. It constitutes a set of structures, the framework within which people, states and other actors operate, where each structure represents a limited totality and where the structures together constitute the system as such.

The former bipolarity between East and West is conceived as a structure, in the sense that it reflected the rules, norms and power relations regulating international economic and political cooperation implemented through different institutions. Some structures are more visible than others. The impact of the (unwritten) rules and norms varies. For some it is heavy, for others light and for some there is no impact at all. Structural adjustment programmes for heavily indebted countries are a case in point. The population of a weak state suffers tremendously from the conditions imposed to gain access to international credit. Stronger states, even if they are more indebted, are less vulnerable, since conditions are often imposed to a lesser extent. One state, the most indebted of them all, does not suffer at all from conditions and demands for structural adjustment, as it for a long time had the strength to provide its own credit and later access to unconditional credit. I refer to the United States. This depends on the possession and use of 'structural power' to which we will return.

## World order and hegemonic stability

For world order stability, conceived as a requirement for international economic cooperation, a strong dominant power is needed to implement agreed rules and norms and to provide sanctions. This affirmation is the essence of the theory of hegemonic stability, focusing on the relationship of a dominant economy and a liberal international system (Keohane 1980), though agreement on the need for hegemonic power and the meaning and importance of hegemony varies between different traditions. The theory does not argue that international economic relations would be unable to exist and function in the absence of hegemony, but rather that a particular type of international economic order, a liberal one, could not flourish and reach its full potential without the presence of such a hegemonic power. Hence, the main role of the hegemon was to be the guarantor of the open world economy.

For the post-World War II world order, coinciding interest between the economic and political elite striving for Atlanticism became decisive. Atlanticism is not only a geopolitical entity but foremost a social system, constituted by a specific phase of industrial development, namely Fordist mass production (Aglietta 1976). The welfare system depended on a strong state capable of maintaining a stable relationship between mass production and consumption at the national level. It depended on liberalised trade and open world markets. The crucial question to be discussed by this study is to what degree disorder could be accepted within the world order without endangering that order itself, and thereby peace and stability. As formulated by Hettne, it is 'a basic premise for all political economists that a market, in order to function, presupposes some kind of order, a concept which contains both coercive and consensual dimensions' (Hettne 1995b, p. 15).

Robert Cox draws our attention to the need to distinguish between the two meanings of 'hegemony'. The realist meaning, which is conventional in international relations literature, is the dominance of one state over others, and the ability of the dominant state, through coercion, to determine the conditions in which interstate relations are conducted and to determine their outcome. The other meaning, found in neo-realist and more liberal thinking, stresses the question of legitimacy (Kindleberger 1973). Political legitimacy may be defined as the 'right to rule'. The governed acknowledge their government as morally right and they are thus duty-bound to obey it. This belief legitimates the rulers' claim to authority and validates the structure of domination (Weber 1964). In the absence of such beliefs and acknowledgements the relationship between the governor and the governed can only be one of power, not of authority, and political legitimacy will be contested. As will be further developed, when discussing legitimacy at the local level, the degree of empathy between the governor and the governed is of great importance for the consolidation of a legitimate relationship. Hence, legitimacy deals with vertical relations. In one sense it is an expression of the relations between the political system at different levels and the citizens, in terms of the relevance and extension of public service and of political representativity and participation. In many countries in the Third World, still on the road to nation building, it is also a question of the relation between society at large and the local communities. But the question of legitimacy cannot be reduced to the explicitly political realm of society. Economic, social and cultural issues are integrated parts of a vertical system of articulation and can also be analysed in terms of legitimacy.

In essence, the Weberian understanding of legitimacy is put on an equal footing with the Gramscian notion of hegemony. Both stress the importance of socio-historical context, something which makes legitimacy more 'a historically contingent, not a universally valid proposition' (Cox 1987, p. 421, n. 20). For Cox, hegemony is a special case of dominance:

> [Hegemony] defines the condition of a world society and state system in which the dominant state and dominant social forces sustain their position through adherence to universalised principles which are accepted or acquiesced in by a sufficient proportion of subordinate states and social forces. This second meaning of hegemony implies intellectual and moral leadership. The strong makes certain concessions to obtain the consent of the weaker. The Pax Americana of the post-World War II era had the characteristics of this Gramscian meaning of hegemony. The United States was the dominant power and its dominance was expressed in leadership enshrined in certain principles of conduct that became broadly acceptable. The economic 'regimes' established under US aegis during this period had the appearance of consensual arrangements. They did not look either like the crude exploitation of a power position or like a hard bargain arrived at among rival interests. (Cox 1993, p. 264)

By bringing in the role of legitimacy for hegemonic maintenance, Gramsci, whose work and concepts will be explored later, made a substantial contribution to our understanding of hegemonic circumstances. However, as Cox reminds us, Gramsci 'took over from Machiavelli the image of power as a centaur: half man, half beast, a necessary combination of consent and coercion. To the extent that the consensual aspect of power is in the forefront, hegemony prevails. Coercion is always latent but is only applied in marginal, deviant cases' (Cox 1983, in Cox and Sinclair 1996, p. 127).

## Power

Power is another fluid concept. Its strength and meaning changes over time, as do its localisation and articulation: from US military power in the 1950s to its structural power in the late 1980s and its more media-linked discoursive power in the 1990s. For international leadership it is a prerequisite no matter whether we are talking about coercive or consensual power. For realist thinkers, the hegemony could only exercise its influence and maintain its leadership through the use of coercive power. A hegemonic state must not only possess enough military power to protect an open world market economy, but must also have control over essential raw materials and in particular technologies, market outlets, finance and credits (Gilpin 1987, pp. 72–80).

Strange (1988) distinguishes between two kinds of power exercised in a political economy – structural power and relational power. Whilst relational power is the power of A to get B to do something they would otherwise not do, structural power confers the

> power to shape and determine the structures of the global political economy within which other states, their political institutions, their economic enterprises and (not least) their scientists and other professional people have to operate ...Structural power, in short, confers the power to decide how things shall be done, the power to shape frameworks within which states relate to each other, relate to people, or relate to corporate enterprises. (Strange 1988, p. 24)

More liberal thinking stressed the consensual aspect of hegemony: 'Hegemony rests on the subjective awareness by elites in secondary states that they are benefiting, as well as on the willingness of the hegemony itself to sacrifice tangible short-term benefits for intangible long-term gains' (Keohane 1984, p. 45). The diffusion of the Western belief system and values is of course important in this regard. Galtung moves gradually from coercive power to consensual power by distinguishing between military power, where the actors are persuaded by violence; political power, where the actors are persuaded by repression; economic power, where the actors are persuaded through incentives or sanctions; and cultural (legitimising) power, where the actors are persuaded of the merits of the belief system and cultural habits of the power holder, in areas ranging from the establishment of a market economy and multiparty democracy to the use of a foreign language as the official language (Galtung 1996).[13]

## Discursive power

Lately the concept of power has increasingly become contested. As discussed above, the traditional analyses of power primarily focus on different strength between actors (relational power) and how such differences can be used in different institutions in applying rules and regulations (structural power) in order to increase influences over states, groups or individuals. More recent power theories underline more subtle mechanisms capable of creating subordination through various forms of discipline. The concept of discursive power is increasingly used in order to pinpoint the power over our thoughts, the formation of prevailing opinions and our actions. Foucault uses in this regard the concept of capillary power (Foucault 1980), a power so present everywhere as to appear not to be present anywhere and which makes us uncritically accept the predominant opinions and societal norms in force.

In this connection, it is important to observe connections and differences between structural power – influences over certain institutions – and discursive power – formation of the dominant opinion. As earlier discussed, the hegemonic discourses in force are shaped and sustained by the political configuration of the historic bloc, its values, norms and security interest. The historic bloc also shapes the institutions, rules and structures required in order to diffuse this discourse and to implement the decisions that can be derived. Hence, the structural and discursive power reinforce each other interchangeably. The structural power (as in influence over the World Bank) is used in order to implement measures and actions according to the discourse and hereby accumulate experiences making it possible to deepen and widen the discursive power. Through discursive power, structures and institutions needed to sustain and to diffuse the discourses are created. However, when a discourse is challenged by an emerging counter-hegemonic bloc and gradually loses its legitimacy, the impact of the structures decreases, i.e. the structural power loses its strength. The USA cannot any longer use its influence over the World Bank in order to pursue its policy if the legitimacy of prevailing opinions and the discourses in force within the institutions decreases and the structural adjustment programmes start to be questioned. In the same way changes of the structures upon which the discourses are founded will also change the discourses. The structures constituting the base for the structural power have their consistency and coherences but also their contradictions. It is these contradictions that over time imply that the political configuration of the historic bloc, and subsequently the structures, will change. Depending on the configuration of the bloc, the structures can be adapted or be replaced by new structures. When a sufficient number of structures has been changed or replaced by others the very foundation upon which the historic bloc and its discourses are based erodes. From this very process discursive transformation and change of power structures is emanating. A new bloc starts to become sufficiently legitimate in order to take over the hegemonic capacity from the earlier bloc. Opportunity for structural change does not necessarily coincide with a transformation and change of the hegemonic discourse. Even if discourses and structures develop and sustain each other in a process of interchange they can also (temporarily) exist independent of each other.

Indisputably, then, structural changes will change discourses over time and vice versa. A discourse without its material and structural embodiment is not socially relevant. Yet it might not be very meaningful for the global justice movement to demand the closure of the World Bank and the International Monetary Fund as long as the historic bloc and its discourse that created the institutions remains in a hegemonic position. The discourse in force will only create other similar institutions and structures, for example on a regional level. Hence a discourse can remain for a while even if the material conditions and structures that created the discourse are no longer at hand. In the same way structures can reside even after the discourses giving them social and political meaning have disappeared. A classic example of this is how the Rhodesian police structures, due to lack of any alternative, were taken over by President Mugabe at the time of Zimbabwe's independence. In the same way the former officials of the apartheid regime in Pretoria continue to this day to have a strong influence over the security and military apparatus in South Africa.

## Hegemonic decline and interdependence

The differentiation between coercive and consensual power is important because it raises the question of consequences when a hegemony is in decline. The conceptualisation of hegemony that stresses a consensual relationship between the leader and the led implies that the power of hegemony can decline as a consequence of reduced legitimacy even if its coercive power remains intact. The question has become topical as a result of the end of the Cold War and the reduced motivation in the United States to maintain its traditional leadership. The debate on US hegemonic decline is crucial because it focuses on the very heart of the current world order; namely, could one of its cornerstones – a liberal international economy and an open world market (i.e. free movement between states of capital, knowledge and goods, but not labour) – remain in place if US hegemony declines?

Some recent realist thinking proposes that the world is in transition to a situation of apolarity and that there is need for chaos management (Crocker *et al.* 1996). A continued decline of US hegemony is thought to be in no one's interest, as this would destroy the possibility of maintaining a liberal international order and an open economy. The realist school fears that protectionism and mercantilism will emerge again.

According to world system theorists, hegemonic decline is something naturally derived from internal rivalry and hegemonic competition. Actors on the regional level have the temporary possibility of exploiting this decline. The liberals consider hegemonic decline to be a consequence of the continued process of globalisation and increased economic dynamics. As Gilpin articulates: 'Thus, an inherent contradiction exists in a liberal world economy: the operation of the market system transforms the economic structure and diffuses power, thereby undermining the political foundations of that structure' (Gilpin 1987, p. 78). The liberals initially agreed with the realists on the need for a hegemonic world order for a liberal international economy and an open world market. However, the open world market not only created contradictions, reducing the hegemonic power, but also created a strong interdependence that could sustain a continuation of the liberal international order without hegemonic power. Hence, according to liberal thinking the world order could be maintained through multilateral agreements on international regimes (regulating, for example, trade and money flow or migration), which are motivated by the interdependence and self-interest of trading partners. Even though Robert Keohane articulated the theory of hegemonic stability, he was himself highly sceptical as regards the conclusions to be drawn: 'there is little reason to believe that hegemony is either a necessary or a sufficient condition for the emergence of cooperative relationship' (Keohane 1984, p. 31). He continues, 'when shared interests are sufficiently important and other key conditions are met, cooperation can emerge and regimes can be created without hegemony' (p. 50). In this regard Keohane draws our attention to the fact that 'cooperation and harmony are by no means identical and ought not to be confused with one another'. He distinguishes between harmony, cooperation and discord:

> If actors' policies automatically facilitate the attainment of others' goals, there is harmony: no adjustment needs to take place. Yet harmony is rare in world politics. … Cooperation by contrast, is highly political: somehow, patterns of behaviour must be altered. Cooperation takes place only in situations in which actors perceive that their policies are actually or potentially in conflict, not where there is harmony. Cooperation should not be viewed as the absence of conflict, but rather as a reaction to conflict or potential conflict. (Keohane 1984, p. 49)

Charles Kindleberger was also influential in this debate. His well-known advocacy of a legitimate and consensual hegemony (although he preferred the term leadership) with strong international regimes was based on neoclassical economic arguments arguing for political actions (Kindleberger 1973).[14] Strengthened international institutional and governmental cooperation was motivated by the need to supply 'public goods', which for obvious reasons the market failed to do, be it in the domestic or international arena. Kindleberger argued that the open world economy, which offered opportunities to all to benefit from increased efficiency in allocation of resources, should be considered a public good in the international realm.

This question of the supply of public goods has given rise to the so-called 'free rider' problem, which has received considerable attention from scholars as it is considered to have an important negative impact on the future possibility of maintaining international regimes. If the costs to the hegemony of maintaining rules and regimes begin to exceed the perceived benefits, powerful domestic groups will start to question their commitment to international leadership. An open world economy is particularly vulnerable to the free rider problem. Concessions made to one member of the World Trade Organisation (WTO) are automatically available to all other members (unconditional reciprocity), even if they are not interested in paying their shares through compliance with the agreed rules.

However, the self-interest of the elite to comply, notwithstanding this problematic, has been reemphasised by Keohane (1984) who demonstrated the possibilities for cooperation based on realist premises, including the empathetic explanation of behaviour.[15] According to Keohane:

> international regimes should not be interpreted as elements of a new international order 'beyond the nation-state'. They should be comprehended chiefly as arrangements motivated by self-interest: as components of systems in which sovereignty remains a constitutive principle. This means that, as realists emphasise, they will be shaped largely by their most powerful members, pursuing their own interests. But regimes can also affect state interests, for the notion of self-interest is itself elastic and largely subjective. Perceptions of self-interest depend both on actors' expectations of the likely consequences that will follow from particular actions and on their fundamental values. (Keohane 1984, p. 63)

The driving force behind the establishment of international regimes stems from prevailing global interdependence. The concept of 'interdependence' usually refers to 'the extent to which events occurring in any given part or within any given component unit of a world system affect (either physically or perceptually) events taking place in each of the other parts or component units of the system' (Oran 1969, quoted in Keohane 1984).

Keohane draws our attention to the fact that the term 'frequently carr[ies] highly positive and egalitarian overtones. Interdependence is not by definition mutually beneficial, it can be negative for both parties or even if beneficial to all parties involved, interdependence can be highly asymmetrical: one actor may depend on another to a much greater extent than applies vice versa' (Keohane 1984, p. 388).

Keohane concludes that the question of asymmetry is politically important. 'Being less dependent than other actors in an interdependent system can be an important source of power' (Keohane 1984). In this connection it is important to stress that economic interdependence could be defined as 'the sensitivity of economic transactions between two or more nations to economic development within those nations', and social interdependence in terms of 'the sensivity of societies to changes taking place in other societies'. Accordingly, Keohane concludes that 'policy interdependence refers to the extent to which decisions taken by actors in one part of a system affect other actors' policy decisions elsewhere in the system' (Keohane 1984, p. 394).[16]

The concept of 'complex interdependence' (Keohane and Nye 1977) further developed the importance of international cooperation instead of conflict by pointing to the multiple channels (governmental as well as non-governmental) that connect societies on a global scale. The agenda of interstate relationships contains multiple issues that are not arranged in a clear or consistent hierarchy. Military force will not be used by governments against other governments when a complex interdependence prevails. Drastic social and political change could, make the use of force an important direct instrument of policy again. A hegemon tries to increase external burden-sharing for its international commitments by using its influence to create rules that satisfy its own interests, thereby trying to liberalise parts of its own financial resources for increasing its internal legitimacy.

The US use of the international financial system to finance its world leadership is an illuminating example.[17] As will be dealt with in the next chapter, this contributed to the first oil crisis in the 1970s, with subsequent recycling of petrodollars, overliquidity on the Euro-dollar market, indebtedness in the Third World and a subsequent need for structural adjustment. Macroeconomic imbalances in sub-Saharan Africa, i.e. deficits in the state budget and current account, needed to be adjusted.

## Conclusion

With these conceptual clarifications in mind, the logic of the framework and the set of concepts describing how I understand the world order can be synthesised and illustrated as in Figure 1.1.

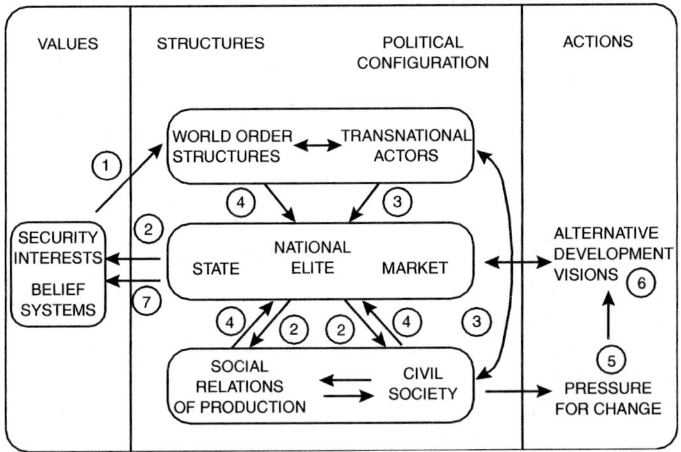


*Figure 1.1*  Synthesised conceptual framework

In Figure 1.1 the world order is conceived as a set of structures constituted by the long-term (Western) values and belief systems as well as short-term security interests of the dominant national elites (1) and reflecting internal power relations within and between the elite and civil society as well as social relations of production (2). The values and interests of the transnational elite groups have a strong influence as well (3). Of crucial importance is whether or not the order is hegemonic and based on consensual power. A hegemonic decline can be compensated for by increased interdependence achieved through interacting structures.

These frameworks or structures can be found at various levels.[18] As a consequence of the ongoing process of globalisation, the impact of the world order structures encompasses both national and local levels (4). Governments acting as 'transmission belts' for world order demands in their effort for external legitimacy simultaneously decrease their internal legitimacy and provoke reactions from civil society (5). However, the prevailing world order structures reduce the room for manoeuvre of alternative development strategies capable of rehabilitating lost social trust (6). Thus world order structures impeding an alternative development strategy are in need of change.

The circumstances that can imply modification of short- and long-term interests (7) and thereby create opportunities for such a structural change are the topic for later chapters.

# 2
# Bretton Woods Revisited

International political economy has devoted substantial attention to the Bretton Woods system, to the role of hegemony and to US leadership in the Cold War world order. Within the field of development theory, the roots of the present financial disorder and the role of the Bretton Woods institutions in debt management have also been fairly well analysed, including their short-term impact on Third World countries.

Few efforts, however, have been made to combine these different areas of research in order to understand the political and economic implications of the fact that the design of the structural framework, within the parameters of which the various social forces acted, was based upon the Roosevelt vision of one world but had to be implemented in a global order characterised by bipolarity.

The aim of the chapter is to analyse these implications. It introduces the argument of how the perceptions of a Cold War reinforced the contradictions which were originally built into the Bretton Woods system. In doing so, the chapter's focus lies on the structures and contradictions in the present world order that are believed to be of importance for the future development of poor countries like Mozambique. Of special importance in this regard is the role of international aid as a tool of US foreign policy.

## From Bretton Woods to Pax Americana

The present world economic order was outlined during the Bretton Woods Conference in 1944, one year before World War II ended. The US Secretary of State invited 44 governments to send representatives for the purpose of formulating definite proposals for an International Monetary Fund and possibly a Bank for Reconstruction and Development. Some economic powers did not participate in the conference, being either occupied (France) or considered enemy countries (Germany, Italy and Japan). Accordingly, the holding of the conference and its decisions were an Anglo-American issue, and an outcome of sterling–dollar diplomacy (Gardner 1969).[1]

During the conference a consensus was achieved on the need to create the proposed international financial institutions, and the USA was asked by its European allies to take on the leadership and to become the main shareholder (Mason and Asher 1973). It took some ten years for the member states to ratify the agreement, and between its conception and implementation the Cold War became a reality. From then onwards, the bipolar world order primarily characterised the national security interests of the two superpowers.

Blueprints for the Bretton Woods system were already being drafted in the early 1940s. In the United States, the Council on Foreign Relations brought together leaders of the American international business and banking community[2] to initiate the development of proposals for a new world order.[2] The American design was based on the need to satisfy its requirements for continued supply of raw material in the post-war period and for access to markets in order to avoid surplus production.

The need to gain a 'Grand Area' constituted the basis of the White Plan (named after chief American negotiator Harry Dexter White), presented at Bretton Woods, and has consequently been perceived as the requirement for continued Atlanticism.

Simultaneously, and partly as a reply to Berlin's proclamation of a post-war plan for a new world order under German leadership, in autumn 1942 the British government assigned to the economist John Maynard Keynes the task of developing a British proposal for the post-war order. Like the Americans, Keynes wanted at all costs to avoid another Great Depression, which in the 1920s had led not only to national misery and mass unemployment but, subsequently, to fascism and war.[3]

While the US was concerned about its large post-war industrial overcapacity, Europe (as well as the rest of the world) was concerned with its desperate need for machinery for industrial (re-)construction and for sources of finance. These coinciding interests within the Atlantic elite, together with their internal power relations, constituted the main driving forces behind the rules and the institutions of the post-World War II world order that was to follow.

The decisions taken at the Bretton Woods Conference were considered purely economic. The reason for playing down the political impact was not only to facilitate getting public acceptance.[4] Cooperation was considered much easier in the economic than in the political field, as the common interests of different national elites could be perceived more clearly in trade liberalisation and an international monetary system.

## The concept of embedded liberalism

Keynes founded his original proposal on four pillars. First, an international monetary regime with a World Central Bank was to provide the necessary international liquidity through issuing the so-called 'Bancor' (the proposed world currency). Second, an organisation, the International Trade

Organisation (ITO), would be established to reinforce international security by supporting the free international movement of goods, services and capital and thereby avoiding the protectionism and rivalry of the past. Third, a strong state should be permitted to develop at national level as the guarantor for national stability through active participation in planning and executing the required public investments. And finally, a comprehensive aid programme would be developed to facilitate the transfer of resources to underdeveloped countries, thereby facilitating decolonisation and modernisation.[5]

It was a true Keynesian attempt to create international security and national stability through sustained economic growth, achieved through free trade in an international environment of multilateralism and a domestic context of full employment under national surveillance.

In other words, an international institutional framework organising a regulated system of trade and finance should enable independent states to concentrate their policy-making on achieving full employment and price stability, rather than on immediate policies aiming at balance of payments adjustments.[6]

Using the language of Karl Polanyi (Polanyi 1957), the aim of these efforts could be described as a form of embedded liberalism.[7] The prevailing configuration of political power within western Europe at the time permitted, in the words of Gramsci, 'a historic bloc' of political alliances between state, labour and capital (Gramsci 1971). This tripartism aimed at creating a welfare state through a market economy that acknowledged social realities and was tempered by stabilising institutions.

World War II obviously played an important role in laying the political foundations of such a 'historic bloc'. Facing external enemies created a strong national unity, and made domestic political conflicts insignificant. However, with the war ended and the external threat fading away, the legitimacy of the state and the foundations of this arrangement could only be maintained as long as the modern state offered its citizens economic growth, security, an administrative and physical infrastructure and material and social welfare.

Hence, at the heart of the economic agenda of the time were the questions of how to create a surplus and how to use it. Production, full employment and the development of the real economy were considered the preponderant issues in maintaining the political base for tripartism.

The experience of the Great Depression meant that few believed in a self-regulating market. In order for international trade to expand a supranational regulating authority was required which would provide the needed financial liquidity, rules of the game, and international stability. Europe's Atlantic-oriented political leaders agreed to exchange some of their national sovereignty for international security under US leadership. It turned out more problematic to convince a reluctant American public that it was in America's national interest to take on a leadership role for making the 'New Deal in

International Economics' possible. This study therefore contends that the Bretton Woods system was originally intended to be a mixed regime, with Keynesian and social democratic stabilisers. However, at the time of its implementation the guarantor of the system, the United States, had little enthusiasm for either abandoning its interpretation of classical liberalism or ceding its sovereignty (Kuttner 1991).

## US leadership motivation

US foreign policy-making shows a strong continuity over time.[8] During most of the twentieth century it has been marked by the traditional effort for a bipartisan consensus,[9] trying to bridge the gap between the positions of US internationalist and isolationist forces. Its main goal has been to defend US national security interests. These interests vary over time in accordance with developments in the domestic production system and its social relations as well as in accordance with the overall geopolitical realities. Behind the short-term national security interests, however, one finds the more long-term need to defend and universalise certain US values rooted in the belief system of the Age of Enlightenment and articulated in American-style capitalism. As this conviction of the supremacy of US values constitutes a cornerstone of the justification of US international commitment it is useful to quote former Secretary of State Henry Kissinger at length:

> Almost as if according to some natural law, in every century there seems to emerge a country with the power, the will and the intellectual and moral impetus to shape the entire international system in accordance with its own values. In the seventeenth century, France under Cardinal Richelieu introduced the modern approach to international relations, based on the nation-state and motivated by national interest as its ultimate purpose. In the eighteenth century, Great Britain elaborated the concept of balance of power, which dominated European diplomacy for the next 200 years. ... In the twentieth century, no country has influenced international relations as decisively and at the same time as ambivalently as the United States. No society has more firmly insisted on the inadmissibility of intervention in the domestic affairs of other states, or more passionately asserted that its own values were universally applicable. Thus the two approaches, the isolationist and the missionary, so contradictory on the surface, reflected a common underlying faith that the United States possessed the world's best system of government, and that the rest of mankind could attain peace and prosperity by abandoning traditional diplomacy and adopting America's reverence for international law and democracy. ... If anything, it has spurred America's faith that history can be overcome and that if the world truly wants peace, it needs to apply America's moral prescriptions. (Kissinger 1994, p. 17)

The consensus on the need to defend and spread these values internationally expressed in the Wilsonian version of 'Manifest Destiny', the so-called 'exceptionalism', was reinforced by Stalin's decision not to join the Bretton Woods system and the Cold War that followed.[10] It became a predominant opinion in the West that alone among the nations of the 'Free World',[11] the United States had both the material power and the moral responsibility to contain communism and thereby to create a just and stable international order, based on American values and national strategic interest. The first post-World War II US president, Harry Truman, made the policy explicit following the decision by the British government to abandon its special support for Greece in early 1947. 'I believe it must be the policy of the United States to support free peoples who are resisting subjugation by armed minorities or by outside pressures' (the Truman Doctrine, quoted in Kennan 1967, p. 320).[12] The US administration therefore considered it necessary to take immediate action wherever necessary in order to avoid communist forces seizing power. Hence, since the days of President Truman, the national security interest of the United States has been complemented by the necessary framework for global anti-communism (the policy of containment).[13]

## Aid as a foreign policy tool

The Marshall Plan[14] became an important US foreign policy tool in this regard, and the logic behind it was important in future guidelines for US aid. The planners behind the plan recognised 'that the communists are exploiting the European crisis and that further communist successes would create serious danger to American security' (Kennan 1967, p. 336). Accordingly, in President Truman's inaugural address in January 1949, following his reelection, the so-called Point Four Program made foreign aid (at the time called 'mutual security assistance') an important tool in US foreign policy-making.[15] This was reconfirmed some twenty-five years later before the US Congress by Secretary of State George Shultz in the following manner:

> Three of the most fundamental goals of our foreign policy are, first, building peace and sustaining the security of the United States; second, fostering a growing world economy and protecting US access to free markets and critical resources; and third, expanding the forces of democracy and freedom. The United States cannot realize these goals unless there is economic growth, peace and political stability in the countries of the Third World. The program you have before you is an essential instrument of our foreign policy and it is directly linked to the national security of the US. (Foreign Assistance Legislation for Fiscal Years 84–85, Hearings before the Committee on Foreign Affairs, 98th Congress, March 1983, p. 88)

As illustrated by the various US post-war study groups hosted by the Council on Foreign Relations in New York,[16] the driving forces behind the need for

US international leadership were not only 'missionary': altruistic or geopolitical. They were also economic and socio-political, based on the USA's own domestic needs.[17] Within the policy-making elite, the so-called establishment, two opinions prevailed on how to avoid the Great Depression of the 1920s.[18] One possibility was to continue the Keynesian policy of national redistribution as manifested by Roosevelt in his 'New Deal'. Another was through the Grand Area referred to earlier.[19] Given sufficient markets and easy availability of raw materials, full employment could be achieved without the need to regulate market forces. This reasoning was synthesised by Dean Acheson before the Special Subcommittee on post-war Economic Policy and Planning of the House of Representatives in 1944:

> When we look at that problem we may say it is a problem of markets. You don't have a problem of production. We have to see that what the country produces is used and is sold under financial arrangements which make its production possible. You must look to foreign markets. If you wish to control the entire trade and income of the United States, which means the life of the people, you could probably fix it so that everything produced here could be consumed here, but that would completely change our constitution, our relations of property, human liberty, our very conceptions of law. And nobody contemplates that. Therefore you must look to other markets and those markets are abroad. (US House Hearings, Special Committee on Post-War Economic Policy and Planning, Washington DC: GPO 1945, p. 1082, quoted in Williams 1962, p. 235)

The initial outcome was based on a compromise. Soon, however, the philosophy of the Grand Area got the upper hand as state interventionism was strongly downplayed.

Hence the perceived external threat and the political need to defend and universalise US values came to be complemented by economic need and gave increased motivation for the USA to take up world leadership. These two interlinked factors would continue to set the parameters for US foreign policy for the next fifty years.[20]

The policy was formulated by the Truman administration in its National Security Council policy paper no 68, approved by the National Security Council in April 1950. This was in between the Mao Zedong take-over of power in China and the escalation of the Korean conflict into war.

The document clearly reflects what came to be known as the Truman–Acheson premises of containment, i.e. revolutionary upheaval and conflict were due to external communist pressures and subversion, and communism led by the Soviet Union represented a monolithic force bent on world domination.[21]

The security policy paper underlined the fundamental importance of the international monetary system and the Bretton Woods system in meeting US national security interests. A framework for open trade and liberalised market economies was indeed a prerequisite for containing communism and securing access to strategic raw materials. Such a world order was also needed in order to give US post-World War II surplus production its required outlet, with the previously well-protected British Commonwealth among the most important markets.

Hence, the mounting communist threat finally forced the reluctant US Congress to accept the proposal of President Truman and his Secretary of State General Marshall to an extensive US commitment to facilitate the reconstruction of Europe. In the eyes of American leaders, the Keynesian welfare state of western Europe was accepted as a 'mal nécessaire', not only to contain communism, but also to advance the spread of the Fordist model of development and defend 'Atlanticism'. In exchange for moving towards trade liberalisation and currency convertibility, the European allies got a twelve-year period of grace (1946–58) to adjust their economies to the requirements of the envisaged open economy.

From the beginning US aid was a fairly cheap tool based on the surplus production in the country since World War II, in agricultural and industrial production. The importance of getting access to outlets for this surplus was made explicit by Nelson Rockefeller, at the time Chairman of the US International Development Advisory Board:

> Improved standards of living of the people of the underdeveloped areas is a definite strategic objective of the United States foreign policy. That grievances are constantly being exploited by subversive forces hardly needs exploration. Soviet agents have been particularly diligent in efforts to propagandize and control industrial and rural workers. ... At present (1949) we are producing approximately twenty billions a year more in goods and services than we consume. We have, in other worlds, about twenty billions a year of excess productive capacity to use in the implementation of our foreign policy – whatever we decide that foreign policy should be. (Rockefeller 1951, quoted in Daniels 1951, p. 26)

Gradually, however, US financial constraints increased and so did the domestic political opposition to aid. In fact, for important political forces in Congress '[Uncle Sam] has become the easy prey of foreign and domestic grafters, vampires and gold diggers ... we are now trying to bribe and govern the world. ... Congress is lost in the dismal swamps of foreign intrigue' (Coffin 1964, p. 71). Though President Kennedy transformed the 1953 Mutual Security Act into the Foreign Assistance Act of 1962, increasing its developmental ambitions, strong emphasis still had to be placed on US national strategic interest. Facing acute aid fatigue in Congress, President Kennedy delivered the following appeal to the press in June 1961:

> I therefore urge those who want to do something for the United States, for this cause, to channel their energies behind the new foreign aid program

to help prevent the social injustice and economic chaos upon which subversion and revolt feed; to encourage reform and development, to stabilize new nations and encourage weak governments, train and equip the local forces upon whom the chief burden of resisting local communist subversion rests. (*The New York Times*, 17 June 1961)

Two years later President Kennedy called the aid programme ... 'essential to the conduct of our foreign policy', and said that if Congress denied him the required means of conducting that policy 'they should recognise that they're severely limiting my ability to protect the national interest' (Press conference on 14 November 1963, quoted in Coffin 1964, p. 71).

## Embedded contradictions

Keynes's bargaining power during the Bretton Woods Conference was limited not only by his dependency on the USA for more and favourable credits to enable the United Kingdom to continue fighting World War II (the so-called Lend-Lease Agreement). His room for manoeuvre was further reduced by the recognised reluctance of strong isolationist forces within the US Congress to accept the establishment of the Bretton Woods institutions. These forces feared that the US government would have no control over its contribution to the Fund and that the Fund's resources would be made unconditionally available according to demands from the British. Similarly, strong domestic opposition had to be faced in the United Kingdom before ratification of the agreements would be possible. The Left was concerned about reduced state interventionism and the impact on full employment, whilst the financial interests of the City of London feared lost financial control when UK pound–sterling diplomacy became replaced by US dollar supremacy (Keynes 1944, p. 40).

The fact that the war situation was still critical together with the need for US international leadership explains why the US got the upper hand. Consequently 'the final result of the Conference bore more resemblance to what was acceptable in Washington than to the pre-Bretton Woods visionaries' (Singer 1995, p. 3).

Thus, in order to preserve US national sovereignty and to avoid over-regulating the banking sector, the Bretton Woods institutions had to be stripped of the powers that they were supposed to embody. Thus the original proposal regarding the creation of a World Central Bank, with a capital corresponding to 50 per cent of world annual trade and with an autonomous capacity to provide international liquidity, was reformulated into an International Monetary Fund (IMF). The primary purpose of such a Fund was to promote international trade and open world markets. This was mainly accomplished through the provision of loans to member countries with temporary balance of payment deficits. The requirement for stability and cooperation within the international monetary system was subsequently to be obtained through the member countries' adherence to fixed exchange rates. The IMF's own capital was reduced to roughly 2 per cent of the value of world trade; instead it was to secure future lending from private American bankers. With this the Fund became exposed to conditions from the financial markets that were incompatible with Keynes's original conviction of the need to guarantee governments' ability to pursue expansionist policies internally.

The proposed Bancor was replaced by the dollar as the international reserve currency, with guaranteed convertibility into gold. The proposed Fund for the reconstruction of Europe was transformed into the World Bank, designed in the USA. The financing of European reconstruction was soon taken over by the United States through bilateral lending and through funds provided under the Marshall Plan, while the aim of the World Bank became to provide Third World member countries with concessional finance for more long-term development. This could be done either multilaterally through the World Bank's own credits or bilaterally by individual states. The bilateral financing was to take place only after the policy pursued by the borrowing country had been certified by the Bank. Hence, the World Bank gradually moved into programme lending with attached conditions on required macro-economic performance, something that never had been agreed upon during the Bretton Woods Conference (Singer 1995, p. 7).

The World Bank's articles of agreement contain a direct link between the two institutions: in order for a country to become a member of the Bank, it must be a member of the Fund (US Department of State 1948). This provision reflected two considerations. First, the IMF was not primarily designed as a lending institution. It was set up to promote international monetary cooperation permitting stable exchange rates and thereby facilitating an open world market. While IMF membership entailed primarily obligations (observance of the agreed rules on exchange rates and currency restrictions), for borrowing countries membership of the World Bank involved only the benefit that membership qualified a country for bank loans. Over time the fund developed into a lending institution. However, neither the fund nor the bank are banking institutions in the sense that savings are deposited and lent out. During the last decade, they have been increasingly dependent for their lending on borrowing from the financial markets or contributions from bilateral donors.[22] As its main financier and shareholder, the United States succeeded in obtaining a voting power considered sufficient for desired influence by the US Treasury in both the fund and the bank. Thus, it accepted the Bretton Woods institutions only because they were well equipped to defend US interests and capable of promoting Atlanticism in a liberalised world.[23]

The coinciding interests behind the creation of the institutions were thus not strong enough, and civil society was not sufficiently involved, to avoid latent contradictions being built into the Bretton Woods system as a result of compromise between these different positions within the Atlantic elites.[24] What is important for our understanding of the origins of the present debt crisis and the subsequent implementation of structural adjustment programmes is that the advent of the Cold War exposed these inherent contradictions and that these contradictions subsequently, albeit gradually, diverted the system away from its original intentions. The lack of domestic consensus on US international leadership that had prevailed during the 1940s, despite the strong advocacy of the internationally oriented elite and the military–industrial complex, was effectively solved by the 'perception' of a Cold War threat. Other contradictions were, however, brought into the system with the advent of the Cold War. As the policy to contain communism put an extra financial burden on the shoulders of the United States that had not been foreseen during the negotiations at Bretton Woods, US power came to provide the stability needed for the IMF since it was the dollar (not the 'Bancor' currency that Keynes imagined) which gave the system liquidity. This turned out to be a political price that the Europeans were prepared to pay for implementation of the US policy of containment.[25]

These contradictions, to which we now turn, were interlinked and reinforced each other over time. It took some twenty-five years for the inherent contradictions to mature and make the system obsolete at the beginning of the 1970s.


## The first embedded contradiction: lack of consensus on financing

The most significant embedded contradiction was the need for a strong American leadership, on the one hand, and the lack of internal US political consensus about how to finance the obligations, on the other. In a Gramscian sense, a hegemonic fit prevailed based upon US global legitimacy and European willingness to be led (Gramsci 1971). However, the hegemonic relationship was questioned from the beginning, not with regard to the USA's capacity to lead, but as to their political will to do so.[26] Despite overlapping interests of the internationalised US business community and the national security planners, foreign policy was in fact perceived by Congress as primarily a need expressed by the business community (Clough 1994). Accordingly, notwithstanding a certain popular support, sufficient legitimacy for domestic financing through taxation or private savings was lacking.

Although various efforts were made to achieve the desired international burden-sharing, it seemed too complicated for any politically acceptable solutions to emerge. On the one hand, according to traditional wisdom, a stable international economic order should be a public good. The hegemonic state must therefore prevent other nations from 'free riding'. On the other hand, the problem for the United States was how to find a formula for burden-sharing without having to share power. During the 1970s, the

Japanese were insisting on increasing their quota in the IMF (implying concrete burden-sharing), but the United States vetoed the increase, since such an undertaking would have reduced US control of the fund (Kojo 1992). One way for the Americans to arrange for burden-sharing was through the mobilisation of international aid (and/or through linkages between military aid and development aid).[27] Considerable efforts to make this possible were made during the Kennedy era, but, it was not until the debt crisis at the beginning of the 1980s that methods for the kind of necessary co-financing could be established.

## The second embedded contradiction: undermined confidence in the dollar

Financial constraints made Congress question actions considered necessary by the US administration for containing communism and consolidating US leadership. The Treasury was therefore forced to adopt an expansive monetary and financial policy that gradually diverted the whole Bretton Woods system from its original intention of 'embedded liberalism' (Volcker and Gyohten 1992).[28] This 'bastard Keynesianism' (Turgeon 1996) came to reinforce the second embedded contradiction, namely the so-called Triffin dilemma. Since budget deficits created by the expansive financial policy were never eliminated through an adequate fiscal policy, the danger of undermined confidence in the dollar increased.[29]

Initially, US provision of foreign currency was considered a privilege, increasing the country's comparative advantages (short-term access to international credits without having to pay any interest): what Charles de Gaulle labelled 'privilège exorbitant'. As long as the Europeans and Japanese tolerated the US current account deficit and held on to their accumulated dollar reserves, the US administration had at its disposal an impressive capacity for a political redistribution of world production in favour of the United States. The Europeans and Japanese obviously accepted these terms as long as they considered the system to be benefiting their needs (Volcker and Gyohten 1992).[30]

## The third embedded contradiction: the creation of economic rivals

During the 1960s, the international liquidity supplied by the US remained in Europe and Asia, substantially increasing the competitiveness of these regions, which were then capable of gradually beginning to challenge American economic hegemony. And with this, the third embedded contradiction became a reality. According to its national security interests, embodied in the so-called Cold War Doctrine, the United States had an interest in ensuring rapid economic growth within its allies' economies, especially in West Germany and Japan. At the same time, such a security policy rapidly transformed political partners into economic rivals.

Simultaneously, the US provision of international liquidity, made possible through increased money supply, created an overliquidity that gradually meant a loss of confidence in the gold convertibility of the dollar. Consequently, history proved Triffin right. At the beginning of the 1970s President Nixon had no other choice than to remove unilaterally one of the main pillars upon which the Bretton Woods system had been based, through suspending the convertibility of the dollar into gold and proclaiming floating exchange rates. Thereafter, the world economy gradually shifted away from its earlier focus on the real economy (investment and employment) towards the financial sphere, since the profits earned from speculation on foreign exchange rate fluctuations boomed.

## The fourth embedded contradiction: diminishing hegemonic capacity

These contradictions were in turn strengthened by yet a fourth embedded contradiction: namely, the fact that the free trade and liberalisation striven at, albeit embedded, gradually created a process of internationalisation which reduced the capacity for state interference and for any nation to assume a hegemonic role, since transnational corporations and the financial markets increasingly took on a larger role in the economic decision-making process.

At the same time, the oil crisis of the 1970s efficiently absorbed the dollar's overliquidity internationally. Thus the breakdown of the entire Bretton Woods system could be postponed by allowing the Third World to become indebted through the recycling of 'petrodollars'.

A number of scholars (Chevalier 1973; Karlsson 1986) draw attention to the fact that the oil price increase in 1973 coincided with two of the US national security interests. From the perspective of US national security there was a need to absorb the dollar 'overhang'. Even more important was, however, the need to reestablish US competitiveness vis-à-vis its new economic rivals and more oil-dependent Japan and West Germany.[31]

However, the problem with dollar overliquidity was only solved temporarily. The recession that the oil crisis brought about reduced economic growth and undermined not only the legitimacy of the state as a consequence of its lost economic opportunities for redistribution, but most importantly the economic foundation and political configuration (historic bloc) that was behind the welfare state. This reinforced the influence of neo-liberal thinking, which reduced the legitimacy of the state even further and subsequently also the hegemonic capacity of the United States itself.

## Intertwined paradoxes

The measures taken to counteract the negative effects from these inherent contradictions led to various non-intended outcomes and paradoxes that over time reinforced the original contradictions rather than resolving them.

One paradox is constituted by the fact that the Bretton Woods system has revitalised the (laissez-faire) ideology of a self-regulating market. This stands in stark contrast to the original Keynesian ideology upon which the system was based, namely, embedded liberalism.

A second paradox results from the fact that the neo-liberal ideology imposed by the Reagan administration as a reaction against previous monetary policies, threatened to reduce US hegemonic power instead of reinforcing it. The neo-liberal ideology was put into practice at a time when the United States started losing its commercial leadership and its ability to fully benefit from the liberalisation in world trade.[32]

Hence, the US reliance on Keynesian prescriptions was considered responsible for the worldwide inflationary conditions that paved the way for the neo-liberal era, at the same time as the continuing US trade deficit made the expansion of the world economy possible in the late 1980s, and Europe and Japan, as suppliers, benefited from the US role as the single largest international consumer with a trillion-dollar credit line.[33]

When Ronald Reagan became president in the beginning of the 1980s, the need for a restrictive monetary policy and severe budget cuts had become unavoidable. According to Paul Volcker, US citizens were consuming far more than permitted by their production, hence 'the standard of the average American has to decline' (Volcker, interview in New York Times, 18 October 1979).

However, from the beginning, the Reagan administration understood the difficulties of trying to convince some of its allies to adopt restrictive monetary policies. In France, for instance, President Mitter and had come to power and was anxious to demonstrate the relevance of a more Keynesian monetary approach. With weak states and divergent political opinions prevailing, it was tempting to let the need for a more restrictive monetary policy be brought about by a deregulated market. This implied a third paradox, since a deregulated financial market at the international level increased monetary supply through the infinite credit multiplier on the Eurodollar market, voiding the results of the restrictive monetary policy at national level. The French government's understanding of this issue explains its initial attempts to use a more Keynesian financial policy.

The fourth paradox is constituted by the fact that the hegemonic financial burden of the USA and its subsequent monetary policy reduced its economic strength and at the same time increased its economic structural power. As outlined in the presidential national security directive, the USA need for multilateral burden-sharing for its international leadership increased over time:

> Given the loss of US strategic superiority and the overwhelming growth of Soviet conventional forces capabilities, together with the increased political and economic strength of the industrial democracies and the heightened importance of Third World resources, the United States must increasingly draw upon the resources and cooperation of allies and others to protect our interests and those of our friends. There is no other alternative. (NSDD 32, 1982/05/20)

However, simultaneously, the monetary policy applied had made it possible for the United States to use the international financial institutions as its foreign policy tool, especially vis-à-vis areas in the Third World of less strategic importance. The reason behind such possibilities was the fact that the institutions, controlled by the USA, had increased their influence far beyond what had been anticipated at the Bretton Woods Conference. Through the recycling of petrodollars via the Eurodollar market, overliquidity had resulted in the debt burden. In order to get access to international credits, the debtor countries had to follow the economic remedies ordained by the IMF and the World Bank.

As a consequence the US Treasury, as the main shareholder in the institutions and provider of the economic securities that the financial markets required, was able to strengthen its worldwide influence considerably during the 1980s. A 'Washington Consensus' between the institutions and the US administration emerged on required measures to be taken by the indebted Third World countries (Williamson 1989). The declining trend of US hegemonic capacity, stemming from reduced direct (in the sense of bilateral) political and economic power, was thus counteracted by the increased possibility of using structural (in the sense of multilateral and institutional) power.[34]

This success enabled the United States to achieve the required financial burden-sharing arrangement for maintaining Pax Americana without needing to indulge in any form of power-sharing.

## The increase of structural power

For an adequate understanding of the underlying mechanisms for US exercise of structural power over the Third World, we must recall how the conceptualisation of development and financial development assistance gradually changed during the 1970s.

When the United Nations initiated the first 'Development Decade' some thirty years ago, it was based on the view that international political and economic stability required a transfer of resources to the less developed world in order to promote its economic development. Having reconstructed Europe, the time was considered ripe to begin building the fourth pillar of Bretton

Woods, namely the decolonisation and development of the Third World countries, facilitated by a comprehensive aid programme.

The predominant development thinking at the time, in the West as well as in the East, was characterised by the supposed blessings of modernisation. Through the intervention of a strong and benevolent state, Third World countries were to catch up with the industrialised world. The African national and political elites, taking over the reins of state power, all maintained that Europe was the model to follow with regard to language, culture and state formation. The process of nation-state creation in a Westphalian sense was initiated, albeit based on the artificial boundaries established during the colonial era.[35]

During the 1970s, the tensions of bipolarity increased. During the Brezhnev era, the East expanded its support to the so-called 'socialist oriented' countries. In retrospect, the geopolitical map of the 1970s illustrates that the capacity of the African countries to exploit this new reality reinforced the power of the elites. Many developed into authoritarian growth-oriented regimes, whilst others concentrated only on self-aggrandisement. As products of the colonial legacy, the administrative capacity and statesmanship of these countries were too limited, the market forces too underdeveloped and civil society too embryonic for more development-oriented regimes to emerge.

Drastically increased oil prices and deteriorating terms of trade, together with low international interest rates following the need to 'recycle the petrodollars', contributed to introducing the ambiguous wish for 'indebted industrialisation'. Expecting a massive transfer of resources, the African continent entered the next development decade with its debt burden growing much faster than its economic productivity.

Gradually, the oil crisis together with the increasing debt burden changed the destination of commercial bank lending, from investment capital for private corporations to balance of payments financing of foreign governments. Official efforts came to focus on enabling the banks to continue lending for balance of payment purposes, but with greater assurance that they would be repaid. Through closer cooperation between the private banks and the Bretton Woods institutions, pressure was supposed to be brought to bear on deficit/debtor countries to bring their external accounts into balance through domestic austerity measures to reduce domestic consumption and the demand for imports. Greater emphasis should be put on the growth of export to help bring trade accounts into balance, and to ensure that the country would earn enough foreign exchange to service its foreign debt.[36]

A reorientation of aid simultaneously became an additional prerequisite for the private banks to recover their loans and, hence, to maintain stability within the international financial system. The World Bank introduced the concept 'structural adjustment lending' and made intensive efforts to obtain finance from the donor community and their shareholders. However, the more multilaterally oriented Carter administration never succeeded in selling the concept to a sceptical Congress, and several other donors showed strong reluctance to subordinate part of their bilateral development assistance to the World Bank ideology.

The Reagan administration came to power at a time when Western-ised development thinking was moving in a more neo-liberal direction, although the axiom of modernisation remained. As accounted for, the military expansionism of the Johnson/Nixon administration, with subsequent international inflation, created an ideological ground for neo-liberalism, which was primarily manifested by the international financial markets upon which the Bretton Woods institutions were heavily dependent for their borrowing. As a consequence, the neo-liberal conceptualisation in the Bank and the Fund was already gaining strength when President Reagan took office. This reorientation was clearly manifested in the well-known World Bank report, *Accelerated Development in Sub-Saharan Africa: An Agenda for Action*, which was published in 1981. The role of the state as an agent for development was called into question, and was now rather perceived as the main obstacle to development.

In Cancun, Mexico, the same year, demands from the 1970s for a New International Economic Order and a massive transfer of resources were removed from the political agenda, as were the other proposals put forward by the Brandt Commission. Instead, the market was considered to be the only force capable of stimulating economic development, provided that the political space in which to operate existed. In her memoirs, Margaret Thatcher explained her concern and stated that 'The intractable problems of Third World poverty, hunger and debt would not be solved by misdirected international intervention, but rather by liberating enterprise, promoting trade – and defeating socialism in all its forms' (Thatcher 1993, p. 170). Most important for the United States was that it should, together with its European allies, succeed in stopping efforts of several member states during the summit meeting to subordinate the Bretton Woods institutions to the United Nations. Such subordination would obviously have reduced US influence over them drastically.[37]

In fact, the World Bank report mentioned above reflected not only a neo-liberal conceptualisation of developmental efforts, but also a necessity felt by the Bank to recuperate the lost legitimacy of aid, otherwise known as 'aid fatigue'. The report, which sought to reinforce the future role of the Bank (Gibbon 1993), should be viewed as a reply to the severe criticism made by the more conservative political forces emerging at the time in Europe as well as in the United States of multilateral aid, in general, and the state-oriented project-lending activities of the World Bank in particular.

Hence, the first half of the 1980s constituted a time when there was a strong need for the World Bank to improve its reputation for economic performance on the international financial markets, in order to counteract the demands put forward by important conservative lobby groups in the United States to reduce the US financial contribution to the institution drastically. Presumably this situation created a strong awareness within the World Bank as to the importance of satisfying as many of its most important owner's political needs as possible.

The Reagan administration took office highly sceptical of the World Bank and other multilateral institutions. It promised dramatic changes in US foreign policy, including a return to bilateral assistance programmes, as such programmes were believed to be more accountable to the American taxpayer and more consistent with US foreign policy interest. However, the intensive cooperation between the Reagan administration and the Bretton Woods institutions that followed does not imply that the neo-liberals within the Reagan administration succeeded in coopting the administration within the Bretton Woods institutions, or the other way around. In fact, it was the Reagan administration that became coopted by the need of the *commercial* US banks to be 'bailed out' from their outstanding claims against indebted Third World countries through increased structural adjustment lending by the Bretton Woods institutions, financed through aid money.[38]

Prevailing domestic financial constraints, hindering the strengthening of US leadership to combat the perceived hostility and expansion of Brezhnev in the Third World (Brzezinski 1983), made it furthermore easier to persuade the Reagan administration of the cost effectiveness of continuing financial support to the Bretton Woods institutions, provided that the administration could use them as important tools for its foreign policy implementation.[39] These emerging coinciding interests between on the one hand, US economic and political elite and between these elites and the management of the Bretton Woods institutions, on the other, were skilfully used by the Reagan administration.[40] Accordingly, the Reagan administration did what the Carter administration failed to do, namely identify strategic programme objectives for US participation in the Bank and convince the US Congress of the benefits of supporting the institutions (Gwin 1994, p. 62). The debt crisis and the need to rescue the international monetary system undoubtedly helped to change the attitude of the Congress:[41]

> Our industries depend on the importation of energy and minerals from distant lands. Our prosperity requires a sound international financial system and free and open trading markets. ... The International Monetary Fund (IMF) is a linchpin in our efforts to restore a sound world economy and resolve the debt problems of many developing countries. With bipartisan support, we implemented a major increase in IMF resources. In cooperation with the IMF, we're working to prevent the problems of individual debtor nations from disrupting the stability and strength of the

> entire international financial system. (President Reagan, printed in US
> Department of State 1984, pp. 11–14)

Simultaneously, as a consequence of the need to improve aid performance in the recipient countries and the (even more important) need to recreate international financial stability, the influence of the World Bank and the IMF over the donor community and the recipient countries increased considerably.

The impressive capacity of neo-liberal philosophy to influence the decision-making process, not least on the African continent, was supported by globalisation at the international level.[42] The internationalisation of finance, production, trade, consumption and communications drastically reduced the room for states to manoeuvre. Simultaneously, the continent's debt burden became unsustainable as a consequence of increased international interest rates and the value of the dollar at the beginning of the 1980s, following the introduction of a more restrictive monetary policy in the United States. The design and implementation of neo-liberal oriented economic reforms was a prerequisite for obtaining future credit from the Bretton Woods system and grants from the donor community. Unlike the reconstruction of Europe, no one saw any reason to pay a political price for a stable and socially acceptable development process in Africa.[43] Hence, the *conditions* of the international private banking sector regarding economic policy had to be applied if any future international credits were to be obtained.

Such requirements were a logical consequence of the US political effort during the Bretton Woods Conference to replace official financing of the institutions by their shareholders, according to Keynes' original idea, with increased commercial borrowing on the US capital markets. In order to satisfy the requirements of the commercial financial markets the World Bank lent out money on the condition that the recipient countries undertook long-term adjustment measures aimed at reinstating macro-economic balance.

Thus, the Bank's lending practices succeeded in developing new activities as important complements to the IMF's more short-term policy-based lending related to stabilisation, which concentrated on eliminating budget deficits and overvalued exchange rates. The bank thus improved its position considerably vis-à-vis other donors. There was of course no point in the Bretton Woods institutions setting macro-economic conditions for lending which could be violated by others. Hence, the need for donor coordination increased, as did the number of joint consultative meetings established under the command of the World Bank and IMF.

These circumstances undoubtedly made it easier for the United States to use the Bretton Woods institutions as tools of its foreign policy and thereby to satisfy its imperative need for burden-sharing.[44]

The fact that the United States used the Bretton Woods institutions as a foreign policy tool is not a very sensitive or controversial issue in the USA. Presenting the US administration's request for the multilateral development banks for fiscal year 1996 to Congress, the Treasury Secretary underlined the importance of the support by referring to 'Cost-Effective Internationalism … supporting Foreign Policy and National Security'. He drew the attention of the Congress to the important fact that the institutions could 'draw in contributions from other countries … four dollars for each dollar we contribute'. If we do this, the Secretary continued, 'We are able to multiply scarce budgetary resources and remain engaged internationally … pursuing our objectives and acting effectively in our own national interest.'[45]

This influence is a consequence of US structural power. As discussed above, the Keynesian multilateral spirit, under which the institutions were originally created, was soon to be replaced by more geopolitical US perspectives due to the emergence of the Cold War tensions. The United States is not only the most important shareholder but its financial markets provided, until the end of the 1970s, the most important lending source for the Bretton Woods institutions. The US exercises its structural power by appointing the president of the World Bank and can, through the localisation of the institutions in Washington, exercise quite an impressive, albeit very subtle, influence over the upper-level management (Mason and Asher 1973; Gwin 1994; George and Sabelli 1994).

For various reasons US influence on the Bretton Woods institutions came under increased stress during the second part of the 1980s.[46] This pushed the Reagan administration to seek reinforcement, not only by building a working relationship between the Treasury and the other G7 countries or with executives on the IMF and World Bank board of directors in Washington, but also by creating stronger alliances with recipient countries when they wanted to reward the country's leadership for doing the right thing, notwithstanding continued economic difficulties or neglect of human rights.[47] Through such achievement, permitting continued multilateral burden-sharing, the United States became more able to implement its foreign policies for the consolidation of Pax Americana in areas of less strategic interest as regards its own national security.

The speech delivered by Chester Crocker (at the time Assistant Secretary of State for African Affairs) in Honolulu before the National Security Committee of the American Legion, August 1981, reflects the thinking within the Reagan administration as regards US aid for Africa, and deserves to be quoted at length:

> We support open market opportunities, access to key resources and expanding African and American economies. … We are concerned about the influence of the Soviet Union and its surrogates in Africa … The United States cannot be the financial 'angel' for Africa any more than we intend to

be Africa's policeman. But we have no intention of allowing this economic threat, any more than the threat of terrorism or subversion, to undermine basic American interest in Africa. This administration aims to meet this threat by emphasizing our strength – specifically by helping bring the poorer African nations more into the mainstream of the free market economy which is the soundest and surest way to growth. ... Our bilateral assistance program will be an indispensable element in Africa during this period. Under the Reagan administration, our bilateral aid will be targeted on areas where our interests are most clearly manifest and focused more to produce policy changes of broad and lasting impact. ... Multilateral assistance agencies, such as the World Bank, provide the bulk of the assistance resources to Africa, far more than we can or need to provide bilaterally. This Administration will play a strong role in these institutions, pushing for combining this aid with the kind of basic structural and policy changes that are essential if Africa is not to reel from one economic crisis to another. We believe that, if helped through this crisis period with the right mix of aid, policy reform, and a strongly reinvigorated role for the private sector, African peoples will opt for growth and the freedom – the personal, economic, and political freedom – that is inherent in the free world's international economic system. (Crocker 1981/08/29 (NSA 01315))

The exercise of US structural power created another set of paradoxes related to the fact that the institutions of Bretton Woods could not be equipped with the power they needed to fulfil their mandates until some 35 years after their creation. Paradoxically, this power originated from the fact that the main pillar (fixed exchange rate) upon which the system originally relied had crumbled, following the expansive US monetary policies of the 1960s and a unilateral abandonment of the gold convertibility of the dollar. The financial crisis during the 1970s (overliquidity, oil crisis and debt burden) ironically did not imply the breakdown of the Bretton Woods system as such, as literature frequently claims, even though the fixed exchange rate was abandoned. However, difficulties in finding adequate roles in a deregulated international financial market, where the limited scope for intervention was occupied by the G7 themselves, together with the threat initially implied by the debt burden of the Third World, made the institutions more concerned with macro-economic stability in the developing countries. Consequently, the export-oriented policies subsequently imposed by the Bretton Woods institutions, aimed at repaying debts and reestablishing macro-economic balance, instead facilitated the achievement of the general goal of the Bretton Woods, namely to create conditions for an open world economy, based on Western values and ideology.

Thus, this study argues that the Bretton Woods system was based upon embedded liberalism and a restricted sphere of influence for its financial institutions, respecting the full sovereignty of its member states. Over time, the system put into motion forces that eroded the system at the same time, and for the same reason, as the sphere of influence of its financial institutions increased considerably. The combination of these factors effectively reduced the sovereignty of some of its member states.

A further paradox is, however, that this process was supported by member countries and political leaderships that had traditionally advocated a strong Keynesian ideology and the sovereignty of small states, and that had opposed the dictated requirements of supranational hegemonic powers outside the United Nations system (e.g. Sweden).[48]

My reading of this situation is that the historic bloc of political alliances, in Sweden for example (forming the well-known 'Swedish model'), was a major beneficiary of the process of internationalisation, at least temporarily, thanks to the comparative advantages of the Swedish export industry. However, the political leadership was eventually forced to sacrifice part of its national sovereignty due to forces outside its control. The only option available was partial subordination to the efforts of supranational institutions to control the increasingly globalised and invisible financial markets. The abolition of the fixed exchange rates in the early 1970s, together with the recycling of the petrodollar via the Eurodollar market, enabled a financial explosion, which no nation-state could possibly control. Decision-makers' ability to address issues in the real economy to resolve the persistent problems of investment or employment was completely undermined by the rapid increase of the global economy of speculation, where access to international credits was far more important for economic performance than were domestic savings.[49] The need for continued access to international credits accordingly gave the Bretton Woods institutions considerable influence over individual nations' economic and political decision-making processes. They have therefore become the most successful instrument to date in homogenising economic policy among nations, and hence comprise the low-cost foreign policy tools that the United States needed for consolidating its world leadership.

## To sum up

The coinciding interests within the Atlantic internationally oriented elite succeeded in creating an unprecedented framework for post-World War II international economic relations during the Bretton Woods Conference in 1944. The coinciding interests were sufficiently strong to embed diverging interests into the agreed articles. Between the conception and implementation of the Bretton Woods system, the Cold War became a reality. The inherent contradictions of the system became strengthened by the superpower rivalry and the subsequent perceived need of protection by Pax Americana. Thus the system became gradually diverted from its original 'one world' intentions. The decline of US relational power was, over time, counteracted by increased structural power. The Bretton Woods institutions became the low-cost tools of US foreign policy at a time when the institutions' influence over the development efforts in the Third World increased considerably.

# 3
# Pax Americana and Southern Africa: Coinciding Interests and Change

Chapter 2 argued that the long-term US interest in diffusing Western values and belief systems was aimed at the consolidation of its international leadership. After World War II, these long-term interests most frequently corresponded to US short-term security interest in the Cold War-based 'policy of containment'. At times the short- and long-term interests diverge to the extent that clear contradictions between the two appear. Measures taken in order to deal with such contradictions simultaneously increase the room for manoeuvre for structural change.

The aim of this chapter is to analytically answer two questions: How did the contradictions embedded in the Bretton Woods system influence US foreign policy towards southern Africa, and what were the implications for future development in the region?

## Hegemony and decolonisation

During the 1950s Africa was never an area of interest for the US policy of containment. The African anti-colonial struggle of the time was not perceived as a threat in Washington as long as it did not endanger the continent's contribution to political stability and economic development in Europe (NSC 68, 1950/04/14).[1] This role of Africa in the world economy was reconfirmed by the White House at the end of the decade. By then, however, the National Security Directives drew attention to possible future threats to US national security interests from increased communist or Islamic influence on the continent (NSC 5818, 1958/08/26).[2]

The maintenance of ties between Africa and Europe was facilitated by the fact that Europe was not forced to decolonise Africa before an African elite had been created, speaking European languages and sharing European thoughts and values. Consequently, at the time of political independence, the challenge for the new African leadership consisted in catching up with Europe as fast as possible through establishing a nation-state capable of pursuing an accelerated process of modernisation.

These African leadership ambitions were strongly supported by the USA, since the spread of the Western development paradigm became both an important tool for and the main aim of the policy of containment (Brzezinski 1963).[3] Accordingly, as far as southern Africa was concerned, US policy was initially focused on its relationship with the white minority regime in Pretoria, considered to be the natural social bearer of these values.[4] Possible anti-apartheid concern was downplayed as long as Pretoria contributed to the consolidation of Pax Americana by sharing its burden of being a bulwark against communism and delivering essential raw materials punctually, not least the uranium oxide required for its nuclear development.[5]

During the 1960s, the strategic importance to the USA of Africa south of Sahara gradually changed. The Congo crisis was interpreted in Washington as being a result of increased Soviet influence.[6] In the long run, such influence could threaten strategic raw material supplies and the security of the transport routes linking the USA with the Middle East.[7] Thus, with the aim of increasing US involvement in Africa, the Kennedy administration introduced the East–West dimension. A memorandum signed by Kennedy in March 1962 advocated that

> What we do or fail to do in Africa in the next year or two will have a profound effect for many years. We see Africa as probably the greatest open field of manoeuvre in the worldwide competition between the communist bloc and the non-communist world. (President Kennedy, March 1962, quoted from Schraeder 1994, p. 15)

As a consequence, US cooperation with the white minority regime in Pretoria became strengthened in various sectors. The USA provided nuclear technology for the civil sector and arms in exchange for facilities capable of tracking Soviet missiles (Mokoena 1993, p. xxi). The strengthened cooperation had profound implications for future development in the region. South Africa not only developed an impressive military industrial complex (Armscor) capable of producing nuclear weaponry (Crocker 1981b), but reinforced intelligence cooperation gave the South African security agencies access to the impressive Western networks.[8] Through the network Western policies towards the region became heavily influenced by Pretoria.

Increased social unrest in South Africa made Secretary of State Henry Kissinger initiate a review of US policy towards the region at the end of the 1960s. The review called for

> broader association with both black and white states in an effort to encourage moderation in the white states, to enlist cooperation of the black states in reducing tensions and the likelihood of increasing cross-border violence, and to encourage improved relations among states in area (Option 2). (NSSM 39, 1969/12/09, p. 14)

The directives turned out to be one of the first political signals of something the White House had gradually come to understand, namely that in the long run the apartheid system was not compatible with US national strategic interest, though the means and time schedule needed to abolish it were still to be matters of much debate. According to the directives:

> the racial problems of southern Africa probably will grow more acute over time, perhaps leading to violent internal upheavals and greater involvement of the communist powers. Though these developments may be years or even decades ahead, US policy should take account now of the risks to our interests and possible involvement over this uncertain future. (NSSM 39, 1969/12/09, p. 4)

Most international analysts misunderstood the 'policy of communication' and overlooked this view. They heavily criticised Kissinger's statement that 'the whites are here to stay and the only way that constructive change can come about is through them' (NSSM 39, 1969/12/09, p. 19), and understood it as only a signal of reinforced US relations with the white minority regime in Pretoria (Martin and Johnson 1981; Minter 1986; Ohlsson and Stedman 1994).

In the mid-1970s US security concern with regard to southern Africa increased with the unprecedented withdrawal of the last colonial power on the continent, Portugal. According to the conceptualisation of the president at the time:

> In 1975, four centuries of Portuguese colonial rule ended in Angola and Mozambique. Now instead of colonial ties to Portugal, both countries have 'friendship treaties' with Russia; they bristle with modern weapons and threaten the whole of what Brezhnev so covetously referred to as the 'mineral treasure house of central and southern Africa'. Together they border on every key country in that 'treasure house'. Just as the Soviets had their eyes on the oil of Arabia when they moved into Somalia and then Ethiopia, they had their eyes on these mineral resources when they moved into Angola and Mozambique. (Nixon 1980, p. 28)

Portugal's sudden withdrawal provoked severe internal rivalry in Angola, supported by various external interests. Through covert action by the CIA and strong support for UNITA, the Ford administration tried to prevent the MPLA from taking power (Stockwell 1978). As a consequence, before the day of independence the MPLA, assisted by Cuban troops, had to combat a South African Defence Force invasion of Angolan territory. Simultaneously, increased social unrest in South Africa culminated in the shooting down of several hundred students in Soweto. As a consequence, Kissinger became even more concerned about the danger of increased Soviet influence than he had been when launching his policy of communication some years before. He now acknowledged the urgent need for majority rule in Rhodesia, the independence of

Namibia and the abolition of apartheid according to an agreed timetable to be drawn up by concerned parties. Consensus had finally been reached in Washington that apartheid was obsolete (NSA 00577, 1976/04/27). Action needed to be taken promptly in order to not endanger Western strategic interests. The following Carter administration immediately tried to adopt a new focus in its policies towards the government of South Africa (NSC-5, 1977/03/09).

## The Rhodesian issue

The coup d'état in Portugal in April 1974 gave immediate impetus to developments in southern Africa and simultaneously increased the region's exposure to international interests. The Angolan experience made Kissinger aware of the danger of a radicalisation of the liberation movements in Rhodesia. Immediate steps were taken to coopt the political programme launched by some black leaders advocating moderate evolutionary reform in the country, as the more conservative Smith regime had become counterproductive for Western security interests in the region.

Consequently, in his Lusaka speech in April 1976, Kissinger promised to support the establishment of a future majority-ruled Zimbabwe as well as US development assistance to its neighbour Mozambique (Martin and Johnson 1981, p. 234).[9] Together with the British, the USA drew up a proposal for settling the Rhodesian conflict, entitled 'Rhodesia–proposal for a settlement' (Martin and Johnson 1981, p. 268).

The British very much shared Kissinger's concern. Since Ian Smith's unilateral declaration of independence in the mid-1960s, Rhodesia had been a pariah, not only for many of the black African states but above all for Britain itself.[10] However, the British had to work hard to navigate successfully between their own short-term national interest of secure access to essential raw material supplies on the one hand and anti-racist obligations stemming from the more long-term interest of keeping the Commonwealth together under British leadership on the other.[11] British concern was additionally rooted in the fact that a radicalisation of the conflict with increased violence could provoke a rapid increase in migration to Europe and the UK. More than 1 million people entitled to British citizenship were living in the region, not to mention more than 600,000 of Portuguese origin living in South Africa. The recent experience in Angola and Mozambique offered a precedent in this regard that the British wanted to avoid (Howe 1994, p. 479).[12]

## Total strategy and SADCC

The policy of the Vorster regime during the 1960s and 1970s was aimed at consolidating the apartheid system in South Africa by pursuing regional détente and economic cooperation with Black Africa, through which it might increase its international legitimacy and reinforce South African leadership on the continent (Hanlon 1986).

In this sense, the Vorster regime's foreign policy was more 'enlightened' than its domestic policy. Provided that guarantees could be obtained that no insurgent activities against South Africa were to be carried out from a majority-ruled Rhodesia, Vorster was willing to support the Kissinger plan for majority rule in Rhodesia, in exchange for a US veto on UN sanctions against his own country (Martin and Johnson 1981).

Vorster's policy of détente was soon replaced by Botha's 'total strategy' facing what he perceived as a communist plot (a 'total onslaught') organised beyond its borders with the aim of overthrowing white rule in South Africa (Hanlon 1986).[13]

The emerging coinciding interests between the black leadership in southern Africa and the main components of political leadership in the West manifested themselves through the establishment of the SADCC, a framework for regional cooperation aiming, among other things, to reduce the dependency of the Front Line states on South Africa.[14]

The creation of the SADCC could have played an important role in establishing alternative transport routes and decreasing dependency on South Africa. However, the main outcome of its creation was that the struggle against the apartheid regime became localised regionally, instead of being conducted mainly by Western anti-apartheid movements.[15] The SADCC did not achieve its objective of reducing dependency on South Africa (Abrahamsson 1989).[16] Pretoria's effort to increase its Sub-Saharan leadership role through a Constellation of States was perceived to be overtaken by efforts to isolate South Africa from the continent, which would immediately increase South Africa's vulnerability to possible international sanctions.[17] Consequently, the intensive economic and military destabilisation of Mozambique was begun. By destroying all alternative transport routing in the region, the Western countries would become totally dependent on the South African infrastructure for their trade with the land-locked Front Line states.

## East–West rivalry in southern Africa

> South Africa may, and I believe will, become as great a threat to the peace of the world in the 1990s as the Middle East is today … conflict there will fragment world opinion, and it is entirely possible – if not probable – that much of southern Africa will fall within the Soviet sphere of influence. (Robert S. McNamara, former President of the World Bank, 21 October 1982)

When the Reagan administration took office in Washington, the conflict in southern Africa was also perceived, at least in rhetorical terms, as having escalated into an East–West conflict. The CIA involvement in Angola in the mid-1970s contributed to this. However, the US involvement is not the only, and perhaps not even the most important factor, in bringing superpower rivalry to the continent.

Of equal importance, as regards Mozambique, was the perceived direct threat to the country's national security constituted by the white minority regime in South Africa at the time of independence in 1975. The developments in Angola, and the subsequent South African invasion and occupation of Angolan territory in the mid-1970s, reduced the credibility of the agreed *modus vivendi* entered into with Pretoria from the Frelimo government's point of view.

Accordingly, with strong support from the Non-Aligned Movement, the Mozambican government tried to increase cooperation with the Soviet Union. The Friendship Treaty signed with Moscow in 1977, following the third Congress of Frelimo, implied that the parties agreed to military cooperation in the case of external aggression. Little is known as yet about the Soviet Union's underlying commitment, and its reason for demanding that the Frelimo liberation movement restructure itself into a vanguard party. Anecdotal evidence points to a need to persuade a reluctant civilian component in the Central Committee in Moscow that Mozambique belonged to the new socialist-oriented countries and therefore deserved support. To the military members of the Central Committee, trained Mozambican troops could mean a contribution to the Soviet Union's global geopolitical strategy.[18] The civilian wing in the Central Committee had the upper hand, and a request from Maputo for increased military support in order to face South African destabilisation was turned down, as was the request for CMEA membership.[19]

There were different opinions in Washington at the time as regards the strength of the Soviet threat. Most political decision-makers in concerned executive agencies agreed with the Western textbooks (Cassen 1985; Kanet 1982; Rubenstein 1989) that the Soviet Union had a minimal interest in the southern Africa region and that Moscow's involvement in the mid-1970s seemed more to be taking advantage of *de facto* circumstances than based upon a coherent strategy.[20]

Few believed that Moscow would challenge US security interests in the region openly. However, as observed by Chester A. Crocker, Assistant Secretary of State for African Affairs during the first and second Reagan administrations, different signals were received from Maputo:

> We may never know whether in early 1983 Machel had already written off Moscow as irrelevant to, or even the cause of, Mozambique's mounting problems. He may, on the contrary, have hoped that his early initiatives with us and with the South Africans would trigger Soviet competitive reflexes and more staunch support. (Crocker 1992, p. 240)

This hesitancy was supported by analysis provided by the US Central Intelligence Agency, which claimed that too little Western support and increased insurgency could force Mozambique to return to the East for military assistance and possibly invite the Cubans (NSA 01797, 1985/04/19). Such statements were made by President Samora Machel from time to time in the presence of the diplomatic corps.

The Reagan administration therefore never downplayed the communist threat. In his National Security Decision Directives of 20 May 1982, President Reagan returned to the language of the NSC 68 from the Truman era. Two of the main goals for US foreign policy were to

> contain and reverse the expansion of Soviet control and military presence throughout the world … and to ensure the US and its allies and friends access to foreign energy and mineral sources. (NSDD 32 1982/05/20 pp. 1–2)

Over time, coinciding interests in reinforced cooperation between Mozambique and the USA improved diplomatic relations between the countries. The Mozambican need for new credits and food assistance became acute, with the worst drought in decades badly hurting the southern part of the country. The message from the leading Western governments became clear during Samora Machel's European tour in autumn 1983: private investment was to be channelled through branch offices in South Africa, bilateral aid required agreement with the Bretton Woods institutions; and increased multilateral food relief depended on acceptance from the USA. In practice, there was no third way available, despite the Socialist International's earlier initiative to create such a road. Simultaneously, US national security interests in the region and the need to challenge the Cuban presence in Angola motivated the USA to redefine its policy towards Mozambique.

Hence, when Samora Machel finally turned to the West for support in 1983, Washington gave its approval, albeit after severe initial doubts and infighting between different interests. In exchange for increased international aid, credits and diplomatic support, Mozambique accepted the US proposal for an agreement with South Africa where both parties pledged not to support actions against the other country from within their territory. The subsequent Nkomati agreement was signed in spring 1984.[21] The US policy goal of befriending Mozambique and motivating the Frelimo leadership to downplay its relations with Moscow was achieved.

## 'Constructive Engagement'

> The rhetoric and style of the new administration suggested a violent swing of the foreign policy pendulum. But it was my goal to build upon – not scrap – the legacy of American policy going back to the 1970s. (Crocker 1992, p. 453)

Few foreign policies have been more criticised and debated all over the world than 'Constructive Engagement' – the US foreign policy towards southern Africa during the Reagan administration.[22] Crocker undoubtedly analysed the southern African conflict in an East–West perspective (Bisell and Crocker 1979; Crocker 1992), and in that sense he lined up behind the Reagan Cold War diplomacy.[23] However, in line with the former Carter administration, over time Crocker increasingly advocated the need to let the Africans find solutions to African problems and to combat the communist threat through increased support for economic progress and social reforms.[24]

In fact, the policy of 'Constructive Engagement' should be conceived as a continuation of 'the policy of communication' elaborated during the Nixon/Kissinger era. Crocker conceived the abolition of apartheid as an historic necessity due to inherent contradictions in the system making it incapable of dealing with the political, social or economic consequences it created. Hence, based on his understanding of US strategic interest in the region, Crocker strongly advocated an 'evolutionary change' towards a non-racial system (Crocker 1981a, p. 324). As regards the question of how a desired change could come about, Crocker ruled out the likelihood of any black revolutionary assault on white power: 'the balance of power remains overwhelmingly in favour of the whites … and although the attitudinal ingredients of a potential revolution may be present, the physical ones are not' (Crocker 1981a, pp. 343–5). Instead he underlined the importance of the kind of 'war of position' that part of the Afrikaner nationalist elite had initiated, and insisted that significant social forces inside South Africa were available that could make the desired transformation of the system possible. According to Crocker, if change was to occur, the Nationalist Party (NP) and the state apparatus itself must be used as instruments. Such a process was already in motion: 'For the past two years South Africa's "new nationalists" have been preoccupied with the task of building coalitions and power bases within the party and government machinery' (Crocker 1981a).

As regards South Africa, according to Crocker the main challenge was to get broader sectors of the Afrikaner constituency involved in a constructive dialogue with the black majority. However, strong internal resistance from the extreme right could be expected. Crocker thus asserted that the desired evolution was unlikely to occur all by itself, but that the USA could contribute to keeping the process in motion through pressure and other means.

First of all, the USA could contribute to providing space and time for change. The government in Pretoria should not be pushed beyond its possibilities. Enough time was required to prevent the right wing being tempted to stop the ongoing reform process. According to Crocker, any external pressure would have to be cautious, bearing in mind South Africa's possession of nuclear weaponry as the last resort for defence.[25] Secondly, the USA could contribute through ways of increasing the awareness of the regional security complex. Crocker agreed with Samora Machel that any conflict settlement must encompass the whole region, notwithstanding the need to use differing tools (Crocker 1992, p. 238). The Cuban presence in Angola, Namibian independence and the process of abolishing apartheid in South Africa were accordingly interlinked issues that could not be treated separately, as clearly demonstrated by the failures so far. Furthermore, they all depended on influencing developments in the other Front Line states, particularly in Zimbabwe and Mozambique. Thirdly, the USA could actively contribute to changing the regional governments' perception of external threats by providing various kinds of support that could create motivation for change. Anti-apartheid movements needed to be persuaded to play down violent actions, and the white minority needed to be made aware that the alternative to apartheid was not necessarily communism. With its support, a capitalist market economy could get the upper hand.

Crocker was well aware of the financing needed to achieve an evolutionary change of the apartheid system and thus the conditions for peace and development in the region. Simultaneous requirements for a more restrictive monetary policy in Washington decreased US financial capacity, and therefore increased the need for multilateral sharing of the burden of implementing its foreign policy towards southern Africa. Accordingly, it became important for the USA to facilitate the access of both the Front Line states and Pretoria to the international financial markets and their credit institutions. However, as will be further analysed in a subsequent chapter, the reasons the US administration brought in the Bretton Woods institutions were not only financial. Two important political reasons were at hand: their involvement reduced interference in the process by Congress, and the multilateral institutions were considered to be more capable than US bilateral aid of bringing about the necessary political and economic reform in the southern African region.[26]

Simultaneously, Mozambique's application for membership of the Bretton Woods institutions and its acceptance of the economic and political values of the West became the proof that Washington needed that the country was in practice changing political allies and moving away from the influence of Moscow. Instead of supporting Renamo, as the right wing in US Congress and the CIA had for a long time been demanding, Crocker succeeded in initiating cooperation with Marxist Frelimo.[27] Soon Mozambique became one of the largest US aid recipients in Sub-Saharan Africa.[28] In the case of Angola, denial of access to the IMF was used as a stick. Despite its urgent need for international credits, the USA blocked Angola's membership of the Bretton Woods institutions until an agreement on the withdrawal of the Cuban troops had been reached.[29] For South Africa, access to the IMF was used as both a carrot and a stick. In 1982 the IMF, under strong protest from the UN, gave substantial credits to South Africa in order to facilitate the implementation of 'constructive engagement' (NSA 01442, 1982/10/21). In the mid-1980s, new credits were denied as a form of pressure aimed at speeding up internal political reforms.[30]

## The ripe moment to abolish apartheid

The achievement of the Nkomati agreement in 1984 was understood in Washington as evidence that the disputed policy of 'Constructive Engagement' had some merits.[31] Through the dynamics put in motion by the agreement, an 'angolanisation' of the Mozambican conflict could be avoided. The USA refrained from official support to Renamo, the Mozambicans from asking for Cuban military assistance and South Africa from occupying the southern part of Mozambique to create a buffer zone.[32]

However, as history shows, the agreement turned out to be an agreement signed by the wrong parties at the wrong moment and was accordingly never implemented. While strictly respected by Mozambique it was violated by South African Defence Force, by governmental and private US organisations and by the 'Portuguese Component' (Nilsson 1992).[33]

The argument that Nkomati was signed at the wrong moment raises the question of when, with hindsight, the turning-point and the ripe moment for abolishing apartheid could have been identified. For most observers, the political struggle inside South Africa played the most important role, especially after the presentation of the new tricameral constitution and the subsequent creation of the UDF as the outcome of a massive social protest. For this development to take place, however, Nkomati played a crucial role in internalising, radicalising and polarising the conflict. This was later acknowledged by the Tanzanian President Julius Nyerere (Johnson and Martin 1986, p. xi), though he had initially been extremely critical of the agreement.

Another factor that permitted the internal unrest in South Africa to grow was the economic restraints resulting from heavily increased military costs incurred because of the Angolan and Cuban military resistance. Cuito Cuanavale is usually considered the military turning point. At the end of 1987, a combination of the Angolan army (FAPLA) and Cuban troops defeated South Africa and UNITA at Cuito Cuanavale in Angola, and thereby changed the military power balance on the ground and the geopolitical realities in favour of the various anti-apartheid forces.[34]

The extra 'tax' imposed by international sanctions was equally important.[35] Not only did the increasing international isolation increase the costs of production for South African industry, but the impact of the precarious domestic economic situation worsened as the country rapidly lost its international credit rating. Pressure from the transnational US elite played a strong role in pushing the US and South African political elites to act. Also important, albeit little understood, was the impact that cultural isolation had on the white minority, especially the lack of access to international sporting activities.

Crocker points to the overstretching of the apartheid bureaucracy in South Africa itself as the main factor behind the ripe moment (Crocker 1992), and his superior, Secretary of State George Shultz, points in his memoirs to the breakdown of the Soviet empire and subsequent changes in global geopolitical realities (Shultz 1993).[36]

Obviously no single factor can be identified as making, in the words of Ohlson and Stedman, 'the actors' fear of continued conflict exceed their fear of settlement' (1994, p. 117). The abolition of the apartheid system was the outcome of an intricate combination of coinciding interests among various actors at different levels, between the economic and political elite in the western hemisphere and the elite in South Africa itself, as well as between these actors and the interests of a committed leadership in southern Africa, and strong social forces at global as well as local level. Hence, the policy of 'Constructive Engagement' intervened in a process that had already been set in motion by the combined forces of the economic elite and social forces at various levels. Its main merit was that through this intervention it succeeded in motivating the political elite, not least the white Afrikaner elite, to enter a dialogue with their adversaries and thus create a space where they could interact with the other forces in play.

## Consensus under stress

The southern African experience shows how long-term strategic Western interests in spreading their values and American-style capitalism contributed to abolishing apartheid. Political stability was both a requirement for, and an aim of, the Western objective of integrating the southern African region more fully into the world economy. In this sense, US foreign policy shows a strong continuity between different administrations.[37]

However, this long-term interest was constantly challenged by two more short-term factors that also interact with, and distort, the policy measures. The first, the perceived communist threat, was also paradoxically the 'raison d'être' that motivated the constituencies to accept the need for long-term US leadership.[38] The second comprises the political forces not easily persuaded of this need for international US leadership, the so-called 'isolationists', frequently reinforcing the difficulties in elaborating a coherent short-term US foreign policy in Congress.[39] Sometimes counterproductive forces were put in motion that temporarily obstructed the long-term interests and policy goals. In the case of southern Africa strong differences both between the US executive and legislative branches and between contending forces within the Reagan administration emerged over time. For the US Department of State, the different short-term US interests vis-à-vis the region and the subsequent lack of consensus on design, financing and how to implement the policy implied that resources had to be mobilised outside the control of Congress. Accordingly, multilateral aid agencies were brought in. By using non-military foreign policy tools in the form of bilateral food aid and influence over the multilateral Bretton Woods institutions, the US successfully tried to motivate regional actors to implement the policy, to get the donor community to pay the main part of the bill and simultaneously to increase its own possibilities of controlling and influencing the future development of the region.

Conflict resolution, however, should be perceived as a process constituted by strongly interacting and interdependent phases. In order for a conflict settlement to develop into more long-term conflict resolution, the roots of the conflict must be addressed and people's expectations of social change and a better life must be partly met (Burton 1990). Inadequate measures brought into the process in its initial stage might endanger possibilities to implement later measures aiming to reinforce local development. In fact, peace and development constitute different sides of the same coin, as peace without development is as inconceivable as development without peace (Galtung 1969; Hettne 1984). This requires a coherent strategy from the very beginning of the peace process capable of increasing local participation and strengthening capacity for local resource mobilisation in order to better satisfy locally identified basic needs, both material and non-material.

In the next chapter, focus will be placed on the implications of the tools used by the USA to implement the policy of Constructive Engagement in Mozambique. It will be argued that both the design of the food aid provided bilaterally by US Aid and the design of the structural adjustment programme brought in by the multilateral Bretton Woods institutions have had a negative impact on participation and local resource mobilisation, and are thereby endangering the peace and stability achieved.

# 4
# Mozambique and the Washington Consensus

## A troublesome relationship

When Mozambique turned to the USA for food aid in April 1981, the answer was No.[1] Relations improved gradually following strong recommendations to President Reagan from Prime Minister Thatcher to improve the dialogue with Mozambique within the framework of the US policy of 'constructive engagement' (Howe 1994, p. 312). The objective of this improved dialogue with Mozambique was, in the words of Crocker, as follows:

> Our priorities in these early encounters were to shift Mozambique away from its self-destructive confrontation with Pretoria, to foster rethinking about its ruinous domestic policies, and to explore its readiness to abandon its close Soviet and Cuban alignment and behave like an independent, non-aligned country. We also sought its help in our dealings with the MPLA regime in Angola.... By early 1983, this dialogue was paying off. In the months to come, US food aid began to flow, and talks were held on aid programme to support the market sector... and to apply to join the World Bank and International Monetary Fund. (Crocker 1992, p. 237)

Hence, coinciding interests between the governments of Mozambique and the USA explain the tremendous shift in their diplomatic relations during the 1980s. From extreme hostility at the beginning of the decade, with Mozambique as one of the few countries on the USA's so-called black list, it became the largest US aid recipient in Sub-Saharan Africa some five years later.[2] In the early 1990s the relations began to deteriorate rapidly again. Thus, during the most critical phase of 'Constructive Engagement' understanding between Washington and Maputo was at its best.

As was the case with US foreign policy in general, the policy of Constructive Engagement suffered from the traditional reluctance towards aid in Congress which irrevocably refused to mobilise financial resources for the implementation of the political and economic reforms needed in Mozambique. According to Crocker, not many policy battles during the 1980s in Washington were more bitter than that over US policy on Mozambique, with constant demands in Congress to abandon and cut off aid to the struggling Maputo regime and help Renamo as 'freedom fighters' under the Reagan Doctrine (Crocker 1992).[3] The logic behind the coinciding interests between the Reagan administration and Frelimo was never fully understood by US Congress, which still conceived it as a Marxist African government.

The strong resistance to increased bilateral aid put up by Congress reinforced the importance for the White House of mobilising contributions from the multilateral institutions. From the point of view of the administration, channelling aid money through the multilaterals was an advantage when trying to avoid limitations and restrictions imposed by congressional scrutiny, though the request for replenishment of capital could have severe drawbacks.[4] Following the debt burden and the Third World's need for fresh credits during the 1980s the traditional use of the Bretton Woods institutions as a low-cost US foreign policy tool complementing US food aid became more intensive. As earlier described, the financial markets placed heavy demands on their creditors to reach agreement with the IMF on the implementation of a structural adjustment programme before new credits could be provided. The USA thus gained access to an unprecedented chance to diffuse its values and to use economic means to contain communism worldwide. In no time in the history of Africa had there been such massive external unanimity regarding the content and direction of economic and social policy.

## US food aid

The difficulties with Congress prevented the Reagan administration from providing urgently needed food aid on a bilateral basis before the Nkomati agreement was signed. However, in order not to lose momentum and to encourage Mozambique to continue its peace efforts, multilateral aid was provided in the meantime. Food that had been requested more than six months earlier from the UN World Food Programme, to deal with severe famine in the southern part of the country, was released.[5]

The food aid to Mozambique provided by the USA was political, and the political objectives in combination with the urgent need for assistance made an assessment of the reasons underlying the famine less important.[6] Hence, US value-based conditionality blueprints were attached to the aid, unadapted to the realities of the countryside in the recipient. The conditionalities were frequently motivated by domestic political causes. They were necessary to satisfy the social forces with direct political objectives behind the development assistance, but there were several examples on how the ongoing process of globalisation had increased political demands by the middle-class constituencies in the North to protect their interests, even if such demands work against the Third World and development aid itself. A classic example is the requirement for protection against cheap imports in combination with various export subsidies to face increased competition on the world market. Another example can be found behind US food aid:

> The agricultural constituencies also became increasingly critical of efforts by the US bilateral assistance agencies during the early 1980s, and by the multilateral agencies to stimulate agricultural production in developing countries that might compete with US agricultural exports. The Bumpers Amendment to the Foreign Assistance Act of 1986 instructed the US AID to avoid supporting agricultural development that would expand competition with US agricultural exports. (Foreign Assistance Appropriations Act of 1987 – section 550)

The influence of the domestic US constituency was a result of the food aid being financed through the Department of Agriculture, with the primary aim of assisting American farmers to find market outlets for their surplus production (cf. Agricultural Trade Development and Assistance Act (Public Law 480 from 1954)).

In order not to enter into contradiction with these strong forces in Congress, the food aid to Mozambique was to be distributed free of charge and through channels separated from the normal commercial structures linking urban and rural areas. State intervention at any level was to be strongly discouraged.

The long-term implications of this were multifold. One important consequence was that the free distribution of food aid destroyed the local markets and reduced peasants' motivation for surplus production in areas where this was possible. There are two different but interlinked reasons for this.

One is that the relief aid was provided by the donor community in kind and not in cash. Hence, instead of buying food from surplus areas inside the country, the donors airlifted in their donated food from abroad. As a consequence, local maize was rotting in warehouses due to lack of buyers, only a few miles away from the airstrip where the chartered aircraft were landing with donated food. Secondly, the requirement of free distribution meant that it competed with the local food provided by the national commercial system. As the commercial network for trade lost its markets, traders began to abandon small-scale rural activities. This increased the vulnerability to future famines.

Simultaneously, the parallel channels created for food distribution by foreign experts gradually drained the country of its administrative skill in this area. The fact is that the donor community intentionally did not strive to develop any Mozambican state administrative capacity, capable of facing future famine. As confirmed by one of the officials within US AID:

> We are fully aware of the shortcomings mentioned. However, it has never been the political and aid-related intention of the US to go in and strengthen Mozambican public administration by helping to

establish a national state organisation to counteract emergencies. Quite the opposite; the faster such attempts erode, the easier it will be for private interest and non-governmental organisations to assume responsibility for the distribution of emergency aid to reach targeted groups. You can quote me on this point. (Personal communication, Julius Schlotthauer, Chief of Mission, USAID, Maputo, 9 April 1992)

Above all the government's crisis of legitimacy was reinforced by the activities of the various NGOs distributing relief aid. *'This food is donated to you by the US government as your government is incapable of assisting you'* was a common expression used in the Tete province by US NGOs in connection with the free distribution of relief aid, according to local officials.

Hence, the different conditionalities linked to US food aid over time had more than economic impact. The political impact became considerable as well.

## Mozambique and the Bretton Woods institutions

It is an irony of history that when the Marxist-oriented political leadership in Maputo finally abandoned its ideology to follow the US policy for bringing peace to the region, and applied for membership in the Bretton Woods institutions (thereby moving into a world capitalist system it had opposed since independence), Mozambique gained approval only after considerable political pressure from the United States. The Bretton Woods institutions initially reacted quite negatively, as they did not find the country's credit rating, or its social or political stability, acceptable conditions for membership.[7]

However, an analysis of the political context in which the application for membership was presented illustrates that the country's economic situation was considered to be of minor importance for the institutions' main shareholder. The aim of the membership and subsequent implementation of the structural adjustment programme, in this specific historical context and in the case of Mozambique, was not primarily to create long-term possibilities for macro-economic balance. Nor was it even primarily to create short-term possibilities for the repayment of outstanding debts, of which the major portion was owed to bilateral and official creditors. The principal goal was political, namely, to create the economic and political conditions that were required by the US foreign policy goals vis-à-vis southern Africa (Constructive Engagement) and to satisfy the demands of its Western allies to uphold the world order (i.e. Pax Americana) and thereby counteract further Soviet expansion in the region.[8]

Hence the Bretton Woods institutions were brought into Mozambique by the US for political reasons, mainly to facilitate the implementation of a liberalised and open economy and Western-style democracy.[9] Membership of the institutions did not only mean coming into the US sphere of interest, but was considered a prerequisite for guaranteeing the financing and implementation of the necessary political reforms.[10]

In addition to Congress's reluctance to increase bilateral aid, the US governmental organisation for development assistance (USAID) was not considered to have the capacity to prepare, or the legitimacy to implement, the economic measures required for the transition from a centralised to a market economy. Through the Bretton Woods institutions the cost effectiveness for the US government could be considerably increased. The World Bank succeeded in mobilising the international donor community on a bilateral basis, yet in direct cooperation with the bank, to provide resources for the implementation of US 'Constructive Engagement'.

At the same time, such bilateral undertakings enabled the Bretton Woods institutions to reduce their own financial exposure to any failure of their programmes. The required burden of sharing for US involvement could thus be achieved. Much of the burden of adjustment was placed on the shoulders of Mozambique as the logic and assumptions behind the structural adjustment programmes came to have a strong influence over the future development of the country.

## The design of the structural adjustment programmes

The immediate objective of the Economic Rehabilitation Programme was to restore short-term macro-economic balance. The programme called for sharp cuts in government expenditure and an end to the attitude that the state would provide for everyone's needs and ask nothing in return. The assumption was that through liberalisation and privatisation the cost-effectiveness of producers and the government would increase, making the country less vulnerable to foreign competition. The market forces were expected to correct the imbalances created by earlier government failures. It was believed that through devaluations, exports would be more attractive internationally and requirements for imports restrained as they would become more expensive. This would effectively reduce the current account deficits. Hence the traditional stabilisation goal of reduced domestic demand, and thereby of imports, was combined with liberalisation and more supply-oriented policies to increase exports.[11]

From the beginning, the Economic and Social Rehabilitation Programme in Mozambique was a race against time. The challenge consisted of creating conditions for increased growth that would permit closing the financial gap through use of the country's resources or grants, or at least through concessional loans before the non-concessional ones came due. Due to the country's import trends (not only of consumer goods, but primarily of raw material, equipment and spare parts for the processing industry), such a strategy would in the short run require increased imports before they could be reduced and substituted by domestic production. The challenge was to increase the exports of goods and services at an even more rapid rate.

The first Bretton Woods missions to visit Mozambique made little attempt to make a real assessment of the roots of the problems before planning the remedies. Consequently, when designing the programme the IMF staff mainly singled out deficiencies in domestic policy-making as the primary and dominant source of the crisis in Mozambique. Difficulties in the balance of payments were due to excessive aggregate demand and domestic credit (IMF report EBS/87/101, 1987). The need to analyse the requirements for a proper rehabilitation and restructuring of the economy that would be able to close the financial gaps was deliberately played down. Accordingly, no risk analysis was presented and the war, still raging in the country, was hardly mentioned (World Bank Report No. P-4100-Moz, 1985).

The neglect of the external factors when analysing balance of payment difficulties and designing remedies has various explanations. One obvious reason was the need to come to grips with domestic economic imbalances. A large metical 'overhang' in the country had meant an overvalued currency estimated to be forty times too high in relation to the US dollar. Inflation was reaching some 100 per cent and the official market could not attract the (decreasing) production and prevent it from entering the informal and, at the time, illegal market.

The other reason was practical. However desirable, Mozambique could hardly influence the world order and the international terms of trade. Hence measures identified for reinstalling macro-economic balances must have their point of departure in activities that were possible to carry out from the point of view of national governance.

A third and more important reason was the political objective behind membership. In order for the USA (in cooperation with the government of Mozambique and supported by committed Bretton Woods officials) to persuade the boards of the Bretton Woods institutions of the logic of initiating economic recovery programmes in a country virtually in ruins and with an ongoing war, an erroneous analysis was made of the main economic constraints, giving too rosy a picture of the possibilities and time needed to come to grips with macro-economic imbalances.[12]

These three reasons linked up to a fourth reason, inherent in the original terms of reference for the Bretton Woods institutions. As mentioned, their main role was to facilitate the expansion of an open world market. Thus the effort of each nation within the system to achieve and maintain a macro-economic balance with stable price levels and a fixed exchange rate (later replaced by a market-based exchange rate) was a requirement for the international monetary system. Accordingly, the possibility for the US as a hegemonic leader of the world order to use the Bretton Woods as a foreign policy tool was a logical consequence of the articles of the institutions.

For political reasons, therefore, insufficient consideration was given to the impact of the South African destabilisation, the consequences of the colonial heritage and the worsened terms of trade. A restrictive monetary policy was ordained, based furthermore on assumptions that overestimated the capability of the private sector and emerging civil society to take over immediately the activities left behind by the withdrawing state.[13]

## The failure of the Washington Consensus

The Mozambican government's strong commitment to the implementation of the structural adjustment programme is acknowledged by the Bretton Woods institutions.[14] In some instances the government moves faster than the conditionality prescribes.[15]

In monitoring the implementation of the programme and assessing its results, the government's main preoccupation seems to be the persistent financial gap and the consolidation of aid dependency and donor influence. The high levels of foreign aid inflows in recent years may not continue and foreign direct investment has been modest so far. The IMF's main concern continues to be inflation and state budget deficits while the World Bank's is lack of supply responses.

The concerns of the Bretton Woods institutions are a logical consequence of the main assumptions behind their models. As explained, the basic assumption in the Fund's model is that the current account deficit results from the country in question living beyond its means. A restrictive policy must be applied with reduced domestic demand and credit. The basic assumption of the Bank's model is that capacity utilisation will increase as a consequence of efficiency-seeking policies. Hence, the withdrawal of the state and privatisation were supposed to bring greater efficiency and more rapid growth.

Domestic policy failures have undoubtedly had a strong impact on economic performance, and perhaps above all on political development. However, the main causes underlying the difficulties in achieving macro-economic balances (for instance, in the balance of payments) are structural, where external factors and the negative international environment must be taken into account. Three aspects merit particular attention in this regard. Firstly, due to structural weakness in the supply side of the economy inherited from the colonial period, Mozambique's modern history is accompanied by a chronic trade deficit. Secondly, this deficit was aggravated through the second oil price shock of 1979–80 (the consequences of which were more severe than the first price explosion of 1973); and thirdly, the deficit was further aggravated through the continued destruction of productive infrastructure for the main agricultural products throughout the 1980s, brought about by South African destabilisation. As a consequence there was a sharp fall in exports (Abrahamsson and Nilsson 1995b).[16]

Failure to diagnose the prevailing economic constraints has meant that the stabilisation programme's current orientation is holding back results from structural adjustment on the supply side, for three main reasons.

Firstly, reduced government expenditure, with decreased budget lines for public as well as donor-sponsored investments, reduces the scope for the rehabilitation of physical, social and commercial infrastructure destroyed by the South African destabilisation, which is needed for supply responses.[17] This so-called 'crowding in' argument (Killick 1995) is obviously even more valid in a war-affected economy in the phase of national reconstruction.[18] Secondly, current credit ceilings make it difficult for private agricultural and industrial interests to participate fully in development.[19] They are heavily under-capitalised due to various constraints, some of which have their roots in the colonial and early Frelimo periods, severely aggravated by the destruction during the war (Abrahamsson and Nilsson 1996). As the monetary policies have resulted in an acute shortage of more long-term credit for productive private investment, this has led to a notable increase in the trade in fast turnover consumer goods.[20] Thirdly, measures to increase exports (devaluations and liberalisations) increase inflation and reduce supply responses even further.[21] This argument goes back to the debate in the early 1980s when the impact of devaluations on countries with a high propensity for imports, a low degree of substitution and low supply elasticities was scrutinised (Tarp 1993). Mozambique is obviously such a case.

Thus the combination and sequencing of stabilisation measures (fiscal and monetary policies) and adjustment (liberalisation and privatisation) have reduced effective demand more than anticipated and simultaneously delayed supply responses. Accordingly, the logic behind the design of the structural adjustment programme in Mozambique, namely the view that achieving a macro-economic balance in the short term is a prerequisite for achieving structural transformation in the long term, must be re-evaluated. Empirical evidence from colonial times, showing that Mozambique's chronic trade deficit was due to distorted colonial economic structures (export earnings rarely reached more than 50 per cent of required imports), suggests that the structural adjustment programme should rather start the other way around. A comprehensive structural transformation of the countryside, with increasing productivity, demand and domestic market expansion, should be carried out before any macro-economic balance can be achieved.

Such a reorientation of current structure enjoys substantial theoretical support. Low-income countries with a substantial informal sector and high unemployment provide a classic dilemma when implementing stabilisation programmes aiming to solve the problem of macro-economic imbalance. In such economies, low utilisation of production factors means a much wider scope for increasing returns to scale and a situation with various equilibrium positions. Hence, there is a risk that restrictive financial policy will bring the economy to an undesirably low level of equilibrium without continuous expansion (the so-called low-level equilibrium trap).[22]

This thinking is more in line with the growth models applied by the World Bank, and explains its concern over delayed supply responses and its favouring of debt forgiveness. Accordingly, the World Bank tends to join the critics of the IMF approach and its analysis that domestic sources of balance of payment difficulties lie in excess demand rather than in structural weaknesses on the supply side. The critics point to the obvious fact that in the IMF model 'no account is taken of the fact that credit expansion may be linked through policy with investment and capital accumulation' (Tarp 1993, p. 63). Hence the assumption that aggregate domestic credit does not affect either real incomes or price levels does not hold true in reality. As Killick points out, 'In most real-world situations we must expect changes in the level of domestic credit to influence the level of economic activity, for example, by influencing the availability and cost of working capital' (Killick 1995, p. 132). The aim of the structural adjustment was, through liberalisation and privatisation, to close down and dismantle economically non-viable production. The intention was to achieve compensation for such job destruction through new investments and job creation in economically viable activities. The reduced availability of credits, following the restrictive monetary policy imposed, has not allowed this to happen. Instead unemployment has tripled.

## The internationalisation of the state

The main problem for the more structural approach of the World Bank is its strong emphasis on the role of privatisation, liberalisation and the role of market forces in coming to grips with economic imbalances. The effort to dismantle the state and transform it into a 'minimalist' state implies more than the reduced 'crowding in effects' referred to. The downsizing and outsourcing of state capacity has provoked a brain drain to the private sector. When the role of the state in providing the institutions and legal frameworks required for the market to function was finally better understood, efforts at capacity-building were hampered by the very design of the structural adjustment programme. As a consequence of tightened budgets for the state, civil servants' salaries are reduced to below the poverty line, and the only way for the remaining civil servants to survive was to abandon their professional ethics.[23]

Gramsci's concern about the passive revolution, based on an elite taking political power without hegemonic capacity, is relevant in this regard. In Mozambique, despite the lack of hegemonic relations of the state, the dominating elite none the less succeeds in navigating around a threatening organic crisis. Both anarchical stalemate with widespread social chaos and development into a highly repressive state have been avoided, at least temporarily. This avoidance has, however, not been accomplished through the emergence of a historic bloc in the Gramscian sense, that is, strong enough to create hegemony in civil society and subsequently enter a war of position aimed at taking state power. An organic crisis has primarily been avoided through aid that, together with weak market forces and subsequent inefficient allocation of resources, provides the emerging national bourgeoisie with possibilities for individual enrichment. The process of privatisation of the banking sector has enabled the commercial banks to grant undue credits to a number of state officials and private actors. Through subsequent allocation of the budget support provided by the donors, the state, when necessary, is rescuing the banks from going bankrupt. Consequently, instead of becoming the enemy of structural adjustment, as the World Bank initially anticipated, this elite became dependent for its survival on structural adjustment and the aid flow that followed. This has postponed Mozambican society being caught in the corporatist trap, in the sense of a more authoritarian and coercive regime.

However, from being a country with a leadership of strong integrity, recent events in Mozambique point to a rapid criminalisation of the state. According to a recent study conducted by the Institute for Security Studies in South Africa, 'there is a lack of political will to fight organised crime and corruption ... [and] ... the relative impunity with which some of the successful [drug] traffickers operate is often a result of their close connections with individuals at the highest levels of government or of the Frelimo party' (Gastrow and Mosse 2002).

One of the most well informed foreign scholars, Joseph Hanlon, not only raises the question but also convincingly argues that foreign aid is inducing corruption. He gives as triggering examples the recent bank scandals, in which least US$400 million have disappeared over the years in bad loans (Hanlon 2002). After the privatisation of the banking sector, imposed by structural adjustment programmes, a number of loans have not been repaid, making it necessary for the government to intervene to rescue the system. Hence state money has been used to cover the losses. This state money is in turn made available through the budget support provided to the state by the donors. Hence, instead of being used in accordance with the agreements of cooperation, donations are channelled to satisfy private needs.

## The pauperisation of the peasantry

What is perfectly clear is that Mozambique in no way constitutes the success story, be it in governmental or in economic performance, that the donors need in order to legitimate the present orientation of the structural adjustment programmes.

On a macro-economic level the World Bank continues to claim that Mozambique over the last decade has emerged as an example of successful reform with an average increase in GDP of some 8 per cent. However, the growth of GDP is limited largely to the surroundings of Maputo, not least in the Maputo Corridor to South Africa. In the countryside, however, recent studies by UNDP show not only decreased growth but also increased gaps in income distribution. On the local level, various surveys of households point to the fact that the majority of the population consider themselves to be in the very same situation as before or being worse off. According to a former governor of the Bank of Mozambique, 'The declared successes have not yet produced tangible results for the majority of the population. Rising unemployment and extremely high levels of absolute poverty are producing among other aspects, adverse social effects and rising crime (Ratilal 2001).

In the rural areas, the transition from a command economy to a market economy is barely visible. Worsened terms of trade have reduced the purchasing power of the peasantry at the same time as traders in many areas consider the operational cost of increased marketing activities to be too high.

A recent assessment of cashew marketing in the districts of Mogovolas, Nampula province, points to the fact that, despite substantial increases in cashew prices obtained by farmers during the last few years, the price of basic necessities has increased at a rate that has not only cancelled out the gains from escalating cashew prices, but completely subsumed them. Whereas one sack of cashew nuts bought 160 kg of salt or 16 litres of cooking oil respectively in 1994, for the same sack of cashew nuts it was possible to buy only 120 kg of salt or 12 litres of cooking oil respectively in 1996 (Owen 1997, p. 38). According to rudimentary research, in 1995 a peasant had to pay the equivalent of 44 kg of maize for a secondhand pair of trousers, while five years earlier the price had been 27 kg of maize. An exercise book for schoolchildren cost 1.5 kg of maize in the late 1980s and 5 kg six years later (Abrahamsson and Nilsson 1996). The explanation lies in the unlimited exploitation in the rural areas to which price liberalisation gave rise, and the disappearance of administrative control of the commercial system. This is also creating a crisis of economic legitimacy, in which the people launch increasingly strong criticisms against traders, in particular Asians. There are various reasons for this worsening situation. In the first place, the prices of consumer goods increased more than those of agricultural products. In the second place, commerce became concentrated among the Asians, who are often outside local social control and who rarely invest their profits in local production and employment. In the third place, the state of existing infrastructures means that the costs of transport are high and the shortage of traders is great. But this crisis of legitimacy for the economy is reflected in the behaviour of the traders. In many places the economy of the rural areas is again abandoning the use of cash. Ten years ago it was the rural population that refused to accept cash when it wanted to sell its surpluses, given that there was nothing to buy. Now it is traders who reduce the use of cash to the minimum, given that the costs related to credits are considered too high. They rotate their own capital at greater speed, forcing the peasants into direct exchange.

As a number of big traders control the local market, all the normal functions of a market economy are neutralised. The wholesalers decide which retailers can operate and decide the prices to be charged. Those who refuse to follow the wholesalers' instructions do not receive the necessary help with transport, credit or access to consumer goods. The majority of the peasantry, living below the poverty line, therefore still tends to be excluded from the market.

The discussion on the political economy of the peasantry in Sub-Saharan Africa during the 1980s has focused mainly on peasant rationality and the perceived dichotomy between profit maximisation and risk minimisation, or between individual effort and loyalty to the community. The literature dealing with the rationality of the peasantry and their price responsiveness is extensive.

Both Chayanov's study of the 'law of subsistence' for the Russian peasantry (Chayanov 1966) and Scott's discussion of the 'moral economy' of the South-East Asian peasantry (Scott 1976) showing how the peasantry opted to minimise risks rather than maximise production in its efforts to survive, have been most influential.[24] According to these theories, existing possibilities for increasing production can only be exploited after the risks are reduced to a minimum and medium term food security is consolidated.

Extensive research carried out in Tanzania (Hydén 1980) gives empirical evidence for such theories. Hydén developed his findings into a theory on 'the economy of affection', where 'economic action is not motivated by individual profit alone, but is embedded in a range of social considerations and reciprocities that allow for redistribution of opportunities and benefits' (Hydén 1980, p. 19). The cultural and informal systems in which the economy of affection is based (for example, what is understood as tribalism or nepotism – e.g. civil servants' need for social loyalty and the ability of a local community elite to use the state for partial satisfaction of its social needs) reduced the state's possibility of forming public institutions and rules systems.

The theory on the economy of affection undoubtedly has a bearing on the social formations in the rural areas of Mozambique. The colonial power was not interested in dissolving the traditional economy, in favour of an expanding market economy. On the contrary, the traditional economy was continuously providing raw material and cheap labour, thus playing an important role for the export oriented and urbanised modern sector.

The peasants were forced to live under this exploitative regime because they were always dependent on a cash income. The fact that the market did not need to expand meant that a civil society did not develop as a form of protection against the social privations usually suffered when market expansion begins. Instead, the value systems and distribution norms of traditional society were maintained essentially intact. Given that the traditional sector was responsible for reproducing the labour force, the peasants were never fully incorporated into the market and the Mozambican political elites maintained their power bases within traditional society.

Neither Frelimo, following independence, nor the Washington Consensus, some ten years later, succeeded in coming to grips with the colonial heritage. They did not perceive the basic structural problems stemming from the limitations of the market, low productivity, limited occupation and reduced purchasing power. Whereas Frelimo gave too much importance to the capacities of the state and the bureaucracy, the Bretton Woods institutions idealised market forces. Frelimo, in ignoring the needs of peasant families (and the degree of colonial exploitation) worsened the classic conflict between mobilisation and accumulation still further. The World Bank in its turn brought about worse terms of trade, in part because the devaluations had serious effects on the imports of the consumer goods that the peasants needed and in part due to the monopolisation and oligopolisation that took place in the commercial network.[25] Both strategies saw rural development as a top-down process of modernisation, financed by external links and international aid. Accordingly, both strategies neglected the local mobilisation of resources. There was therefore no need for local identification of needs or peasant participation.[26]

The low productivity in the economy of affection explains partly the lack of interest for rural agriculture among the political leadership. It was (and is) considered hopelessly backward. The rural areas should be modernised and urbanised as soon as possible. The experiments with reallocation of the population into collective villages, in order to improve supply of social service and to introduce the cooperative ideas for mechanisation of agriculture, show how the socio-cultural patterns linked to the economy of affection made this transformation difficult. The peasants lived at the margin of their survival capacity, to the extent that they were not prepared to take any risks. Awaiting new political solutions for this dilemma, the political decision-makers left the rural areas to their own destiny. The peasants did not get any access to inputs for agricultural production, nor the consumer goods necessary as incentives for an increased surplus production. As a consequence, the peasants withdrew from the market, at least temporarily. This was possible since the economy of affection still offered sufficient reproductive conditions.

The common image that the state after independence continued to exploit the family peasants through non-beneficial pricing has been taken for granted, though in southern Africa this image has never been seriously investigated. Our experiences from Mozambique rather point in the opposite direction. The costs of import of consumer goods necessary as incentive for increased peasant surplus production, together with costs of marketing, transport, warehousing and distribution were often higher than the price the state marketing company Agricom could demand from the consumers. The problem was not primarily linked to the necessity of supplying food with reasonable prices to the urban population, to avoid social disturbances. The problem was mainly that Agricom had to compete with the world market prices, which were (and still are) artificially low due to the European and North American subsidies to their farmers. Decreasing internal commercialisation increased import needs, which reduced the scope for imports of necessary consumer goods. This increased family peasants' feelings of marginalisation.

The foodstuff production diminished increasingly, and the vicious circle was aggravated by the ability of the state to maintain physical and social infrastructure in rural areas. The difficulties in supplying public goods rapidly came to reduce the legitimacy of the state.

Hence the low productivity of the economy of affection, and its continuing marginalisation not only has macro-economic implications: The implications are, above all, socio-economic and political. The dissolution of a state providing security and thereby consolidating the legitimacy of the political system, the absence of a functioning market offering individual opportunities and a rural community incapable of social protection have in combination begun to deprive the economy of affection of its most important cornerstone, namely social trust and linkages of reciprocity. Consequently, both the legitimacy of the political system (the vertical relationship between the individuals and the state) and the social trust (the horizontal safety network) have been eroded.

The forms of horizontal safety networks in Mozambique vary. Family relations and relations among different lineages are often important components. These relations coexist with other types of relation that are conducive to social trust, for example organisations such as religious communities or others by which people try to defend their interests. The war, the period as refugees and the resulting social turbulence have broken down much of the old social trust that is currently badly missed in the attempts to normalise life. The reestablishment of this social trust is intimately linked with the non-monetarised parts of the family economy, i.e. the possibilities for families to keep up and consolidate their social obligations, mutual help and informal credit systems.

## Social distrust and increased illegalities

The importance of political legitimacy and social trust for economic development has been a subject of debate in recent years, particularly following the study on development in northern Italy by Robert Putnam (1993).

In his study on the democratisation process in Italy, Putnam emphasises the inability of the Italian state, for historic reasons, to offer the inhabitants of the Mezzogiorno (southern Italy) protection and security (Putnam 1993). The study tries to show the importance to stable democratisation of the role played by emerging civil society. While trust and social involvement over hundreds of years had created far-reaching civil horizontal communication networks among citizens in northern Italy, the boss–subordinate relation and vertical communication networks has dominated in the south. As earlier discussed, the appearance of a civil society requires a strong state. One of the reasons for the appearance of the Mafia in Sicily was precisely the existence of a weak state, and, unlike civil society, the Mafia came to stand in opposition to the state. In the north of Italy the state was stronger and enabled the growth of a civil society.

In the south, the poor peasants struggled bitterly among themselves for access to sufficient land. The vertical relations between the poorest peasants, the local representatives of the feudal lords and the lords themselves who owned the land but lived on the mainland, became far more important to poor peasant survival than horizontal relations, and it was very difficult to break with the boss–subordinate relation. Over time, these vertical relations also contributed to creating considerable social distrust.

The socio-cultural context in which the Mafia emerged in southern Italy is naturally different from the context characterising Mozambique today. Contrary to the situation in the Italian south, the economy of affection is widespread in Mozambique's rural areas, and reciprocity and cooperation outside the family are still of importance, though apparently declining. Yet there are, similarities to the experience of the Italian south. The failure of the westernised modern project and the structural adjustment programmes to mobilise enough resources to establish the legitimacy of the state and the market economy (and with this the appearance of a civil society) has created a vacuum which has led to a dilemma from the security policy point of view.

## Poverty and conflict – an ambiguous relationship

The restrictive policy of the structural adjustment, in combination with its demands for democratisation and privatising property, could mean that the violence that characterised the rural areas in so many countries in Africa in recent years is becoming permanent.

In order to understand the relationship between poverty and conflict, it is important to expand the meaning of poverty to include the concept of relative deprivation. Commonly, relative deprivation, or frustration, is interpreted as an effect of disillusionment, when aspirations or expectations are not fulfilled. But, according to recent research by Anders Nilsson (1999), relative deprivation is not always limited to a comparison between what people want to have, and what they get. Here the concept has its main focus on the difference between what we consider to be our socially justified right to have, do, receive, believe, and, on the other hand, our *perception* and understanding of what we are permitted by other people, or institutions, in terms of capacities to satisfy these justified needs for ourselves. In short, it could be described as the *perceived* gap between expectations/aspirations and the capabilities for their satisfaction. In the text that follows, the gap will be called a gap of frustration.

As Nilsson further pinpoints, everybody can develop a high degree of relative deprivation, independent of their class and social strata – from people with a very low degree of basic human needs satisfaction, to people very rich in material terms. Relative deprivation and frustration may emerge at any level of societal hierarchy. It should be emphasised that relative deprivation in our meaning embraces both material and immaterial conditions (Nilsson 1999).

Of strong importance in this regard are two interlinked and conflict-creating processes. The first is what Nilsson calls politicisation of identity. By this he refers to a kind of bottom-up process, in which a group of people may start to develop political claims based on a specific identity. It could be that people are living in precarious conditions, or feel their long-term survival threatened, or live in a state of cultural or religious marginalisation. Since identities are fluid and transformative, political claims could be made in the name of any kind of identity, which coincides with the extension of the perceived problems.

The second process is what Nilsson calls instrumentalisation of politics, which is a top-down process, originating principally among marginalised elite, feeling they have less room for affirmation in terms of economic, political, social or cultural needs and to improve their capacity for competition against other elites. A marginalised elite which thus feels it a necessity to expand and reinforce its social base, or constituency, may start to formulate political claims in terms coinciding with the claims of a group identity which is being, or already is, politicised. It is the point in between, when the process of politicisation of identity from below meets and interacts with the process of instrumentalisation of politics from above, that the situation will be explosive and prone to violent conflict. Accordingly, it is one of the main arguments of this book that in order to create conditions for peace and development, measures must be taken in order to close the gaps of frustration prevailing in society. In fact, this must be one of the main objectives for any alternative development strategy.

The conventional, and hitherto dominating, view on the poverty-conflict relation limits the analysis of the actors in the sense that elites and their role in violent conflicts are excluded. Evidently since elites normally have no place within a quantitative concept of material poverty. With an expanded view on poverty, as I propose, such groups may be included in this context.

In this regard, identity is a crucial component of our understanding of violent conflicts, not least in terms of its importance as regards mobilisation emerging from the meeting points between politicised parts of the population and frustrated elite groups. Feelings of exclusion among elites often have deep historical roots. As discussed, these deep-rooted grievances must be adequately addressed in order for any development efforts to contribute to conflict resolution and sustainable peace, since they keep on appearing again and again.

Let us take a brief look at the deep-rooted identity of actual elite groups in Africa. Many of the pre-colonial states in Africa could be compared to the pre-Westphalian empire states. Their political and economic reach varied, both between different states and over time, and therefore also the character of the relations between the imperial centre and the subordinated units. Often a certain political, social and cultural autonomy was 'traded' against regular payments of imperial taxes.

However, early relations between African political units and the colonial powers rested on an alliance between colonial representatives and the African power structure they were facing, i.e. the centres of power of the emperors and kings. The subsequent arbitrary drawings of colonial borders, and their splitting of national identities, were also based on the fact that the colonial power expanded from geographically relatively limited urban concentrations, within the occupied pre-colonial kingdoms. From these centres the colonial power expanded militarily, and incorporated new geographical areas, over which they in fact had a very limited control. The political leaderships who took over after independence often had their roots in the administrative centres, which implied a continuation of the low priority as regards development and political control over the peripheral areas, which had been militarily incorporated. The Congo kingdom in Ovimbundu-land in the high plateau or of the Gaza-empire in Niassa (province), are examples of peripheral areas from Angola and Mozambique. This situation explains much about the feelings of marginalisation, the rivalry and the conflict that excluded elites maintain with the political power centres.

The early efforts of the Portuguese to take over the River Congo basin was built on an alliance with the Congolese kingdom, and its power centre in today's Angolan city of M'banza Congo. The extension of the kingdom diminished with distance, and the different political units then existing within the today's borders of Angola had different relations to the kingdom. The power of the centre was diluted with distance, and the areas between different empires' spheres of influence offered a relative degree of autonomy.

A similar situation is found in Mozambique, where the relations between the colonial power and the pre-colonial political units in Mozambique have shifted over time. Initially, the challenge for the Portuguese penetration was to establish a stronghold in the Arab-dominated areas of commerce along the northern coast of Mozambique. Only after the Berlin Conference 1885 did the Portuguese start to worry about the Emperor of Gaza, Gungunhana, who had extensive diplomatic relations with British colonists in the era of Cecil Rhodes. While the Emperor himself was singled out as a military target, his population, later on, came to be a favoured group in the south of the country, when the focus of economic activities had shifted southwards to establishing commercial links with South Africa. The fall of the Gaza empire allowed previously dominated areas to search for new positions, within the borders of the colonial dominance.

Taking into account the importance of analysing identity in its role as a base for mobilisation, we may be able to identify a number of identities (with language as a main indicator). Seeing languages as often territorially anchored, we may admit that these identities only change slowly over time.

The introduction of colonial logic, both in the political and economic spheres of reality, heavily affected two important pillars of these identities. First, the relative power balance between pre-colonial political units was abruptly changed. The empire state's political logic was broken down, and new relations between different identities had to be searched for, within new physical borders, and a new political logic with another configuration of identities. This meant that new political centres were created. Political units at the outskirts of the empire's logic were subordinated to other political centres, now seen as allies to the colonial power. Former peripheral political units lost also the relative autonomy they had enjoyed due to its weak links to dominating empires. Second, the patterns of the colonial economic exploitation contributed to a new kind of differentiation based on exclusion and inclusion. Although there was nothing close to development or benefits coming out of colonial exploitation, the differentiation as such probably contributed to differentiation of elite aspirations and expectations before independence.

After independence, most new governments opted for an accelerated modernisation and industrialisation. This struck against the possible territorial bases of accumulation, which could have remained a vision for some elites, and it reinforced the demands for a political, social and cultural homogenisation within the modern nation-state.

Under the rhetoric of national identity, post-independent development strategies (both market and socialist planning oriented) have contributed to a multifold differentiation, which has very little to do with conventional social differentiation, but is based on political and economic processes of inclusion and exclusion. This constitutes a strong undercurrent in most African countries, and it is a strong source of identity mobilisation (Nilsson 1999).

The danger lies in the politicisation of identity as a consequence of continued unequal development and the limited possibilities of implementing alternative economic programmes, combined with the destructive role that can be played by 'demobilised' soldiers if they are not demobilised, in the true sense of the word, and given the chance to reintegrate into normal civilian life. The traditional mistrust in relation to authority that has been present since colonial times, rapid privatisation and the speed with which the economy of affection can break down and be replaced by an individual struggle for access to land and property constitute other areas of concern. Here too vertical relations (particularly with international aid organisations) may become more important than horizontal, solidarity relations.

A 'godfather' system is emerging in commerce, at the same time as the privatisation process and the absence of a functioning state and implementable legal norms are quick to create the need for private protection based on organised violence. It is becoming increasingly easy to buy these private protection services (including, on a large scale, from 'demobilised' soldiers). As a result of the reciprocal need of the population and the political elite for alternative social protection, separate from the state, and the fact that it cannot be satisfied through legitimate or socially legal means within the framework of a civil society, a kind of perverted economy of affection has emerged. It is based on important features of the extra-economic value system and distribution norms, but these become perverted when they are integrated with the accelerated neo-liberalisation of an economy that had previously been planned at central level. The cultural and informal systems in which the economy of affection is based always made it difficult for the state to establish the public institutions and norms required for a market economy to be able to function. The perverted economy of affection, with a considerable number of illegal aspects, is making it impossible (Abrahamsson *et al.* 2001).

In Mozambique this situation is made more acute by the parallel development of events in South Africa. In South Africa illegal activities are increasingly extensive (or at least better documented) and the network of contacts with organised crime at international level has deep roots. It began as a necessity for South Africa to mitigate the effects of international sanctions. The interests that have difficulty in accepting change and a black majority regime, or in integrating themselves into legal social development, are trying to keep up their contacts with actors with the same attitudes who were affected by the peaceful developments in Mozambique. KwaZulu-Natal province in South Africa is described as a bastion of illegal activities of all kinds, with ramifications inside Mozambique.

Added to this are developments at international level linking the traditional contact networks of organised crime with new networks of so-called unconventional contacts. These networks appeared following the fall of communism and are nourished by liberalisation. Some former KGB and Stasi agents are reported to have developed private commercial interests in Africa with the help of old contact networks. They continue to have ramifications within the Soviet Mafia and are establishing new contacts for the international arms trade. The Italian Mafia used to be partly financed by the Christian Democrats, in order to keep the communists in control. While the financiers are behind bars, accused of corruption, the Mafia seeks new contacts. The meeting point of these networks, and what enables international crime to expand so greatly, is liberalisation and privatisation at international level together with the internationalisation of electronic communications systems.

In the former eastern countries and the former Soviet Union, as in Mozambique, liberalisation has meant that national industrial production has been exposed to greater international competition. Investment needs are great, but the will to make private investment is very small due to the high costs of capital and burgeoning political uncertainty. On the other hand, activities that are often illegal in the fields of commerce, transport and speculation are highly profitable. When the international creditors are hanging back, collaboration with organised criminals at international level becomes an alternative for various elite groups within or outside the government.

Just when structural adjustment, with its liberalisations, created conditions for criminal expansion, the restrictive monetary policy of the structural adjustment programme and the demands for debt payments created the need for these networks of contacts to unite. Other countries will suffer from the so-called boomerang effect of this development, which is becoming increasingly evident.

## The trap of low-level security equilibrium

By putting the recent development in Mozambique into a historical context, it becomes evident that the pre-colonial structural obstacles for peace and development have not been overcome. Instead, after independence the country has become even more rooted in something that I suggest could be called *a trap of low-level security equilibrium*. The different forces and circumstances creating the trap of low-level *security* equilibrium can be illustrated as in Figure 4.1.

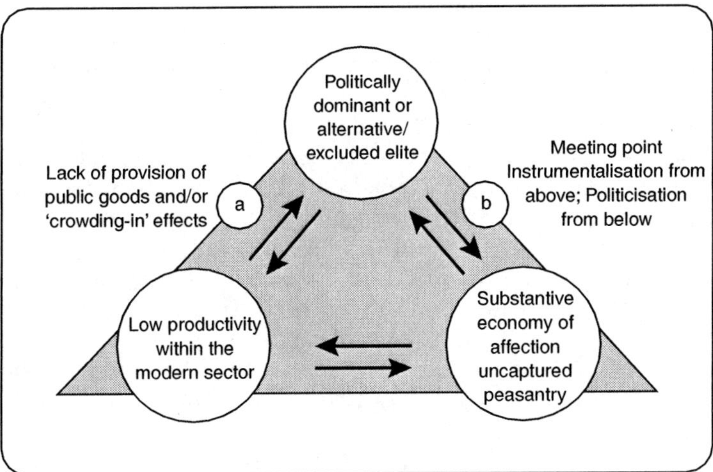


*Figure 4.1*   Trap of low-level security equilibrium

Figure 4.1 illustrates (axis a) how the political and economic elite in control of the state apparatus implement a strictly functional development policy, thus marginalising the peasantry. The lack of public goods in terms of consumer goods and social service makes the peasantry withdraw from the market. Their productivity is still low, thus the income/tax base of the state does not increase. The economic development is being blocked, and we enter a situation, which Keynesian economists call attention to – namely the trap of low-level equilibrium. The balance between supply and demand is established at a level of a too low (and thereby non-dynamic) utilisation of the productive capacity. Both employment and purchasing power is held back at a low level.

This situation is further complicated by the political dimension (axis b). The economic blocking is being used (rhetorically) by any alternative elite feeling excluded from the societal development. They use their traditional links with the economy of affection, and mobilise support for political resistance (possibly organised violence in the long run) among the parts of the population still living in the economy of affection, but feeling excluded and thus fuelling a gap of frustration. The social differentiation of the economy of affection should also be noted. Contrary to the teaching of conventional economy, it is not the poorest people who, having nothing to lose in a rebellion, are primarily mobilised. In our view, they have everything to lose – in the sense that they are living on such a thin margin of survival that they cannot risk anything. At the same time, research carried out by Nilsson shows that the poorest are most vulnerable to violent recruitment (Nilsson 1999). Neither do the richest layers of the population lend themselves to mobilisation for violence. They have too much to lose in a rebellion. Instead it is the population which has still not been able to anchor or root itself in the social hierarchy, and which still has strong expectations for a different and better future. Thus, it is primarily among frustrated youths, without direct responsibility for the family's survival, that we find the base of recruitment for active participation in violence and resistance.

Together the pre-colonial and colonial socio-cultural context have maintained political and economic fragmentation, which in its turn creates the basis for relative deprivation. This triangular relation reduces the critical mass in the historic bloc. The created contradictions do not permit any hegemonic discourse (national consensus) to grow, and society moves into organic crisis (Gramsci 1971), discussed earlier (pp. 6–7). This is the situation that I want to call the trap of low-level *security* equilibrium. This means that even if a ceasefire is established, the frustrations which have fuelled the conflict are still present and constantly threaten the sustainability of the peace agreement.

This situation makes the African continent especially vulnerable to conflicts, due to the historical context we have discussed. Furthermore, the trap of low-level security equilibrium has been reinforced since independence.

In Mozambique, the development strategy, sometimes called 'gigantismo' and based on a rapid mechanisation of agriculture and industrialisation, linked to an urbanisation of the countryside, was early on confronted by problems such as described above. The legacy of Portuguese colonialism meant that very few people had the education and experience needed to manage the many 'giant' projects. The development strategy had thus to rely on educated Mozambicans of Portuguese descent, or so called 'assimilated' black Mozambicans. The regional bias in educational facilities within the country further reinforced a long-established inclusion–exclusion pattern.

Two issues at the local level reinforced the sense of exclusion that accompanied with this centralised development approach. With the dismantling of the colonial politico-administrative structure all Mozambicans who had been part of this structure at the local level lost their influence and were portrayed as traitors and counter-revolutionaries. As this local elite normally belonged to influential families, its members came to develop deeply felt grievances around their entire life situation. Furthermore, in building a new district administration, the representatives of the state in the districts were systematically placed so that no one should have a position in his mother tongue area. This was aimed to be a step in the nation-building process, but had, among other things, the consequence that they could not communicate with the peasantry without an interpreter.

On top of the political-structural issues, with a direct bearing on the inclusion–exclusion process, came the fact that the implementation of the functional development strategy and its objective of rapid modernisation did not improve the situation. The expected benefits from economy of scale were largely unrealised. Where benefits were seen they were not distributed regionally. On the contrary, rapid 'villagisation' reinforced an exclusion of the poorer strata of the population, who 'lost' productive capacity because of increased distances between homesteads and fields, and increasingly had to survive as day-labourers. The consequence was a growing marginalisation of the peripheral areas within the country.

Hence, the perspective of exclusion–inclusion may help us to see how consequences of a certain development strategy affects people at different levels of society, and how it may create an integrated dynamic force which contributes to a kind of multi-layer reaction. Extensive research shows that the war in Mozambique at the local level to a great extent was a war of the poor – the locally marginalised people – supported by the excluded local elite (Nilsson 1999). At a national level, frustrated elites based on sub-national identities did not to any great extent participate actively in the war (South Africa's orchestration made Mozambican direct participation operationally unnecessary), but could at least be described as 'passive' in relation to the Mozambican needs of defence mobilisation during the war.

Most of these underlying patterns of inclusion–exclusion are still active in the public debate. While the government is internationally praised as a structural adjustment success story, it was on the brink of losing the 1999 general elections, with a territorial voting pattern, confirming both the historical roots of division and the perceived actual regional inequalities. Now, the opposition is threatening to divide the country along the same lines as the voting pattern (Renamo won an overwhelming majority in the centre and the north). This acute threat of violence may develop further, if this claim does have a vulnerable audience in the rural population, who have not benefited from the extraordinary figures of national economic growth.

Applying the same kind reasoning to Angola will make it clear that, although diamonds and oil are the main sources of financing the war, its old patterns of grievances are still intact. The two inland kingdoms – Kongo and Ovimbundu – and their respective relations to Kimbundu, are still marked by historical events, unequal development and multilevel experiences of exclusion and inclusion. This, however, does not imply that the conflict should be described as an ethnic conflict. There is a 'hierarchy' of identities, which potentially may be relevant for continuous conflict, and new ones may emerge. The MPLA–UNITA divide is often portrayed as an ethnic Kimbundu–Ovimbundu conflict. But the underlying reality is not so clear-cuts. What will, for example, be the future role of the Bakongo people, whose interests are ignored in the peace process? The conflict could equally be described as a centre–periphery exclusion, or a littoral–hinterland issue. Frustration gaps at all levels of Angolan society have also developed during the years of war. Within a basic general pattern, the Angolan society could be described as an assembly of different group interest identities, with a high degree of relative deprivation.

As will be further illustrated, the pockets of frustration in a given society and the dangers of being caught in the trap of low-level security equilibrium have multipled through the process of corporate globalisation. The new information technology, often described in terms of the 'CNN' factor, is indisputably increasing aspirations and requirements for what could be considered a decent life. At the same time, however, the exclusive character of the process of globalisation reduces people's expectations of being able to satisfy such requirements. It is in fact this situation, in combination with increased poverty-related ecological constraints, which creates the paradoxical situation whereby globalisation carries the seeds of its own destruction.

However, as will be the focus of Part II, the paradox is in fact a double paradox. Poverty and violent conflict cannot, in a global era, be contained through repression and/or fortress actions. They can only be dealt with through development. This fact partly justifies why in the second part of this study, the present room for manoeuvre is discussed in terms of historic opportunity for structural change.

# Part II

# Understanding Structural Change – and the Way Forward

# 5
# Theoretical Guidance

## Describing forces of change

In coining the maxim 'Pessimism of the intelligence, optimism of the will', his programmatic slogan in 1919, Gramsci wanted to underline the importance of Machiavelli's realistic approach to achieve social change and the need for active and realistic politicians to *combine* the pessimism of the intelligence with an optimism of the will (Gramsci 1971, pp. 174–5). However, today pessimism of the intelligence still prevails. The TINA syndrome (There Is No Alternative) has made it difficult even to conceptualise structural change, let alone identify the forces and actions required to achieve it. Normative approaches to future prospects for development are at most viewed as a required rhetoric that is conveniently used at international summits.

The main argument of Part I was that the evidence of modern history does not support this pessimism with regard to human action. The objects of our study, namely the Bretton Woods Conference during World War II, and the abolition of apartheid in the early 1990s, constitute encouraging examples. Coinciding interests in avoiding the Depression experienced between the wars succeeded in establishing an unprecedented framework for post-World War II international economic relations. The development in South Africa during the 1980s also showed how coinciding interests can become strong enough to shape history into a more human orientation. An obsolete apartheid system challenged internal social forces as well as Western long-term security interests and had to be abolished. Hence, pessimism of the intelligence can be combined with optimism of the will and thereby achieve structural change, provided the conditions are right.

Yet even if this is so, there is need for caution. Optimism of the will must not be allowed to take the lead and transform intended actions into mere utopianism. As the experience from southern Africa has taught us, optimism of the will is not enough to resolve conflicts. Conflict Resolution is constituted by different interacting phases. The approach used in one phase has a bearing on the outcome in the next. The experience from Angola and Mozambique is illuminating. Development strategies imposed by Western political interests have reinforced social disorder at the sub-national level, which in the long run threaten peace and development in the highly interdependent region of southern Africa.

As will be argued in this part, these problems are simultaneously interacting with ongoing processes at global level. The contradictions built into the post-World War II economic order have been activated by the end of the Cold War, and are now threatening the survival of the system. Strong elite groups in the western hemisphere are consequently trying to grapple at global level with the same problems which were manifested at local level in southern Africa. A new coinciding interest for structural change has thus emerged between the international elite and the national elite, increasing national governance's room for manoeuvre.

In a post-Cold War era, a structural opportunity for reactivating politics at various levels is at hand. It is an open question, however, if such an opportunity can be seized. The answer depends on how the elites at various levels can reinforce their links with global civil society and local social forces capable of bringing such structural change about. For this good theory and analytical tools are needed.

## Towards a critical international political economy

Theory is formed in interaction with reality. It provides the possibility of changing reality through its influence on the dominant thoughts and understandings shared by the social actors who reproduce reality. Accordingly, I conceive of theory as a framework assisting me not only in understanding and interpreting my empirical findings and the reality I am studying, but also possibly in contributing to its development and change. In that sense I agree with Robert Cox (Cox 1995) that theory is always for someone and for some purpose.

The theoretical framework needed for this undertaking can be found within Peace and Development Studies and its sub-disciplines of International Relations, Conflict Resolution and Development Studies.

The discipline of International Relations is a social science discipline that, since its inception, has been characterised by tension between realism and liberalism. The main area of tension relates to whether foreign policy, like any other state action, evolves in response to social demands: is it society that moulds the state or is it the other way around, i.e. is the dynamics created mainly by political or economic factors, by the struggle for power or for wealth, or, if you wish, by state-centred actors or other actors? The relationship between the two ideological positions is further complicated by its multi-dimensional character. One dimension is constituted by the tension between realism and idealism, i.e. should one describe the world as it is, or as it ought to be? Another dimension is the international versus the domestic; is the national foreign policy essentially determined by the global environment or are policies primarily the outgrowth of national political processes? These dimensions are characterised by the conceptual and consensual development of the question of international regimes and interdependence, which concepts have a long-standing tradition within the discipline. It has roots in the science of International Law and the legal institutional approach of Woodrow Wilson, a quest to prevent war by international treaty and negotiation (Halliday 1994, p. 10). For classical realists, stressing the inevitability of conflict in an interdependent world, such an approach was considered to be utopianism. Their mechanism to regulate conflict was balance of power. For liberals the idea of peace through interdependence and international law has, however, been fundamental. In the 1970s the realist approach developed into a more neo-realist and somewhat less state-centred variant. Through the work of Krasner (1983) a bridge was built within the discipline to the more transnational and liberal approach elaborated by Robert Keohane and Joseph Nye (Keohane and Nye 1975). Through their concept of complex interdependence they strove to combine the neo-realist perspective with a commitment to liberal international economic arrangement (transnational liberalism). The classic tension between realists and liberals displayed in such academic debates as that on the role of the state versus the market, political versus economic interests, or national versus international priorities is in practice frequently downplayed by the stronger actors being in a hegemonic or leading position, enabling them to benefit from liberalism without having to diffuse power and accept decreased sovereignty. Hans Morgenthau, who, in his academic capacity, symbolises the realist school, both personifies and illustrates that in political decision-making there are, at times, no clearcut incompatibilities between liberalism and realism. In his classic work *Politics among Nations* (Morgenthau 1948), considered for decades to be the main realist textbook, he discussed at length how the UN system ought to be organised. The same kind of convergence between realism and liberalism can be found with Henry Kissinger. Despite being a well-known realist, he nevertheless, in his capacity as a prominent member of the Trilateral Commission, strongly advocated liberal economic approaches to increase the room for manoeuvre for various transnational business interests (cf. Gill 1990). The diverging perspectives can be related more to means than to goals. For realists, as Gill observes, 'strong political and military foundations are conditions of existence of a liberal international economic order' (Gill 1990, p. 17).

In my view, the discipline of International Relations has so far contributed little to Development Studies. The mainstream of International Relations is mainly concerned with the interaction between states and non-state actors or 'transnational' relations across nation-state borders. Thus the discipline aims to study the operations of the international system as a whole. However, the questions of social movements and society at the local level have not been integrated into the analysis. Hence, the efforts to move towards a multilevel approach have not been sufficient to inspire a substitution of the too state-centred thinking characteristic of the field of Development Studies, with a more dynamic approach to development as advocated by Hettne (1995, p. 154). In my understanding, the main reason for this omission is the continuation of the predominant top-down perspective characterising the discipline of International Relations, partly explained by its determin-istic and somewhat 'immanent' approach to the development process as such. Of special importance in this context is the failure to integrate the criticism of the orthodox approaches to development launched by Burton in his 'World Society' (Burton 1972), notwithstanding the great importance given to his analysis. Through his vision of a 'world society' Burton broke completely with the state-centric view and gave more importance to indi-vidual actors interacting in a global cobweb that was constituted by specific issues of interest to the various actors. Burton emphasised the global charac-ter of this cobweb, its interdependency and the subsequent need to analyse and understand world society as such. Instead of integrating Burton's think-ing as an independent and separate strand, as it deserved, the discipline of International Relations subsumed his contribution in the emerging transna-tional liberalism approach, and its concern with interdependency. On the other hand, the points made by Burton did not attract much attention from the field of Development Studies and failed to become an issue of interest for its, at the time, much too state-centric models of development. Hereby, both disciplines missed Burton's important contribution to our understanding of the process of development, namely that development is a multilevel process constituted by the interaction between human needs, articulated at the local level, and the structures permitting or constraining the satisfaction of these needs on the global level.

During the last decade, the impact of globalisation has become clearer (e.g. deepened integration and interdependence on the one hand and con-tinued inequalities and growing income gaps between rich and poor in the international political system on the other). As a consequence, the traditional area of tension within the discipline of International Relations between the realist and the liberal approaches has been complemented by two dimen-sions. One relates to the need to revitalise the earlier Political Economy, integrating the domestic and the international in order to understand more fully the social order linking the issues and levels. The other dimension refers to the question of value neutrality, the motives that lie behind theorising and how political the study of International Relations can be, and if 'as someone once said, the purpose of understanding the world is to be better able to change it' (Cox and Sinclair 1996, p. 35).

The first dimension implied the emergence of a new research area for Inter-national Relations called International Political Economy (IPE) dealing with 'the way the world economy is organised politically' (Hettne 1997, p. 1). The basic traditions from the study of International Relations are still its main pillars, although some efforts have been made to achieve a synthesis (Strange 1988). The fundamental research problematic continues to be the motives that underlie state action (realist), adjustments in the international arena (pluralist), and increased inequalities (globalist), and the concept of the dynamics for societal change in terms of force (realist), actors (liberal or pluralist) or economics (Marxist or globalist).

However, these new approaches failed to elaborate the concepts and tools required for coming to terms with the dynamics of international relations. The traditional approaches upon which the research field of International Political Economy was constructed were too structural, too economistic, too deterministic (realism and Marxism) or too actor-oriented (liberalism) to solve the actor–structure problem adequately. Hence, instead of analysing factors contributing to structural change, the conventional approaches were caught in the trap of system maintenance.[1] This gave rise to a new debate bringing in the question of value neutrality. In fact, peace and development research is normative by nature. However, the more intentional Development Studies also started to lose its normative strength following the growing irrelevance of its nation-state approach in an increasingly globalised world (Hettne 1997). Difficulties in coming to terms with the multilevel dynamics reinforced emerging doubts during the 1970s about whether development as such can be influenced intentionally as the 'acceleration of history' has made it more or less immanent. Through this debate questioning value neutrality (an important concern within the discipline of International Relations) a more normative and hereby critical approach of International Political Economy has been brought back into the field of research.[2]

Indisputably, and notwithstanding its own tendency towards deterministic structuralism, the modern world system theory ploughed new ground by bringing the French historian Fernand Braudel and the Hungarian anthropologist Karl Polanyi into the discipline as its main sources of inspiration.[3] Through their work the question of civil society was introduced as a research area. The focus gradually shifted from the state as the unit of analysis to the inclusion of non-state actors, either local or transnational. In this context, the works of, Antonio Gramsci took on great importance. The discipline gained the knowledge it needed for multilevel analysis of structural change, and became able to identify the existence of and dialectics between social movements for change at the local level and constraints and room for manoeuvre at the international level. It became possible to start developing theories and strategies on how to bring structural change about.[4]

Robert Cox is a key contributor to this endeavour and considered to be one of the founders of what has become a critical International Political Economy.

In reasoning historically and in explaining and promoting social change, the main influence of critical International Political Economy stems from historical materialism. Accordingly, Cox identifies some important features that characterise the theory and that distinguish it not only from realist and liberal approaches but also from the so-called structural Marxism that dominates much of Marxist thinking within the field. Critical IPE is a dialectical approach in the sense that it sees contradictions and conflicts as possible causes of structural change. The theory aims to escape from the horizontal dimension of rivalry among the most powerful states by bringing in a vertical North–South dimension of power. It also tries to enlarge the orthodox IPE perspectives through its concern with the relationship between the state and civil society. Finally, as historical materialism, critical IPE focuses upon 'the production process as a critical element in the explanation of the particular historical form taken by a state/society complex' (Cox 1987).

Cox analyses forms of states, in a Gramscian extended sense, and how these forms change under pressure from forces from above (world order) and from below (civil society).[5] The basic unit of such an analysis is constituted by the totality of the social relations configured by social structures rather than by individual actors whether political, social or economic, governmental or non-governmental.


## Problem-solving versus critical theory

The multilevel analysis and holistic approach that critical IPE provided became paramount. 'Critical theory is directed to the social and political complex as a whole, rather than to separate parts' (Cox and Sinclair 1996, p. 89). The critical dimension that Cox brings to the more conventional approaches reflects his conceptualisation of the role and objectives of the theory. He distinguishes in this regard between what he calls problem-solving theory and critical theory. The former takes the existing world order and its structures as the given framework for action. The aim of the theory is to correct any dysfunctions, thereby making the system work more smoothly and efficiently. Critical theory, on the contrary, searches for contradictions in the framework and questions the structures *per se* by asking how they came about and what the possibilities are for changing them. In Cox's own words: 'the first is concerned with specific reforms aimed at the maintenance of existing structures, the second with exploring the potential for structural change and the construction of strategies for change' (Cox and Sinclair 1996, p. 32). The critical theory aims at more long-term change and 'takes a bottom-up view, privileging the concerns and interests of the less powerful while not ignoring the constraints imposed by the more powerful' (Cox 1997, p. xviii).

In this regard Cox is a close follower of Gramsci in the sense that he agrees with Gramsci's famous striving 'for optimism by will and pessimism by intelligence': 'Critical theory allows for a normative choice in favour of a social and political order different from the prevailing order, but it limits the range of choice to alternative orders which are feasible transformations of the existing world …. It must reject improbable alternatives just as it rejects the permanency of the existing order' (Cox and Sinclair 1996, p. 90).

The question remains open, however, whether the kind of structural change envisaged by this study would have been understood by Cox as a problem-solving measure or as a more critical approach. The question is legitimate, as the empirical findings of the study will argue that it is in the interest of various elite groups to support the envisaged structural change in order to avoid global chaos and an organic crisis of the whole system. Hence, there is reason to believe that Cox should have considered the structural change envisaged by this study as a problem-solving measure for maintaining and consolidating more overall existing global structures.

In fact, in one of his first essays discussing how one could use Gramsci in the analysis of International Relations (Cox 1983), Cox comments upon the concept of self-reliance as follows: 'The notion of self-reliance, for example, began as a challenge to the world economy by advocating endogenously determined autonomous development. The term has now been transformed to mean support by the agencies of the world economy for do-it-yourself welfare programmes in the peripheral countries. These programmes aim to enable the rural populations to achieve self-sufficiency, to stem the rural exodus to the cities, and to achieve thereby a greater degree of social and political stability amongst populations which the world economy is incapable of integrating. Self-reliance in its transformed meaning becomes complementary to and supportive of hegemonic goals for the world economy' (Cox 1983, p. 64).

However, recent writings by Cox make the distinction between problem-solving and critical theory a bit more fluid and point, thereby, to his awareness of the fact that long-term dynamics for change can also be created by problem-solving measures. Talking about the future of institutionalised forms of multilateralism, Cox introduces the concept 'incremental change' for actions that take 'international organisations as givens and consider how these might be changed so as to improve their functioning' (Cox 1997, p. xvi). The difference between incremental change and a critical approach is 'in part one of time frame. The incremental approach has a medium-term time frame and the structural approach a long-term time frame. The two are different but not mutually exclusive. In considering strategy, some combination may be appropriate' (Cox 1997, p. xvii).

A more rigid distinction between problem-solving and critical approaches is accordingly problematic as it misses the dynamics that will be injected into the process through these problem-solving measures and which in their turn may facilitate a structural change in the long run. The implementation of the structural adjustment programme in Mozambique earlier described assists us in visualising these dynamics in more concrete terms.

For most Sub-Saharan countries their relationship with the international political economy manifests itself in concrete terms when a westernised and more conventional development strategy (i.e. an outward export-oriented market economy) is imposed through various conditionalities, most frequently framed in a structural adjustment programme. During the Cold War one of the objectives with such programmes was long-term inclusion of the aid-recipient countries into the US sphere of interests. However, the efficiency of the programme's implementation and degree of fulfilment depended on active participation of decision-makers at the national level and popular participation at the local level. The former was facilitated through the internationalisation of the state and the emerging business structures earlier referred to. The latter proved from the very beginning of the implementation of the programmes much more difficult to obtain. Hence, the development strategy had to be complemented with efforts to increase efficiency in implementation.

At times the efforts to strengthen central and local participation through increased 'ownership' and 'empowerment' respectively set in motion unforseen local dynamics. In Mozambique various problem-solving measures striving for decentralisation and democratisation could provoke an activation of civil society (i.e. the local community and its various 'social movements') with increased demands for satisfaction of locally identified basic needs. Obviously, the conventional development strategy, based on mainstream development thinking, has severe difficulties to cope with such demands. Local measures need therefore to be taken to approach development from another angle and form a counterpoint to mainstream development thinking. Accordingly, one can expect social pressure on the state and national governance to facilitate such efforts. If the national leadership needs to rehabilitate its internal legitimacy, the demands raised have to be taken into consideration. This in turn could gradually set in motion a process that confronts and thereby makes visible the limits of existing world order structures in this regard. The final outcome of such an interactive process depends very much upon the strength of the coinciding interest between the transnational and national elites, wanting to improve efficiency in programme implementation and the local population wanting to increase its basic need satisfaction. Here, the dynamics that are created at national and local level through increased ownership and empowerment are of great importance as they might imply improved legitimacy for national governance. Such dynamics are in fact a vital requirement for the achievement of a more encompassing structural change, something to be discussed in the chapters that follow.

## The agent–structure dilemma

Cox's aim is not only to understand forces of change in a given 'historical structure' but also contribute to bringing about change in a Polanyian sense, i.e. through the self-defence of society. Such an approach and ambition brings in the agent–structure dilemma or, as Cox calls it, 'the chicken-and-egg proposition' (Cox and Sinclair 1996, p. 494).

As discussed in the preceding chapter, actors and structures are two independent units of analysis in interaction. The structures make action possible but also constrain action. As the structures do not exist as physical things but only in the minds of the actors, they will not change by their own force. The structures are changed by actors. Motives for change are provoked by actors through their interaction and their intersubjective meaning and making of reality. However, as every action is influenced by structural factors this interaction of structural change is not carried out under conditions determined only by the actors. Hence the importance of the dynamics of this interaction.[6]

This classification is important as it enables us to analyse processes of change through identification of structures under stress in specific issue areas and the strength of social forces capable of introducing counter-hegemonic structures. In addition to Braudel, both Polanyi and Gramsci provide some useful historical insight. Polanyi studied forces for change in rural areas of the United Kingdom during the eighteenth and nineteenth century, whilst Gramsci's concern was how to recapture the state after the Fascist take-over in Italy in the early twentieth century. As earlier described, Polanyi conceived structural change as a counter-reaction by social forces against further market penetration. These collective and organised defensive reactions led to the emergence of a civil society. He called the market-led 'disembedding' of the socio-economic relationship in a given society, which exposed the people to forces over which they had no control, the first phase of a 'double movement' (Polanyi 1957, p. 155). Society's response constituted the second phase of the same movement.

With the term 'structural change', I mean an intentional transformation of the structures constituting the regimes of the world order as such (i.e. the pattern of rules that constitutes the framework and the realities within which the various actors at various levels are acting). These structures have been created through their interaction over time and reflect prevailing power relations. In Braudel's sense we are talking about 'historical structures' that take considerable time to create and consolidate. I do not necessarily mean by a change the slow-moving structural change envisaged by Braudel, the so-called secular trends (*longue durée*). What I am aiming at is structural changes that transcend Braudel's daily events and reach the level of conjunctural time with a life-span of around 20–50 years. The end of the Cold War should in this sense be considered a structural change, fundamentally transforming the room for manoeuvre and development prospects in the Third World, not least for southern Africa.[7]

According to the logic of Cox, a 'historic' structure is to be conceived as a 'picture' of a particular configuration of forces:

This configuration does not determine actions in any direct mechanical way but imposes pressures and constraints. Individuals and groups may move with the pressure or resist and oppose them, but they cannot ignore them. To the extent that they do successfully resist a prevailing historical structure, they buttress their actions with an alternative, emerging configuration of forces a rival structure. ... the method of historical structures is one of representing what can be called limited totalities. The historical structure does not represent the whole world but rather a particular sphere of human activity in its historically located totality. (Cox 1981, 1996, pp. 97–100)

Following on from this affirmation, and at this specific level of abstraction, by 'structural change' I mean a transformation of the global framework and its rules that increases the room for manoeuvre on the part of national governance in countries like Mozambique and thereby facilitates the implementation of an alternative development strategy, if such an implementation is desired. It can be argued that such structural change, its importance for Sub-Saharan Africa notwithstanding, is nothing but a Coxian problem-solving measure to avoid global chaos, if seen in the perspective of the totality of the world order. Such an argument is, however, totally dependent on the level in focus. While the envisaged structural change's impact on the social relations of production can be expected to be marginal on the global level at least in the short term, its importance for local social relations of production can be great depending, on how the structural change will be used and the alternative development strategy designed. As has been stressed, 'problem-solving measures' may, under certain circumstances, initiate dynamics that in the long run will lead to a change of some of the prevailing structures on the local level.

## 'War of position' versus 'war of movement'

Gramsci's concern was what he called the passive revolution (Gramsci 1971, p. 59) which was created by an elite taking political power without hegemonic capability. Hence, popular participation was missing and critical citizens became marginalised or coopted into the dominant coalition of the ruling elites (*trasformismo*). This enabled the Fascists in Italy not only to take over power but also to continue the *trasformismo* (Cox and Sinclair 1996, p. 130). In order to regain power a 'war of position' had to be initiated that slowly built up the strength of the social foundations of a new state. According to Gramsci, a social force that has political aspirations to take over state power must work through a prolonged war of position to strengthen its influence in civil society, in order to gain a dominant position in relation to the forces that have been the basis for the existing state power (Gramsci 1971, pp. 238–9).

Gramsci distinguished between 'war of position' and 'war of movement' (or 'war of manoeuvre', as Gramsci also called the more frontal attack on power he envisaged). The distinction is based upon Gramsci's analysis of the power structure prevailing in Europe at the time (Gramsci 1971, pp. 229–40). Whereas civil society was strong in western Europe under the bourgeois hegemony and therefore could endanger a success of the revolutionary movement's frontal attack on power, the more fragile civil society in Russia could not effectively resist the disciplined Bolshevik vanguard party which thus was able to overwhelm the state in a 'war of movement' (Cox 1983; 1996, pp. 127–8). The difference between western Europe and Russia that can explain the need for a strategy based on a 'war of position' in the former and on a more frontal attack or 'war of movement' in the latter can be found in the relative strengths of the state and civil society.

Following this argument a number of African states could be subject to a 'war of movement' launched by alternative elites challenging the prevailing power. The historical record confirms this. However, two aspects emanating from the globalisation process are believed to have changed the conditions for some Sub-Saharan countries during the late 1980s and early 1990s. Firstly, the democratisation imposed by Western interests, together with the increased access to international communication, has implied a more open society, the dubious impact on legitimate power-holding notwithstanding. Coupled with the reinforced financial constraints, this has also implied a lowered degree of militarisation. Secondly, increased aid-dependency and the vested interests of the donors in the consolidation of political stability have decreased the possibilities for the external support required to launch a 'war of movement'. Hence the strategy of a 'war of position' is believed to have become more relevant in the Sub-Saharan context.

With the concept 'war of position', Gramsci aimed at a political process capable of building alternative structures within the established structures, without entering into any bargaining with the established elite that could endanger the ultimate goal of replacing the existing structures. In order to create new structures strong enough to replace these already existing, Gramsci pointed to the need to create a new historic bloc based on counter-hegemonic forces where the role of the organic intellectuals would be paramount (Cox 1996, pp. 124–43).

## Structural change of a limited totality

Cox identifies three kinds of forces interacting in a historical structure: material capabilities; ideas; and institutions (Cox and Sinclair 1996, p. 98). He conceives historical structures as 'objects for transformation when material circumstances have changed or prevailing meanings and purposes have been challenged by new practices' (Cox and Sinclair 1996, p. 514). As regards the transformation of more short-term conjunctural structures, Cox stresses the importance of contradictions within them, as well as the impact of social forces. Ideas constitute an important sphere of tension in this regard. The above-mentioned inter-subjective (collective) meanings, giving the structure its hegemonic consensual character, are constantly challenged and opposed by rival collective images representing a counter-hegemonic structure. 'The idea of a society which produces in its structure the antagonisms that lead to its modification appears as an appropriate model for the analysis of change in general' (Cox and Sinclair 1996, p. 514). Cox points to the need for a multilevel analysis and places his three identified interacting forces (material capabilities, ideas and institutions) in a broader analytical framework constituted by three interacting, interrelated spheres in the social world, i.e. social forces, forms of states and world orders (Cox and Sinclair 1996, p. 100). One important structure for developments in southern Africa that we can identify and evaluate through this method is the Cold War, a limited totality which left its mark on a number of institutions (Bretton Woods, World Food Programme), ideas (total onslaught, SADCC) and material capabilities (food aid, nuclear weaponry). The structure thus had an important impact on social forces (apartheid, refugees), forms of states (authoritarian security regimes with reduced legitimacy) and world order (bipolarity with its Warsaw pact and NATO).

Although Cox includes the emerging transnational elites as important social forces and opens up the possibility for structural change from above, he basically considers the process of change a bottom-up process. 'By analysing the dynamics of the restructuring of social relations on a world scale, it is possible to see how changes in production become the basis for social movements for change, and for new forms of state and world order' (Cox 1996, p. 192). Hence: 'The social forces generated by changing production processes are the starting point for thinking about possible futures' (Cox and Sinclair 1996, p. 113).

In his search for forces behind a Polanyian 'double movement', the most important social configuration capable of resisting continued globalisation in the short run identified by Cox is a corporatist process underpinning state-capitalist development, constituted mainly by national political and economic elites and workers forming a new 'historic bloc'. The political motives for such a configuration however remain somewhat unclear.

The conclusion to be drawn on the essence of the process corresponds to the point made by Björn Hettne on the gradual integration of the counterpoint into the mainstream, albeit the other way around (Hettne 1995, pp. 163–7). Thus, structural change should be conceived as a process in which the counter-point gradually substitutes the mainstream. New structures from 'within' take over old structures and become dominant even though parts of the old structures will remain.

The change of one structure or one set of structures in the system (a limited totality) will furthermore open up possibilities for further changes of other structures in the system. In that sense a structure can be conceived as an 'overlay' in the words of Barry Buzan (Buzan 1991). Its removal will bring new contradictions to the surface and change the power relations that constitute the basis for the maintenance of a series of other structures. The end of the Cold War as a clearcut example of this process is a key starting-point for the study and its search for opportunities for other structural changes.

Drawing from these theoretical guidelines, three forces appear that may possibly contribute to the creation of a structural opportunity for change. The first is contradictions within the system affecting what Cox calls the 'material capabilities'. The second is social forces within civil society, as well as different elite interest, that react against these contradictions, thereby constituting, respectively facilitating, the second movement in Polanyi's double movement. The third force consists Gramsci's 'organic intellectuals', who can use the contradictions and political pressure from civil society to initiate a 'war of position' aimed at changing the constraining structures. In the next chapter we will look more closely at all of these forces, in constructing an analytical model for understanding structural change.

# 6
# An Analytical Model for Action

## Identifying forces of change

Assisted by the conceptual framework and theoretical guidelines predominant within critical IPE, a set of 'core concepts' can be elaborated and developed into an analytical model designed to study processes behind structural change. In this chapter we will develop and discuss such a model, drawing from preceding chapters dealing with the Bretton Woods Conference and the abolition of the apartheid system in South Africa. We will also revisit the process around the demands for a New International Economic Order (NIEO) during the 1970s as an illustration of the forces at work. These demands, which were raised by the Non-Aligned Movement in the mid-1970s, envisaged a similar kind of structural change as this study. An assessment of the background to and outcome of these demands may therefore contribute important empirical experience of structural change:

1. The first core concept is that of *contradictory circumstances*. By this I understand contradictions that are embedded in the current world order that may reach a non-manageable level, i.e. when it is no longer possible to tackle them within the framework of prevailing structures. The contradictions may have a negative and a destructive impact on future political and economic development.
2. The second core concept is that of *coinciding interests*. i.e a situation in which the interests of various groups of political and economic elites are temporarily congruent as the dysfunction of the system is becoming counterproductive for all parties. This congruence of interests creates a 'ripe moment' for change since the contradictions referred to earlier imply a stalemate that is mutually destructive.
3. History related that elite interest seldom is the subject behind social change. Structural change requires pressure from below and interaction with social forces. Hence, the third core concept is that of societal *vertical links*, and the interaction between the elite and civil society.

In what follows these core concepts, which are the cornerstones of the proposed analytical model, will be further developed.

Although the main focus lies on the first two concepts of importance for structural change (the contradictory circumstances and the coinciding interests of the elites) the interlinkage and triangular relationship between the three concepts are both creating a 'structural opportunity for change' and the possibility of using such an opportunity. The concepts are thus inseparable. Nevertheless, the study will argue that whilst the two first concepts of change constitute the opportunity as such, the third concept, albeit not fully explored by this study, constitutes a prerequisite for whether a 'structural opportunity' will be taken advantage of or not.

## Contradictory circumstances

For Cox the social material framework and the social relations in which historical actions take place have a decisive impact for structural change (Cox and Sinclair 1996, p. 52). This understanding made Cox enlarge the realist perspective with its focus on power relations with a more historical materialistic approach. For historical materialism, the role of contradictions and conflicts as sources of social change constitutes the point of departure for its dialectical approach to the study of societal transformation. Cox thus broadened the range of determining forces beyond social change and state power to include the state/society complex. He labels this effort to synthesise historical materialism and realism 'new-realism' (Cox 1997). New-realism differs from neo-realism in its concern with structural change and the fact that this change is understood in historical terms (Cox 1997, p. xvi).

Historical materialism is, furthermore, primarily 'sensitive to the dialectical possibilities of change in the sphere of production which could affect the other spheres, such as those of the state and world order' (Cox and Sinclair 1996, p. 97).

This study's focus on contradictory circumstances as one of the driving forces for structural change takes a slightly different approach as regards two important aspects. The first relates to the content of the contradiction as such and the second relates to the importance of how the contradictions are *perceived* in relation to the short-term and long-term security interests of different actors.

As regards the content of the contradictions, it is obvious that the contradictions in the sphere of production continue to play an important role for change. However, the contradictions inherent in the present structures of the world order, and not necessarily immediately visible in the sphere of production, can at times assume equal importance. These contradictions arise from the fact that prevailing power relations seldom permit a desirable consensus on optimal long-term solutions to possible sources of conflict to be reached.

The negotiations on economic cooperation during the Bretton Woods Conference are a case in point. In fact, limited freedom of action for policy-makers is more often the rule than the exception. Negative outcomes of this lack of consensus will thus have to be counteracted through various methods of conflict management. This is essentially how I understand the Coxian notion of 'problem-solving' measures, with its aim of smoothing the functioning of the whole (Cox and Sinclair 1996, p. 89). However, through such management measures and actions, self-propelled dynamics are at times put in motion that in their turn can create various paradoxes, i.e. outcomes that conflict with preconceived notions of intention and desirability. These non-intentional outcomes may reinforce the original contradiction and transform it into a non-manageable and unsolvable situation within the existing structures. Hence a more critical approach in a Coxian sense will be called for 'that allows for a normative choice in favour of a social and political order different from the prevailing order, but it limits the range of choice to alternative orders which are feasible transformations of the existing world' (Cox and Sinclair 1996, p. 90). This area of tension between a reinforced contradiction and a non-manageable conflict constitutes what I term a contradictory circumstance. Figure 6.1 illustrates the relationship.

Measures taken to cope with the inherent contradiction (1) imply different non-intentional outcomes (paradoxes) (2). These non-intentional outcomes can in fact reinforce the original contradiction (3), and hereby create a contradictory circumstance. Possibly, these reinforced original contradictions cannot be kept manageable through continued problem-solving measures. Hence a structural change is called for (4).

This is not to say that the contradictions built into the present world order structures are not rooted in the social relations of production. The very structures of the world order are here described as being constituted by the values and interests of the dominant elites, in so far as they reflect internal power relations within civil society and the social relations of production. The influences of the various elite groups – not least the transnational elite – have, however, increased as a result of interdependence and globalisation. This

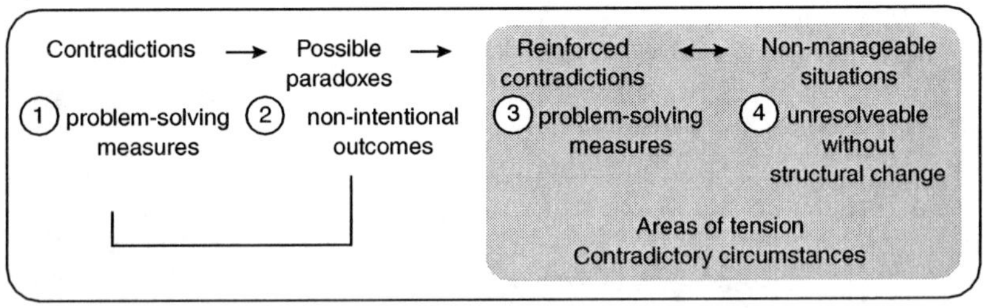


*Figure 6.1*   The dynamic between contradictions and paradoxes

has led to a shift in the balance from the national level to the transnational. Hence, the contradictory circumstances in question also originate from actions of these various elites carried out in the financial sphere, which at times is delinked from the domestic sphere of production. These actions are taken to consolidate the regimes, rules and conformity of the world order as such. The structural adjustment programme themselves, with their focus on macro-economic balances, contribute to this neglect of the real sphere of production. As Strange argued, capitalist accumulation has entered a phase where access to cheap credits has become more important than returns and rates of profit (Strange 1988). Accordingly, the contradictions within the system can be conceived as an outcome of the interacting dynamics within the 'limited totality' of the world order/state/society complex, i.e. the whole context of ideas and institutions within which the production of material goods takes place. Hence, 'contradictory circumstance' is a relative and subjective concept, which is foremost dependent on how the problems that the contradictions provoke are *perceived* by the elite and civil society respectively.

## Coinciding elite interest

These contradictory circumstances indisputably have significant influence on the interests of the elites at various levels. These interests vary between different kinds of elites. This study distinguishes between interests representing the elites in the north and the south respectively, between economic versus political elites and between national versus transnational oriented elites.

Elite groups with enlightened self-interest are here understood to be not merely the part of a social group's political and economic leadership that has a comprehension of the long-term challenges and the political motives required to try to come to grips with the contradictory circumstances, but rather the ensemble of different elites that for various reasons realise the necessity of change. Following Gramsci, the elite must furthermore have the capacity to be an organiser of society in general (Gramsci 1971, p. 5) and also, according to Cox, to lead hegemonic and counter-hegemonic formations (Cox and Sinclair 1996, p. 9). The Gramscian notion of 'hegemony' is important in this regard as it highlights the question of legitimacy. The legitimate social base of the elites must be sufficiently large for them to be able to influence the prevailing structures. The existence of counter-hegemonic formations points to the role that can be played by an alternative elite, that is at present excluded from power-sharing, but that has sufficient legitimacy and social base for challenging the political system.

Hence, the study of elite interest as a driving force for societal change requires a careful typologisation of elite interests based upon their needs of accumulation – externally versus internally oriented as well as productive versus speculative-oriented allocation. The type of accumulation of the elites determines their need for market access and purchasing power, something intimately linked to the question of legitimacy and stability of the political system. The case of Angola shows clearly how domestic elite groups in need of internal accumulation can become active actors in the peace-building process. Hence, whether the historical role of the elites in societal change is conflict-prone or peace-inclined must be contextualised and based upon their present situation.

The coinciding interest between different elites is important in the sense that it constitutes one of the bases for interdependence. The Gramscian notion of 'hegemony' also contributes to understanding how increased interdependence has reinforced the need and strength of coinciding interests of different elite groups at all levels. As earlier discussed, hegemony in a consensual Gramscian sense does not only require the capacity to lead but also the capacity to be led. As a consequence of the process of globalisation and the subsequent increased interdependence, hegemonic relationships are required for all levels simultaneously. Political instability and social disorder on one level may easily spill over to other levels. This is an important point to make since it underlines the need of the transnational elite to cooperate with legitimate elites on the national and local level. It is thus that the coinciding interests of the elites to create world order structures that permit such legitimacy increases.

The self-interest of nation-states as a driving force behind international cooperation has been analysed by different scholars. Realists conceive the principal actors in world politics – states – as rational egoists pursuing objectives based on their own self-interest, security and welfare. Increased interdependence has complemented this perspective with the concept of mutual interest. One partner's security and well-being is dependent on the others (Keohane 1984). Self-interest has become common interest or shared interest. Keohane distinguishes between interests that are situationally interdependent and interests that are empathetically interdependent. By the former he understands actors having interest in the welfare of others because improvements in others' welfare improves their own and vice versa. By the latter, he understands actors interested in the welfare of others for their own sake, even if this has no effect on their own material well-being or security (Keohane 1984, p. 122). Many interests today are instrumentally interdependent or strategically interdependent. Actors are interested in the welfare of others for fear of retaliation, or for long-term strategic reasons.

Central to this study is the identification of conditions under which interests of the elites coincide. Is the dysfunction of the system unifying or splitting the interests? If congruent, are they sufficiently strong to be able to contribute to a change of the existing structures? Such strength is what is understood by coinciding interests.

With the concept of coinciding interest, reference is primarily made to the interests emerging out of a situational interdependence. The question of empathy is deliberately left aside, giving the concept of interest a flavour of realist assumptions about human nature. This is in order to make the motives behind the interests clearer and to find out if and when coinciding interests for coming to grips with world poverty exist independently of altruistic, ethical or empathetic explanations prevailing within the different elite groups.

The concept 'coinciding interests' should not be confused with 'harmonizing interest' as developed by Carr (Carr 1939, p. 41). Coinciding interests consist of objectives and aims simultaneously articulated by various groups at a given time that – in spite of different background and origins – temporarily converge. If they remain congruent, the coinciding interest will be transformed into common interest. However, these interests tend to diverge after the objectives have been partially achieved, because the various elite groups usually react to the contradictory circumstances for different reasons. As a consequence they also strive for different solutions. These coinciding interests represent a force of change, the strength of which is dependent on the degree to which the elites are motivated to enter a process of negotiation with the aim of revising international policies and the reformed or new institutions, including the power relationship governing these institutions (Cox 1979).

### Reinforced vertical links with civil society

For the actor-oriented approach within the discipline of International Relations the task of the elites is mostly conceived as channelling the dissatisfaction articulated by society. As earlier discussed, the main social forces for change are to be found within society and change is partly considered to be a bottom-up process, initiated by various social movements.

A more comprehensive analysis of the role and strength of civil society in the north and the south respectively is for obvious reasons beyond this study's scope. However, it is important to observe the factors contributing to the strength of the vertical links between elites and civil society which enable the elites to involve society more in decision-making and to gain popular support. Here the importance of the involvement of the elite is approached from another angle. It is not only a question of how the elite can channel pressure for change articulated by civil society in a bottom-up process. It is also one of how the elite can take initiatives and mobilise such pressures to merge with the strivings of the elite, giving rise to a kind of two-way top-down-bottom-up process.

It is not the contradictions as such that constitute the main driving force of change even if they constitute the sources of conflict. Rather it is how these contradictions are *perceived* and the subsequent measures taken to manage these contradictions that lead to paradoxes and contradictory circumstances. Civil society is heavily influenced by these contradictory circumstances, something that implies a demand for action posed on the state and on the political leadership from below. The argument of this study is, however, that the process of globalisation, with its subsequent influence on market forces and the 'invisible hand', has increased both the role and the need of elites for structural change. In an increasingly interdependent world, the decision and/or power centres that the social forces in civil society are able to confront alone have become less visible, let alone accessible. This development tends to diffuse the TINA (There is no alternative) syndrome and thus reduces requirements for collective action and strengthens individual searching for solutions. Such developments explain the constrained possibility for social forces being mobilised (the necessary requirement for a Polanyian 'Second Movement') without an 'injection' from the political leadership – either from the elite in power or the alternative elite challenging the power.

The political elite's difficulties to maintain internal legitimacy and a domestic political base may, together with the interests of the economic elite, increase these elites' need for structural change. The elite of society thus develops a self-interest in coming to terms with the contradictory circumstances. Hence, the vertical link between the leadership and civil society is strengthened by the interaction between a pressure from below and from above mutually striving for coherence in problem formulation, identification of solutions and internal mobilisation. The structural opportunity for change is created when such double pressures are present on the different levels in the system.

Understanding of the multilevel requirements for legitimacy, and the subsequent interests of the elite for societal change, make the classic dichotomy between top-down and bottom-up perspectives irrelevant. A top-down perspective is understood as pressures from established political authorities, whereas bottom-up perspectives normally focus on the concerns and interests of the less powerful. The strength in social change lies in the interaction between top-down and bottom-up processes. Hence, the attempt must be made to keep the relations between the central level and the bottom level of society sufficiently dynamic and 'organic' to consolidate the coinciding interests that enabled the national historic bloc to emerge in the first place. It is through the maintenance and reinforcement of such a national historic bloc that the social forces at different levels will be able to dismantle developmental constraints imposed from above or from below.

## The core of the model

Accordingly, a set of 'core concepts' constituting the cornerstones of the analytical model, has been identified to assist in analysing the origin and impact of the rules and the power structures of the present world order and under which conditions that change can be brought about. In illustrating their triangular relationship, Figure 6.2 suggests some crucial interaction between the various components of the conceptual framework. The prevailing contradictions in the system in general and in the sphere of production in particular

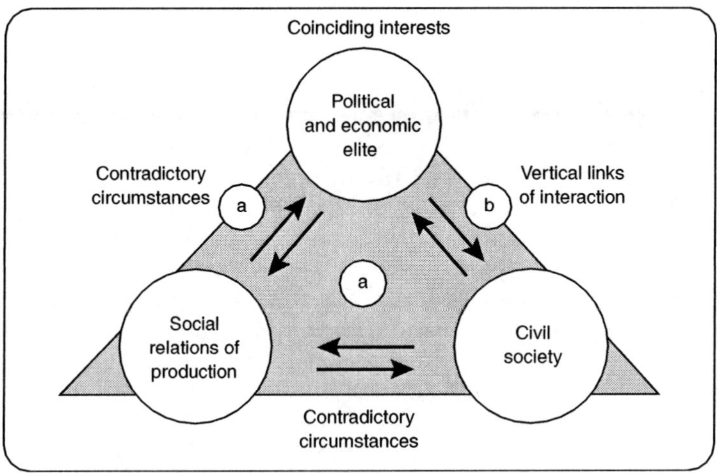


*Figure 6.2*   Analytical model

are *perceived* as non-manageable for the state and/or for the transnational elite as well as for civil society and constitute what we have called contradictory circumstances. If various elite groups are exposed to the same complex of problems, a coinciding interest for change will occur. Such a situation creates a structural opportunity for change (a). Some of these elite groups and social forces might have a congruent interest in reinforcing their vertical links (b) in order to increase interaction and mobilise forces within society as a whole, be it in the rural areas of Sub-Saharan Africa or the civil society of the Western world, which are required to seize the opportunity and to bring about structural change.

These three different forces of change are, in conjunction, a prerequisite for the analysis of processes of structural change. The reason is that they all constitute important links between different units included in the Gramscian 'historic bloc' that at a given historic time shapes the state/society complex. Hence, except in the case of an organic crisis, the social and political foundation of society is always constituted by a historic bloc, although its political configuration varies with the social relations of production and the formation and nature of the state.

## The analytical model with an African Prism

Applying our analytical model in a southern Africa context the existence of a structural opportunity can lead to four different outcomes, depending on the prevailing political configuration:

1. *Organic crisis.* In this situation, sufficient coinciding interests for change have not yet emerged within the elite behind the first movement. Neither

has a sufficient second movement developed. The historic bloc cannot deal with the situation. The opportunity for structural change is not seized – society is moving into a situation without political leadership and control, i.e. 'organic crisis' in the terminology of Gramsci. With an organic crisis we understand on the one hand a crisis of legitimacy for the functions of the state, and on the other the inability of civil society to articulate and take action. The concept overlaps with what the literature at times calls 'failed-state' in that the institutions function in the social sense and hereby permit some kind of political decision-making at the local level, even with weak institutions at the central level. Logically, where the state is not present, people have their own rules of governance. Society has in other words not degenerated into what the literature sometimes calls 'collapsed state' or 'black hole'. Angola is a society which can be considered to be in an organic crisis.

2. *Problem-solving reformism.* Here we understand a situation when the first movement has not yet lost its potential for market expansion. Subsequently, the second movement is still too weak and there is no political momentum to seize the opportunity for a more radical structural transformation. The enlightened elite is however sufficiently strong to conduct a series of problem-solving measures not to avoid the organic crises. The situation prevailing in Mozambique, where the apparent positive results of the economic reform programme at macro level has brought the international community to talk about a success story, is a good example of problem-solving measures. As discussed, these measures do not come to grips with the structural transformations required for moving the country out of the risk zone of a low-level security equilibrium trap. Accordingly, Mozambique is rapidly approaching an organic crisis, where demands for a territorial division of the country is on the agenda and the possibility of renewed violence and war cannot be excluded.

3. *Structural change – transformation.* Here, strong coinciding elite interest for change prevailing within the first movement conduct together with and supported by an activated civil society (the second movement) a war of position through which the power relationship within the historic bloc as well as its created structures are gradually transformed. A Great Compromise could be reached capable of reestablishing the political equilibrium. Although the counterpoint (i.e. the second movement) is absorbed by the mainstream (i.e. the first movement) it nevertheless changes its content and direction. As has been discussed, South Africa constitutes a clearcut example of such a development. It also constitutes an example of the danger that the development can regress rapidly and subsequently approach a situation of organic crisis if the new historic bloc is not capable of delivering what is required to consolidate the Great Compromise.

4. *Structural change – rupture.* Here a strong second movement has emerged but no enlightened elite interest is at hand to constitute a base for a Great

Compromise in Gramscian terminology, the war of position is transformed into a war of manoeuvre and a revolutionary situation emerges. The structural opportunity is used for a sudden and radical break with existing structures. Such a situation is at hand when the democratic institutions in society prove incapable of dealing with gaps of frustration and relative deprivation among different social group. In such a situation, instrumentalisation of politics from above can more easily link up the politicisation of identity from below. In the sudden break of the structures that such a situation creates, instrumentalisation of politics could take two different directions. In the first case, the second movement is crushed and dismantled by non-compromise-willing and more fascist-oriented (totalitarian) elite. In the second case a contra-hegemonic historic bloc emerges, driven by alternative elite capable of integrating the second movement and thereby substituting the former historic bloc – radical revolution. The case of Laurence Kabila in the Democratic Republic of the Congo constitutes one of many African examples of the latter development. The case of President Mugabe in Zimbabwe some twenty years earlier is another. The latter constitutes an example of how organic intellectuals can gradually loose their organic relationship with society, becoming more instrumental and less legitimate. It also points to possible political consequences when very radical initiatives are considered necessary to recapture internal legitimacy.

Our main point is that the Great Compromise should be understood as a transformation. It constitutes something different from pure reformism, but also from radical revolutionary change. The two given historical examples illustrate the point. The structural transformations that followed the Bretton Woods Conference and the abolition of apartheid fifty years later were necessary for the system as such to find its point of equilibrium. These transformations never threatened the economic system as such – on the contrary they created conditions for a continuity that problem-solving reforms couldn't obtain. Accordingly, by problem-solving we refer to change within the given structures. Structural transformation means changing the structures in the system whereas revolutionary ruptures change the system as such. In the terminology of Braudel, we could understand transformation as a change of structures 'conjuncturelle', and rupture as a change of structures with considerable *longue durée*.

## A historical example: the demands for a NIEO

Searching for historical experiences of how these forces of change have operated in practice could be an important contribution to our understanding of how the processes work and of the kind of analytical tools that are required for a more comprehensive identification of present opportunities.

Turning to the example of the demands for a new international economic order, Robert Cox provides us with some illuminating reflections on structural opportunity for structural change that at the time could not be seized (Cox 1979). Cox conceives the demands for a NIEO as a negotiating process, broadly speaking between countries of north and south. This process was concerned with the possibilities of agreement on both revised international policies and reformed or new institutions (including the power relationships governing these institutions). In those terms, the demands were aiming at a structural change. The structures to be changed did not only concern the international framework (i.e. the Bretton Woods system), they also linked the local and global, thus enabling the policies of the World Bank to interact with local development. They further relate to the dichotomy of urban versus rural development and the crucial question of regional balance between different geographical areas. As these structures are a product of the modernisation development paradigm a change in them logically also questions the universality of this paradigm. Although it has undoubtedly been emancipatory for some, it has created misery for others.

Three intertwined areas of tensions, or contradictory circumstances, of particular relevance can be identified as the antecedents to the demands raised for a more global economic equity. Subsequently, these contradictory circumstances were also influential on the various reactions the demands provoked in the industrialised countries in the late 1970s (cf. the UNEP/UNCTAD's symposium in Cocoyoc, Mexico, October 1974; the so-called Cocoyoc-Declaration and the Brandt Commission 1980; Singham and Hune 1986).

The first contradictory circumstance relates to the state, market and society complex. The role of the state was preponderant for the smooth functioning of the post-World War II order. The aim of the state should be to provide its citizens with a social security net and to buffer its national economy from external disturbances, without sacrificing the benefits of the liberal international order.

The French regulation school drew attention in this regard to the importance of a functioning mode of regulation to maintain stability in the process of accumulation.[1]

The role of the state as the redistributor of income was considered a prerequisite for a stable relationship between mass-consumption and production at national level. However, the political decision to create an open world economy with free trade put in motion a process of internationalisation of production, which gradually changed the role of the state and reduced its capacity for economic intervention. Through the internationalisation of production the state lost its capacity to influence, let alone control, the level of interest rates, the rate of profits and even the level of salaries (Bernis and Bye 1977). Thus, the crisis in the sphere of accumulation became structural.

In the USA, the crisis was intertwined with the perceived US hegemonic decline. In a special issue of *Business Week* (30 June 1980) a programme for 'The reindustrialisation of America' was proposed. A new social contract was called for, on which a new partnership between labour and management could be built in order to reconstruct the USA and adapt the levels of consumption to the requirements of investment. The need for and suitability of a 'code of conduct' for international enterprises became relevant, in order to facilitate the required coordination of industrial activities on a global scale.

The second contradictory circumstance concerned the need and scope for global governance. The decreased influence of nation-states, together with the hegemonic decline of the USA, raised the question of global governance. Global economic integration had to be coupled with a similar development as regards world politics. In order to reverse the international economic crisis, someone somewhere had to be willing and able to plan. Such international coordination was, in fact, the aim of the newly created Trilateral Commission.[2]

Private global industrial and financial interests, mainly of American origin, strove to maintain the international framework of global Fordism (Bernis and Bye 1987). In order to compensate for the decreased economic strength of the USA, Atlantic cooperation needed to increase and to encompass Japan (Gill 1990).

This effort for increased global governance was shared by a majority of the Third World countries and articulated through the Non-Alignment Movement (Singham and Hune 1986). Diverging opinions existed on the extent to which such governance should be based on strengthened multilateral cooperation within the UN system or rather on reinforced coordination between the main capital and financial interests in the world economy as envisaged by the Trilateral Commission. Initially, the balance was in favour of the former, not least through the support of the European social democratic elite (cf. Brandt Commission 1980). A decision was made to create a research centre linked to the UN which should focus on the surveillance of transnational corporations and the identification of suitable 'codes of conduct' for them. The aim was to strengthen the influence of the host governments vis-à-vis the transnationals.[3]

The need for international coordination and regulation was primarily provoked by the internationalisation of the financial markets and the need to come to grips with the international monetary system which had broken down as a consequence of Nixon's unilateral decision to suspend the convertibility of the dollar into gold on 15 August 1971.[4]

Various forces, among them the so-called 'establishment', which had been striving for deregulation in the first place, were now calling for some kind of regulation of the Eurodollar market (Volcker and Gyohten 1992).

The third emerging contradictory circumstance created by the lack of governance, be it on the national or global level, concerned the troublesome increased inequality gaps. In fact, the demands for a new international economic order should be understood as an outcome of the increased frustrations of the Third World elite. These elites had become more and more marginalised in the world economy, their efforts to adopt the Western development paradigm notwithstanding. Their demand was for a new international division of labour that could reduce the existing inequalities, to be brought about through a massive transfer of resources and industrial productive capacity.

The concern about increased inequality was, as discussed, traditionally shared by parts of the elites in the northern countries. A quote from the speech of Robert McNamara at the Board of Governors of the World Bank, September 1972, illustrates the logic behind this preoccupation of the Western elites:

> When the highly privileged are few and the desperately poor are many – and when the gap between them is worsening rather than improving – it is only a question of time before a decisive choice must be made between the political costs of reform and the political risks of rebellion. That is why policies specifically designed to reduce the deprivation among the poorest 40 per cent in developing countries are prescriptions not only of principle but of prudence. Social justice is not merely a moral imperative. It is a political imperative as well. (Robert McNamara, quoted in ul Haq 1976, p. 10)

The apparent paradox of the simultaneous existence of unsatisfied basic needs in the Third World and unemployment in the rich world reinforced the concern. Order should be created out of the prevailing contradictions, based on existing 'mutual interests' (Brandt Commission 1980):

> At the time that the demands for a NIEO were raised, the elite in the Third World was interested in using the newly emerged opportunity for changing the asymmetric relationship of power between themselves and the industrialised countries. This opportunity was brought about by the oil crises. The demands were supported by the social democratic elite in Europe which was concerned not only with increased inequalities between rich and poor countries, but also in challenging US hegemonic influence on the global level. The demands were further supported by the so-called 'establishment' in the United States, i.e. the internationally oriented US economic and political elite. Besides concerns of declining market outlets, they were also concerned from a security point of view by the widening gaps between poor and rich countries. This elite accordingly realised the need of some changes in relative incomes in favour of the poor countries, though without a clear opinion on the scale of such changes. The Brandt Commission thus stressed the common interests for structural change. (Brandt Commission 1980)

The so called 'Fourth World', generally considered 'a welfare burden', gave rise to a special establishment concern articulated by organisations like the Trilateral Commission and the Council on Foreign Relations. It is noteworthy that the establishment of the time was able to accept more inwardly oriented strategies in order to increase local food production. In the view of the US establishment it was a necessary evil to be understood 'as a complement to the pattern of growth through an open world economy to be applied by the impoverished sector of world population that does not participate directly in this pattern of growth' (Cox 1979, pp. 271–2).[5]

The concern of the 'establishment' for the well-being of the Fourth World undoubtedly derived from a belief in the progressive nature of a world capitalism capable of bringing about a new international division of labour. In that sense their recommendations, aimed at reducing inequalities, could be regarded as examples of 'problem-solving' measures in a Coxian sense.

Various factors explain why the structural changes envisaged by the demands for a NIEO never materialised. The contradictions in the system manifested in growing inequalities of North and South never challenged the survival of the system as such. The poor people in the Fourth World could be excluded since they were not needed as either producers or consumers. At the same time, the coinciding interests of various elites encompassed international economic interests and the political elite in the South together with international Social Democracy and a more liberally-oriented elite in the North. However, the coinciding interests never included the political elite of the more realist school of thought in the North. Instead, this latter elite was brought to power in its respective countries based on a more parochial and nationalist-inspired policy formulation. Two different but interacting factors of importance for our study explain this state of affairs.

One reason was that the contradictions arising as a consequence of the internationalisation of the time, though not threatening the survival of the system as such, threatened the national interests of the middle and working classes in the North. The inward-looking reaction of these social strata originated within the internationalisation process, which had not as yet reached the qualitatively different form of globalisation.

The importance of the involvement of civil society was stressed in the response to the NIEO demands. The Brandt Commission report concluded that the 'haves are rarely willing to relinquish their control and their resources and share them with the have-nots' (Brandt Commission 1980, p. 65). This dilemma could only be dealt with through involvement of civil society and increased solidarity: 'Therefore we speak of solidarity as something that goes beyond mutual interests' (Brandt Commission 1980, p. 64). According to its terms of reference, the Commission should above all strive to 'convince decision-makers and public opinion that profound changes are required in international relations, particularly international economic relations' (Brandt Commission 1980, p. 11). However, the elites never succeeded in anchoring the demands in society in order to obtain political support and increased pressure. The demands remained elite demands with a low degree of vertical links, because of an absence of a sufficient number of simultaneous articulations of such demands at other levels in society. Civil society had not been sufficiently brought into the process of creating foundations for a global civil society and a 'global village' consciousness. Hence, the majority of civil society in the North (with the exception of the solidarity movement and some committed NGOs), was barely exposed to the debate on the demand for a new international economic order and subsequently not asked to participate in the negotiations. It did not exercise any pressure for changing the international structures, but instead oriented its frustrations towards change of the national policies.

Another reason the demands never materialised was the emergence of the second Cold War and the termination of the era of détente which drastically changed global geopolitical realities (Halliday 1983). Based on a revitalised security threat and the need to revive the policy of containment, the European political elite not only accepted but also encouraged the efforts of the United States to maintain its role of world leadership. As a consequence the European elite started to accept a certain burden-sharing to facilitate the consolidation of US hegemonic power. With regard to areas of secondary strategic concern for the USA, the Bretton Woods institutions within control of the US administration could thus increase their influence considerably, instead of reinforcing the institutions of the UN system, as initially proposed and advocated by the international social democrats and the Non-Aligned Movement (Brandt Commission 1980; Singham and Hune 1986).

## In conclusion: structural change in retrospect

We conclude with a quick review of how the core elements of the analytical model were present in the processes of structural change described in Part I. As discussed, coinciding interests between the political and economic elites explain the unprecedented international agreement on world economic cooperation achieved during the late 1940s and 1950s following the Bretton Woods Conference. The underlying motives developed out of a fear of a repeat of the post-World War I contradictions, with the subsequent Great Depression, and went on to include the perceived communist threat. A common denominator for these interests was the desirability of diffusing Western values and development thinking worldwide. However, the vertical links between the US internationally-oriented elite and civil society were not strong enough to obtain domestic US consensus on how to finance its international leadership. New contradictions with subsequent paradoxes were thus built into the system. These contradictions explained why and how the USA could use the Bretton Woods institutions as its main foreign policy tool in areas of minor strategic importance.

Similar coinciding interests between various elites also contributed to the effort of social movements to abolish apartheid in southern Africa some forty years later. Here, strong vertical links between the elites and different parts of the civil society were present, albeit on a racial basis. The interests were motivated by non-manageable racial contradictory circumstances and fear of a radicalisation of the anti-apartheid movement. The contribution of the Reagan administration consisted in creating a space that made it possible for such coinciding interests to emerge.

The empirical findings from the Bretton Woods Conference as well as from southern Africa during the 1980s pointed to the fact that it was only when the contradictory circumstances became non-manageable, and the elite therefore had a self-interest in change, that the vertical linkages between the political leadership and civil society became sufficiently strong for coinciding interests at various levels to emerge capable of bringing structural change about. Such an affirmation does not imply that it is the elite that is *the* subject of historical change, but that the elite is *one* of the subjects required for change. In order to seize the opportunity for change, however, the interaction between the elite and civil society is a prerequisite: political pressure for change from below is required. Such a situation was not at hand when the Carter administration tried to push the apartheid system to an end.

# 7

# A Globality with Contradictory Circumstances

The analytical model elaborated in the previous chapter, aiming to identify forces of change, suggests different outcomes depending on which part of the world is analysed. Nevertheless, it is the argument of this chapter that at a rather higher level of generalisation and in general terms the global contradictory circumstances have been reinforced during the 1990s.

The geopolitical considerations engendered by the Cold War strengthened the US long-term interest in diffusing Western values, as this became an important part of the policy of containment. It was primarily the demands put on the indebted countries to implement economic and political reform programmes under the auspices of the Bretton Woods institutions that contributed to this diffusion of values. The lack of internal consensus in the United States on how to finance its international leadership had forced the administration in Washington to implement expansive monetary policies. This created a troubling excess dollar liquidity, which in turn contained the seeds of destruction of the monetary regime. Consequently, at the beginning of the 1970s the fixed exchange rate agreed upon at Bretton Woods had to be abandoned. The effort to sterilise the excess dollar liquidity in connection with the oil crisis, and the subsequent need to recycle the petrodollar, gave rise to the debt burden and the structural adjustment programmes that followed. As the excess liquidity was used mostly for speculation, the financial markets exploded. Productive investment and employment started to decrease substantially. We moved into an era of 'casino capitalism' (Strange 1988). At the same time the misuse of the monetary regime devalued the relational power of the United States, something that the Washington administration tried to compensate for through increased use of its structural power (Strange 1988). Thus, the Bretton Woods institutions became important tools for foreign policy implementation (Abrahamsson 1997).

The USA could obtain the multilateral burden-sharing desired without any corresponding power-sharing. Consequently, it succeeded to 'embed' some of the contradictions into the overall framework of Pax Americana. These embedded contradictions and the paradoxes that developed out of them have, over time, interacted with the globalisation process and influenced the articulation of globalisation. The contradictory circumstances that motivated the demands for a NIEO were, consequently, reinforced by the structural change of the political world order that followed the breakdown of the Soviet Union. The increased concern over these areas of tension, manifested by the international political elite, can be explained by a growing awareness of the risk that the contradictory circumstances will gradually evolve into a non-manageable situation, if not properly counteracted.[1]

In this book we will not make any attempt to analyse these contradictory circumstances in depth. They are used as illustrations of some of the consequences brought on by the contradictions embedded in the Bretton Woods system. Together these contradictions constitute the framework within which the forces required for structural change may emerge. In this sense, these more global contradictory circumstances can contribute to increased room for manoeuvre for national governance and thus open up for implementation an alternative development strategy in poor countries like Angola and Mozambique. It is therefore of importance to make a brief assessment of the present state of these areas of tension before proceeding any further.

As regards the state, market and society complex (the first contradictory circumstance accounted), the post-World War II compromise between the New Dealers and more neo-liberal forces in the United States resulted in the so-called embedded liberalism that came to characterise the Bretton Woods system. This compromise illustrates how the political balance temporarily shifted in favour of authority and state intervention as a reaction to the Great Depression and the Cold War. The role of the state changed from institutionalising and promoting the self-regulated market to a role of regulation and redistribution.[2]

The free trade regime initially meant increased worldwide competition, something that reinforced the tendency for capital to be concentrated in the hands of the Transnational Corporations (TNCs). In order to attract foreign capital and maintain domestic employment the nation-states transformed themselves from the intended filter (aiming to absorb or neutralise external shocks) into a kind of transmission belt trying to facilitate foreign penetration of the domestic political and economical system (Cox and Sinclair 1996). Production and finance became increasingly internationalised. Following the erosion of the national system of production and thus of the prerequisites for the national historic bloc, the state's intervention and redistributive capacity became an empty shell. The main consequence of liberalisation, deregulation and privatisation, following the imposed economic and political reform programmes designed in Washington, turned out to be problematic as national governance eroded before any mechanisms for increased global governance were at hand. With the end of the Cold War, the final 'disembedding' of the system became possible. The political system has lost vital parts of its social contract and consequently its legitimacy. The subsequent social disintegration is threatening the capitalist system (Soros 1998).

As regards the demands for global governance (the second contradictory circumstances brought up with the demands for a new international economic order earlier discussed), indisputably such demands increased during the 1980s. Consequently, the Brundtland report (1987) as well as the Carlsson independent commission (Carlsson and Ramphal 1995) articulated these concerns.

Simultaneously, the US hegemonic capacity that had already come under stress was substantially reduced with the end of the Cold War. As a consequence, the US public motivation for leadership decreased and the world did not change to a unipolar world under US auspices. The capacity of the inter-state and multilateral system within the UN framework was called into question by the reduced role of the nation-state, following the pursued internationalisation of the state on the one hand, and the rapid increase in complex multi-dimensional relations between actors at the sub-national and transnational level on the other. Instead of moving towards a multipolar world under the hegemonic leadership of the UN we are rapidly moving towards an apolar world order with increasing elements of disorder. This disorder became especially notable within the international financial markets after the deregulation of the late 1980s.

Through launching its war against terrorism after 11 September 2002, the Bush administration tried through its new identified threat, to regain sufficient legitimacy and to strengthen its hegemonic leadership. However, due to strong reluctance, not only manifested by traditional Western allies but also in the rest of the world, as regards the effectiveness in dealing with terrorism through repression and bombing only, the US initiative has not met with the desired responses. Instead Pax Americana continues to move from a more consensual and hegemonic leadership to one based on dominance and balance of terror.

The increased disorder has rapidly been exploited by increased illegalities at the international level meeting the reduced control by the nation-states and a greater freedom of action that has been the result of the globalisation process and market integration. The development of information technology has facilitated administration and contacts among the international mafia network, e.g. links between American and Sicilian Mafia, Chinese triads, Japanese yakuzas and Colombian cocaine cartels (Sterling 1994). Furthermore, the privatisation process of the huge resources of the former USSR created immediate coinciding interests between the international Mafia and the Russian Mafia in taking full advantage of this unique opportunity (Vaksberg 1991). The joint activities of these criminal organisations were fomented even further by the transition process the country was undergoing, related to the adjustment from a planned to a market economy (UNRISD 1995). Thousands of former civil servants, with internal contacts, information and scientific knowledge were eager to cash in on their assets.

The scale of these international illegal activities has developed so much during recent years that some scholars speak in terms of a 'Pax Mafiosa' as the replacement of the former Pax Americana as a more adequate characterisation of the present world order (Strange 1996).

The international community's main concern about these illegal activities was the effects of the drugs and arms traffic, the uncontrolled storage of toxic waste and the 'laundering' of the dirty money derived from such transactions, the so-called narco-dollars (USIA 1997). The UNDP has estimated the value of the drugs and arms traffic alone to be equal to 25 per cent of the value of the international trade in goods (UNDP 1994). Africa is rapidly becoming involved in this illegal circuit through similar processes of liberalisation and privatisation on the continent. Money laundering activities are complemented with arms trafficking, production of cannabis and transit services for harder drugs coming from the Asian countries en route to the USA and Europe. The tragic dilemma for Africa is that integration into the international illegal economic network has not resulted in any similar integration into the legal world economy. Lack of infrastructural and administrative capacity, as well as skilled labour and sufficient markets has deterred foreign and private capital flows from contributing to modernisation and decreased global inequalities. The geographical concentration of capital flow suggests, on the contrary, that the process of globalisation itself contributes to increased inequalities.[3]

Turning finally to the question of increased inequality gaps (the third contradictory circumstance referred to), the Third World elite's striving to reduce the increasing inequality gaps between the poor and the rich countries through a new international order and a massive transfer of resources was supported by important parts of the elite in the developed countries. This support was motivated by a mutual dependency that stemmed from unsatisfied basic needs in the South and untapped resources in the form of unemployment in the North.

However, changed geopolitical realities following the emergence of the second Cold War in the late 1970s gave, as discussed previously, the more conservative and neo-liberal-oriented elites the upper hand in foreign policy-making. Despite the fact that the inequality gap, identified at the summit meeting in Cancun, Mexico, in the beginning of the 1980s, was estimated to have increased to 1:30 (UNDP 1992), the demand for a New International Economic Order was taken out of the international political agenda. Following the shift in favour of a more neo-liberal policy, the market and private investment flows were subsequently supposed to take over responsibility for closing the gap from state and international aid.

For the USA, the post-Vietnam War political need to 'roll back' communism in the Third World by mainly diplomatic and/or economic means the debt crisis became extremely useful. Simultaneously however, this need undermined the post-World War II consensus established in the mid-1940s that the adjustment burden should rest with the industrial world (Toye 1994, p. 19). Through imposed structural adjustment programmes, the western hemisphere transferred the costs for the adjustment required to maintain the international monetary system to the indebted Third World countries.[4] Hence, the neo-liberal policies pursued by the conservative governments in the West did not facilitate the Third World countries' efforts to reduce the inequality gap.

The Earth summit in Rio in 1992 focused on ecological constraints as a future challenge to development. At that time, the gap between the poorest 20 per cent and the richest 20 per cent of world's population was continuing to grow, and had reached a ratio of around 1:60 (UNDP 1992). Methodological ambiguities aside, the calculations indisputably showed a relative increase in the unequal distribution of global income. The concern of the transnational-oriented elite for the potential political risks of social upheaval and rebellion by the poor increased. The roots for such a concern became dramatically evident following the terrorist attack on the World Trade Center and Pentagon, 11 September 2001. In Monterrey (spring 2002) the transnational elite with enlightened self-interest again pointed to the need to fight poverty in order to reduce risk for future terrorism. Simultaneously, the Monterrey Conference did not address the issue of trade, nor the question of debt forgiveness. These issues were postponed to the meeting in Johannesburg, autumn 2002 (the so-called Rio plus ten meeting), and subsequently postponed to the following WTO meeting in Cancun in autumn 2003.


## Reinforced contradictory circumstances

The continued and intensified process of globalisation has made these contradictory circumstances visible. Instead of the increased political democracy and economic efficiency strived at, the ancient political institutions for national as well as for global governance have eroded. Consequently, and in combination with the privatisation of security and availability of all kinds of surplus arms, the state has lost its monopoly of organised violence. Instead, the increased disorder and illegalities have led to what has been called 'world society conflicts' (Nilsson 1999) or 'new wars' (Kaldor 1999).

These kind of wars, albeit with strong local dynamics, have a strong global presence. Various international security or peacekeeping consultancy companies are actively involved for commercial reasons. They are commonly staffed with former intelligence officers, following new security requirements in the post-Cold War era with subsequent privatisation of military and security forces. These local wars have also a strong global impact through related refugee-flows and cross-border illegalities to logistically sustain the warfare. Hereby they reinforce prevailing global disorder and instability.

Another reason for the strengthening contradictory circumstances in the 1990s is the fact that long-term and relatively slow-moving ecological processes of change have gradually come to interact with the more short-term economic and political contradictions dealt with earlier. Such slow-moving ecological processes have so far been more difficult to manage due to the lack of efficient transnational institutions, the simultaneous downgrading of national state intervention capacity (increasing the free rider dilemma) and the prevailing perception that possible negative effects of these processes are more long-term and may be counteracted in the future through technological innovation.

The meeting-point between the two processes is increasing inequality. The impact of short-term political and economic processes on the more long-term ecological processes has been fairly well understood. Increased development gaps between the haves and the have-nots have aggravated the latter's misuse of renewable resources (Brundtland 1987). Strong evidence of correlation exists between high population growth and poor living conditions, especially for women. Hence increased inequalities and poverty have aggravated the ecological threats that are more local in nature, if not in impact. Population growth combined with the prevailing traditional modes of production have reinforced deforestation, land erosion and desertification. This is one of the reasons why during the last ten years the global development environmental threats, in the form of global warming, depletion of the ozone layer, air pollution and anticipated scarcity of non-renewable resources, have been complemented by the more locally felt scarcity of renewable resources such as water and food supply, or what I would like to call poverty-related environmental threats (Ohlsson 1999).

Through this interplay between global development environmental threats and local poverty-related environmental threats, history has caught up with the limits of environmental space. Earlier slow-moving ecological processes, leading to long-term reduction of the environmental space, have over time become integrated with more accelerated and poverty-related ecological processes.

Hence, the present challenges being faced by humanity are not primarily the question of how to substitute non-renewable resources but, first and foremost, how to avoid scarcities of renewable resources such as water and land (Ohlsson 1999). There is an acute need for measures that come to grips with the ecological long-term processes of change.

These different kinds of ecological threat cannot be dealt with separately. They are highly interlinked. Decreased global environmental space means that the western hemisphere's lifestyle has a direct impact in the southern hemisphere. Global warming, originating from air pollution, increases drought in Sub-Saharan Africa and thus contributes to water scarcity and land erosion. Land and water resources required for the planned modernisation of modes of production compete with local needs for food production. This is why the south's growing population cannot satisfy its aspirations for a better life without increased global environmental space. Global ecological interdependence, i.e. the global impact of the more local, poverty-related ecological constraints, could imply that local strategies for immediate survival create unexpected boomerang effects in the form of storage of toxic waste, arms and drug trafficking, illegal migration and so forth, which are inimical to the security interests of the rest of the world.

This logic draws attention to an important point, namely that the relatively more slow-moving ecological processes that are now becoming acute have not only started to interact with but have aggravated the short-term political and economic processes. The environmental space has begun to be reduced to a level below what is required not only for global poverty elimination but also for the global sustainability of the economic market system.

## Coinciding elite interests

The important question is to what extent these challenges will provoke a modification of predominant values, belief systems and national security interests constituting the very underpinnings of the world order. The agendas for different world summits and various UN conferences during the 1990s provide strong indications of the perception of the threat that these contradictions imply for important parts of the transnational elite.

Drawing upon our earlier discussion, four main developments are of special importance for the emerging coinciding interests between different elite groups in the western hemisphere. Firstly, the changed power balance resulting from the end of the Cold War did not result immediately in the expected creation of an unipolar world. The difficulties for the United States in consolidating its previous international leadership without its bipolar rival, and the subsequent apolarity, increased the social and political instability as well as the space for international organised crime. This development threatens the long-term interests of important elite groups dependent on economic and political stability. With the end of bipolarity national security interests are changing. The reinforced process of globalisation, together with increased need of multilateral burden sharing related to international leadership has made the security interests more global and mutual than national in character. Hence joint action is called for at various levels. These threats to consolidating the sustainability of the market economy, and therefore to long-term interests, are further aggravated by the environmental constraints. Measures needed for coming to terms with such ecological processes will necessarily have to be based on the establishment of a transnational institutional framework. When such institutions have been agreed upon and established, they will also be able to provide conditions and means for tackling the driving forces behind the more short-term economic contradictions. This kind of converging problem-solving measure will increase the scope for and strength of coinciding interests between different elite groups, and likewise the impact of the joint actions.

Secondly, an urgent need for financial stability and re-regulation of financial transactions has emerged on the political agenda. The political elite strives to rehabilitate its legitimacy and hold on to power through enhanced social security and economic protection. Strengthened opportunities for increased employment and domestic resource mobilisation must be provided in order to reduce new security threats in the form of various cross-border illegalities. At the same time, the financial elite is preoccupied by extraordinary financial losses stemming from financial turmoil, whether in Mexico, South East Asia or Russia.

Thirdly, the need to come to terms with growing global inequality has won high priority on the international agenda for action. Continued economic growth is taken as a condition for the redistribution of resources that is called for, but the continued marginalisation of the world's population by world financial markets creates political resistance to the Washington Consensus. The point is that as Western values are unable to deliver, the transnational elite, with its dominant Western inspiration, starts to lose allies, which in turn forces the transnational elite to be much more open to multicultural approaches.

Fourthly, these demands for joint actions are rooted in short-term political considerations. The transnational elite is not sufficiently strong, and is also starting to lose legitimacy within civil society, complicating implementation of its global vision. The threat is twofold. On the one hand, market fundamentalists advocate that market forces will themselves come to grips with the contradictions, if only permitted to continue with business as usual. The failure of the inter-state development cooperation to spread Western values should be compensated for by more fully enabling the TNCs to influence national decisions through the establishment of a Multilateral Agreement of Investment (MAI). On the other hand, the transnational elite faces strong opposition from various national alternative elite groups not in a position to extract any gains from the process of globalisation. This national elite is getting more isolationist and parochial, due to the increasing international interdependence that creates fear for some kind of global governance to replace national state sovereignty. In the West, this elite is not willing to give up its lifestyle and tries to consolidate its superior position in the world hierarchy through various kinds of parochial actions.

## Global development and structural change

It should be evident from the discussion above that whether the part of the transnational elite with enlightened self-interests will succeed in mobilising sufficient understanding and support for its vision of a more inclusive process of globalisation depends very much upon whether measures can be taken to bring about a more equitable distribution of the gains from globalisation. The global and national redistribution is not only a political demand raised from below but also a prerequisite for poverty reduction, political stability and market expansion. The implementation of such measures depends to a great extent on the vertical links between the ruling elite and civil society.

Two points deserve mention. One the one hand, the global reformist elite has somewhat paradoxically contributed to a development that has de-ideologised and de-politicised important parts of civil society. This combination of ignorance and arrogance about the importance of a permanent dialogue with civil society has created serious problems and given rise to individualistic approaches to needs satisfaction. The economic consequences of globalisation has increased the gap between the excluded citizens' aspirations for quality of life and their capacity to obtain it. The relative deprivation of ordinary citizens and the subsequent frustration have prepared the ground for renewed conservative nationalism with links to political fascism. Insecure in the private world, we are afraid of the Other in the public sphere. The global cultural meeting is not conceived as an opportunity but as a threat. In the vacuum, increased organised violence makes people call for law and order and for a strong political leadership.

On the other hand, the increased exposure of civil society to the process of globalisation through the development of information technology, with its combination of the CNN factor and increased access to the Internet, has made the arrogance and/or ignorance of the ruling elite vis-à-vis civil society visible and therefore unsustainable. Hence, the new information technology plays an unpredictable role in changing *attitudes* and individual aspirations within both the elite and civil society.

The global network created by various social movements to bring the multilateral agreement on investment (MAI) to a halt, as well as the ongoing campaign for international debt forgiveness and restructuring of the World Bank and the IMF (Jubilee 2000), illustrate how the ruling elites have been forced into dialogue with civil society through the activation of the latter.

The important point is that the emerging global civil society will have to carry out two-front 'wars of position'. Firstly, the global citizen striving for a respectable and decent life must combat both the market fundamentalists and the more xenophobic, parochial and isolationist forces, both amongst the elite and in civil society at large. Secondly, civil society has to exert pressure on the transnational elite in order to seize the opportunity for structural change in such a way that global citizenship of the global village can become possible. Such actions by civil society will only be successful through 'bringing politics back in'. It is only through launching 'wars of position' that prevailing contradictory circumstances can be changed. A development vision with a coherent strategy is needed in order to make the constraining structures visible. Civil society must be capable of identifying breaches in the structures and coinciding interests with the ruling elite, in order to use such entry points to exert pressure for change from below as well as from above.

The implementation of Agenda 21 could turn out to be a critical weapon in this regard and serve as an illustration to my argument. Environmental stress and increased awareness of the borderless world create a new need for the ruling elite and civil society to reinforce connecting links. At the same time, implementation of the Agenda at the local level could create an organic space, illustrating the global interlinkage with the local through the concrete opportunity to show the interaction between development-related environmental constraints and more poverty-related ones. The question of gender equality could prove equally important for loosening up constraining structures by bringing in new perspectives.

## Confrontation or dialogue

The lack of will and capacity among leading actors to come to terms with issues of global justice has during the last decade given shape to a global counter-reaction involving a broad spectrum of old and new social movements articulating various demands and interests. In the south the local impact of requirements from the WTO and from the Bretton Woods financial institutions – not least the access to land for the poor peasantry – has lately resulted in social upheavals involving several hundred thousands of people. Through global, Internet-based networks these movements have strengthened their cooperation with various social movements and solidarity groups in the north with similar concerns about globalisation and its repercussions. Some of these movements are pushing for offensive global projects (e.g. fair trade, global taxation or debt relief) to create a more inclusive process of globalisation. They share to a large extent the formulation of the problem provided by the elite groups with enlightened self-interests, although their solutions to the problems are far more encompassing and radical questioning the very structures constituting the fundaments for the present market led globalisation. Due to the uneven distributive effects of globalisation between social groups and geographic areas, other social movements constituted by more anti-global and xenophobic political forces have been pushing hard for more parochial actions.

Thus contemporary globalisation involves both a global market expansion and a socio-political reaction to the effects of this expansion. These two sides of globalisation can be understood in the theoretical framework of a 'first movement' and 'second movement' (Polanyi 1957). Polanyi pointed out not only the importance of social movements but also to the role of the elite in facilitating the growth of a second movement. It was the enlightened self-interest of the enlightened elite for financial regulation that created a space of resistance against a deregulated market, which over time culminated in the Bretton Woods Conference. Such a Great Compromise indicates a sort of institutionalised equilibrium of forces in both movements, which also determines the degree of political influence on the market forces. But a Great Compromise is only one possible outcome of the interaction between the two movements. Other socio-political reactions to the deregulated market were the communist and fascist movements.

Of importance is the fact that the meeting point where these different social forces interact has become a new global arena outside the control of the nation state. The direction of the double movement depends very much upon the interaction between elite groups and transnational networks of social movements, and whether or not the global arena can be used as an arena for dialogue concerning different global problems and propositions or whether the interaction only will imply reinforced clashes and confrontations. The recent summits, whether in Seattle, Prague, Nice, Göteborg or Genoa illustrate the difficulties in channelling people's concern with globalisation in a non-violent and peaceful direction. The crises of legitimacy and the immense gap of mistrust between the political decision-makers and the critical social movements have reduced the possibility for a serious dialogue. Instead the movements have opted for more drama-oriented actions, be it carnival or war-inspired dramas (Vinthagen 2002).

In this connection it is important to distinguish between different kinds of dialogues. The problem-solving and more reformist approach is characterised by the consensus-oriented dialogue. Through a negotiating process the dialogue aims to create some kind of consensus as regards required reforms of existing structures in order to increase the sustainability of the system. Such an approach diverges radically from the more revolutionary approach when the dialogue between contending forces for obvious reasons is non existent.

Presently, there are indications pointing to the fact that the intensified process of globalisation and the emergence of a new global arena for political confrontation has opened up for a more transformative and a confrontative dialogue between the ruling elite and various kinds of social forces. The reason for the elite to indulge in such endeavour is increased awareness of present contradictions and the need to reform some of the structures. It is my understanding that such enlightened interests could possibly increase the political room for manoeuvre and intensify the ongoing war of position in the global arena. Accordingly, whilst refusing any kind of cooption by the elite some of the social movements have opted for a strategy of interaction with the elite. They realise that the question of global justice cannot be dealt with through street violence. The transformation of the envisaged power structures is more linked to what is called discursive power, i.e. the dominant opinion prevailing in a society, and requires strong public involvement and support to be changed. The aim of the radical social movements to use such a confrontative dialogue in their struggle is to make structures and diverging political positions visible as well as to develop alternative visions and strategies. The confrontative dialogue challenges the constellation of political forces in the ongoing war of position. Through political mobilisation and new (albeit temporary) political alliances a Gramscian counterhegemonic bloc is aimed at sufficiently strong to transform part of the structures (cf. the limited totality) and thereby to decrease the degree of structural violence in society. Although, the confrontative dialogue transcends the problem-solving approach this will not imply an abolition of the whole set of structures and thereby the whole system, as it would in the more revolutionary situation.

It should be noted, however, that the aim of the confrontative dialogue is not only to identify diverging opinions and the different values and priorities lying behind present world-order structures. The confrontative dialogue aims to identify areas of coinciding interests between different parties that can be used as entry points to initiate a process of gradual structural transformation. The question of debt cancellation and the Tobin Tax (a Tax on financial speculation), which both aim at some kind of a regulation of global financial flows, are two examples. Different social actors are for different reasons, and consequently only temporarily, pushing in the same direction. If such different forces could be identified possibility to seize the historic opportunity for structural change would increase.

# 8
# Towards a Structural Opportunity for Change

In this chapter, the different threads presented in the preceding chapters will be brought together to assess the room for manoeuvre for future national governance in southern Africa. The main argument is that Sub-Saharan Africa presently faces a structural opportunity for change. In the post-Cold War era, coinciding interests at different levels have emerged striving to come to terms with the interacting global and local contradictory circumstances, thereby increasing the political room for manoeuvre. The question in focus here is the circumstances permitting such an opportunity to be seized.

First, an assessment of the interests of various elites at the international level as regards Sub-Saharan Africa will be presented. It will focus on current identifiable trends in the response of the transnationally-oriented elites to the challenges imposed by the present stage of globalisation and new geopolitical realities.

Secondly, the possibility for the African national elite to use such increased room for manoeuvre will be discussed, as will various outcomes if such an opportunity cannot be seized.

## The interests of the transnational elite

The conditions for structural change vary depending on which part of the world is in focus. The local and regional implications of global networks and interlinkages based on commercial relations are different from those based on multilateral and/or bilateral international development assistance. Accordingly, the future room for manoeuvre for national governance in Africa depends very much on how the transnational elite on the one hand, and the national political and economic elite in the Western countries on the other, will perceive the present phase of globalisation in relation to their own short- and long-term security interests. Different and contradictory tendencies can be identified as regards the present relationship between the western hemisphere and the African continent.

The economic decline following the second increase in oil prices in the early 1980s was soon accompanied by a gradual marginalisation of Africa in the world economy. Towards the end of the 1980s this tendency was reinforced as national strategic interests in the West changed. With the breakdown of the Soviet Union, the danger of Communist expansion on the continent became part of history, reinforcing existing difficulties in mobilising popular support and tax money for international commitments. Geopolitical interests shifted as a result of a decreased need for supplies of raw materials. Despite the fact that the Bretton Woods institutions have achieved their main objectives in defending the US world leadership fairly well, the US Congress began to question the underlying rationale for future US participation in the institutions. Political instability, unreliable infrastructures, a lack of skilled labour and limited markets in Africa reduced the commercial interest of foreign investors even further. Consequently, capital flows and trade have decreased significantly, and are currently no more than one or two per cent of the world total. International aid decreased from US$17 billion in 1990 to some US$12 billion ten years later.

The marginalisation of Africa is reflected in various contributions from different think-tanks striving to formulate new security interests for the US in a post-Cold War era. Most of the private and non-governmental foreign policy establishment argues for selective US engagement (Brzezinski 1993). In a much discussed article in *Foreign Affairs*, the American historian Paul Kennedy argued that 'The United States should adopt a discriminating policy toward the developing world, concentrating its energies on pivotal states rather than spreading its attention and resources over the globe' (Kennedy *et al.* 1996). Pivotal states were states considered big enough to contribute to both stability and instability in a given region. In Africa, Algeria, Egypt and South Africa were designated pivotal states. A self-proclaimed non-governmental Commission on America's National Interest (1996), involving several important think tanks, such as the Council on Foreign Relations, Harvard University and the Nixon Center for Peace and Freedom, argued that the United States is 'adrift in the world, bereft of a clearly focused foreign policy and undecided about its national interest' at the same time as the American public has turned inward, less concerned about international affairs than at any time in over sixty years. 'If it continues, this drift will threaten our values, our fortunes and indeed our lives' concludes the executive summary to the report. Africa was not mentioned by name. Another report published by the ODC in Washington, *The Partnership Imperative*, concludes that though the communications revolution and market-based economic growth have been accompanied by an international diffusion of

Western political and social values, with the end of the Cold War the public's concern has shifted from national survival to personal quality of life, giving most foreign issues a low day-to-day salience (Blechman *et al.* 1997). Africa was not included among the international future challenges mentioned.

This diminished interest in Africa is not only illustrated by the parochial trend in the US Congress; Europe shows the same development. Africa is not on the public agenda and various opinion polls show that although development aid is still a concern for European citizens, assistance to the countries in east and central Europe is normally ranked as the most important priority (European Union 1996).

This attitude reflects the ongoing transformation of the global production structure. Present industrial development is adapting itself to an increased number of poor people with too low a purchasing power to be included in the market economy. Accordingly the production moves from a more horizontal expansion of productive capital engaged in mass production (cf. Fordism), into a more vertical process of production mainly designed according to pre-vailing purchasing power and pattern of consumption of the middle and upper class. The exclusive process, coined 'global apartheid' (Cheru 1997b), obviously reduces even more the general applicability of the theory of fac-tor price equalisation and reinforces the unevenness of globalisation (UNDP 1997).[1]

## The articulation of enlightened self-interest

The marginalisation of Sub-Saharan Africa was initially perceived by Western Africanists as an opportunity for the continent to find its own path towards development.[2] Soon however, the marginalisation of Africa started to pro-voke a counter-reaction. The international economic elite began to see it as a threat. However marginal, Africa is still needed to provide some essential minerals, specific crops or market outlets. Social unrest and political insta-bility that would make such a commercial relationship difficult to maintain are seen as a danger. This economic elite strives for continued official devel-opment assistance, not only in the form of short-term humanitarian aid but also as credits for the needed rehabilitation and maintenance of outdated infrastructure. This is why, in the ongoing discussion of why the USA should care about Africa, one can find the following argument, delivered by Booker (1996) at the Council of Foreign Relations:

> The US should acknowledge that many of its Cold War policies – which shaped US relations with Africa from the era of independence until this decade – have done considerable damage in a number of key African states. We should feel a national obligation to help the people and governments of these countries to recover from the devastation that superpower rivalry inflicted upon them, and helped them to inflict upon themselves.

The Western political elite's concern has also increased. History points to the danger that the difficulties in providing the African population with food and security could result in an increased number of civil conflicts, mass migration, the diffusion of AIDS and environmental destruction. In order to prevent expensive peace-keeping interventions demanded as a result of the 'CNN factor', this elite tries to mobilise public support for continued involvement in African affairs. They point to the possibility that knock-on effects from the African danger could not only spread into neighbouring countries but also increase social instability in the Western countries.

These threats, considered capable of endangering global security, are also articulated in the efforts by US administrations to redefine the national security interest in the post-Cold War era. The national security directives on Sub-Saharan Africa during the 1990s therefore point to the need for continued US involvement. The altruistic concern for the well-being of the poor is now complemented with concern for the protection of US citizens. Hence, the articulation of security interests is beginning to be based on the interests of individuals, as the interests of the nation become difficult to identify. The thinking was formulated by George Bush when presenting his National Security Directive, December 1992:

> The dramatic changes underway in post-Cold War Africa present unprecedented opportunities and challenges for US policy. Africans, seeking economic progress and democracy, are beset by ethnic tensions, economic decline, environmental degradation, and new threats from AIDS and narcotics. Progress and stability will require a long-term effort both by the international community and by the Africans themselves ... We must reduce terrorism and narcotics trafficking in Africa, counter the proliferation threat, and limit subversion by radical regimes (e.g. Iran, Iraq, and Libya) that consider Africa a priority target and that are inimical to our interests. (NSD 75, 12/23/92)

These new security interests were clearly highlighted during the Africa Conference organised by the White House in summer 1994. The central national strategic interest of the United States vis-à-vis Africa, with the probable exception of security in oil supplies, is to avoid the danger of a spillover from a continent embroiled in chaos that would endanger social stability in Europe as well as in the United States. The question of what could be done to keep African problems in Africa was loudly asked. The policy of containing the communist threat gradually became transformed into what could be called 'the policy of containing the African danger'. Susan Rice, the Assistant Secretary for African Affairs, US State Department, consequently explained in a speech in October 1999 the necessity to let American policy towards Africa rest on two pillars: '[W]e seek to accelerate Africa's full integration into the global economy ... [and] we must defend the United States from the threats to our national security that emanate from Africa ... Terrorism, international crime, narcotics, weapons proliferation and disease.' These security interests, which came to dominate the White House Conference, are not only rhetorical. They have developed into American policy. The guiding principles decided by the US Congress – African Conflict Resolution Act (1995) was reconfirmed within the framework of Congress's approval of the Africa Growth and Opportunity Act (May 2000). Dissemination of AIDS is now classified as an American national security problem. The influence of the Ministry of Health on the American aid budget has consequently increased considerably. A 'democratic enlargement' has taken form, based on a new geo-economic synthesis. Only democracy and economic growth are considered to be able to create conditions for the search for political stability. The largest problem for a strong, but selective, US engagement is its financing. The aid fatigue in the US Congress is at least as palpable as in Europe.

According to conventional wisdom, stability could only be achieved through the logic of an expanding market economy enabling private actors and a process of democratisation to reduce scope for self-enrichment and misuse of power. In order to make the required integration into the world market possible the macro-economic balance must be reestablished. The role of development assistance became paramount. The involvement of the Bretton Woods institutions was a requirement for producing a regulatory framework motivating increased foreign capital flows. Increasing human and social capital and the rehabilitation of physical and commercial infrastructure required external resources which were not easily mobilised through private foreign investment flows. This conceptualisation was articulated by the US Treasury Secretary when addressing a seminar in Washington DC on increased commercial cooperation between the USA and Africa:

> Africa's growth and prosperity can be viewed as a moral imperative, but even leaving this aside, while Africa's growth and prosperity certainly is in Africa's interest, it is also very much in America's interest. A critical challenge for those in this country who recognize this identity of interest is to build among their fellow Americans a better understanding of the numerous dimensions of that identity of interest. A growing and dynamic Africa – an Africa committed to democracy, economic reform, sustainable development, and investing in human capital – will provide higher standards of living for its people and be more stable politically and socially. That, in turn, will present American businesses and workers with new opportunities to expand trade, create jobs and increase standards of living in this country, and will strengthen our national security, as stability in any part of the globe contributes to our national security. … In an era marked by true global interdependence, our economic success, our national security, our environmental protection, and our health are linked to a successful international economy, international political stability, effective environmental protection and health care throughout

the globe…let me turn to the United States and what we need to do to support the reform efforts of African nations and Africa's economic growth. …First, we must fully fund our commitments to international organisations such as the World Bank, the IMF, the African Development Bank and the United Nations to do our fair share and to maintain our leadership in shaping the global economy. In no other part of the world are these institutions more important than Africa. It is also very important that the World Bank and the IMF look closely at their programmes in Africa to make sure that they are working and are supporting Africa's boldest reformers. More generally, these institutions have their problems, but they are working to address those problems. …Second, we must continue to provide leadership to relieve unsustainable levels of debt. Africa's debt burden is now almost as large as its total GDP – the result of a lot of mistakes made by too many countries and by too many leaders. …Third, just as it is in the interest of African countries to open their markets to world trade, so too must we work to maintain United States' traditional openness to trade. …Fourth, we should utilize to the fullest extent that we can the agencies and programs we already have established to promote trade and investment. (Rubin 1997)

In order for the political elite to pursue such a policy, the social forces wanting to reduce bilateral aid and withdraw from the multilateral institutions must be counteracted. This requires stronger support from US non-governmental organisations and increased involvement of the US business community to influence the domestic political constituency and compensate for decreased government budget allocations for foreign aid.

Consequently, the Clinton administration strengthened its advocacy of the benefits of improved commercial relations with the continent. According to a report submitted by the President to the US Congress early in 1996, decreased aid should be counterbalanced through increased private capital investment.[3] The report points to high returns for American multinational firms in natural resources, manufacturing and services, reaching an average of 25 per cent in Africa in 1993 compared to 16.6 per cent and 8.6 per cent in all developing and developed countries respectively. According to the report, the US government would 'advocate actively on behalf of US companies seeking contracts in Africa'. Of special importance in this regard was the US administration's continued possibility of using the Bretton Woods institutions not only as foreign policy-making tools but primarily as US commercial tools.[4] The report refers to the US$700 million deal ENRON signed with the government of Mozambique to develop the Pande gas field as one of two examples illustrating the success of such advocacy.[5]

From these points of view, the current orientation of the economic and political reform programmes carried out in Africa is becoming counterproductive as no enabling environment for business is created. The economic difficulties encountered and the political instability created are not only causing security concerns and impeding world market integration, but the social unrest following restrictive policies risks being exploited by the regimes inimical to US security interests, namely Iran, Iraq and Libya, i.e. the Islamic factor.[6] Accordingly, the concern of the Western elites about the African danger manifests itself in a need to reformulate the development paradigm predominant within the Bretton Woods institutions.

## Global security interests and the World Bank

Over their fifty years, the Bretton Woods institutions have achieved their main objectives of defending the Western development paradigm in general and US world leadership in particular reasonably well. The affirmations made by the US Treasury, have recently been reconfirmed by the General Accounting Office.

It is therefore not very surprising to find that the security interest of the Clinton administration was well reflected by its new leadership in the World Bank as well as by its executive directors on the Board. Developmental ambitions, together with present difficulties with the long-term structural adjustment programmes, have made the World Bank understand the importance of 'ownership' and legitimate governance. Increased partnership and involvement of Africans is a prerequisite for the needed success stories.[7] Debt forgiveness is on the agenda (albeit on the basis of case by case) and NGOs are invited to assess the structural adjustment programmes critically and to propose alternatives. Given current population growth, poverty alleviation is of major concern, not only with the aim of environmental protection but also because social injustice presents one of the major challenges to stability in the world today:

> We must be aware of the close relation between peace and development. ... It strikes me as bitterly ironic ... [that] the threat to development assistance has never been greater ... [but] we must explain that world citizenship has a price ... private investments are not yet the answer for the poorer countries. (Wolfensohn 1995, pp. 10–12)

This new approach of the World Bank, though merely problem-solving in the terminology of Cox, is of utmost importance as it may open increased room for manoeuvre for national governance in the recipient countries. However, the World Bank leadership faces various challenges when getting its new policy ready for implementation. Strong reluctance is expected within its own organisation, which will require extensive and expensive internal restructuring. Prevailing attitudes within the donor community will have to be changed to facilitate future financing and implementation of the proposal for debt forgiveness. The World Bank is more dependent on its constituency and on taxpayers' money for its lending in comparison with the IMF, whose lending draws from the quotas paid by the member states and which can more readily get access to financial markets. As a consequence, the present World Bank leadership also needs urgent support from the business community and NGOs to mobilise public pressure on the various shareholders to enable the financing and implementation of its new policies.

Such support, however, contains a delicate incompatibility for the World Bank leadership to balance. On the one hand, support from the business community depends very much on how the Bank succeeds in creating an enabling environment, and thus motivates increased private involvement and expanding market forces. The World Bank must therefore be able to present various success stories to convince the traditionally somewhat reluctant financial markets that the macro-economic policy of the Bretton Woods institutions is correct and that opportunities exist for profitable private investment.[8] However, successful development in this regard may simultaneously hamper the effort to alleviate poverty and provoke criticism from the more human needs oriented NGOs. The NGOs also have a problem which is that they are incapable of offering the long-term continuity that rehabilitated confidence and social trust at the local levels requires. Those incompatibilities underline the probability that the coinciding interests between these forces only are temporary. The NGOs need to articulate their standpoints in such a way that their reluctance for structural adjustment does not turn out to be counterproductive. The strong criticisms, and the legitimate questioning of the programmes of the Bretton Woods institutions formulated in the recent NGO campaign '50 years is enough' is a case in point. The campaign, involuntarily and somewhat paradoxically, linked up with and considerably reinforced totally opposed interests representing the strong forces of reaction in the US Congress which wanted to withdraw future US financial support to the multilaterals.[9]

However, such a withdrawal or reduced commitment from the United States could provoke some of the main shareholders, particularly the European political elite, to search for development alternatives. Their efforts to regain control of market forces through increased regional cooperation, together with fear of the spill-over effects from an Africa in chaos, can put into motion a dynamic that gradually leads Western-based regional development banks to evolve into logical successors of the multilateral institutions. For Africa, such a development should not necessarily be conceived as a threat, as the geographical proximity and historical ties between Europe and Africa could make the coinciding interests for an alternative development even stronger. The question whether Europe is prepared to enter into such a new partnership remains to be answered.

## Towards a new partnership for Africa

These different tendencies in most of Western countries as regards future relationships with Africa, have been clearly illustrated in a multiplicity of recent 'partnership' seminars and conferences.

Indisputably, the political decision-makers involved in international development issues have all reason to consider the impact of development assistance to be in a situation equivalent to the metaphor 'up the down escalator' eloquently used by the President Norman Manley of Jamaica (Manley 1987). The flow of aid continues to support this view. Some $10 billion is transferred to Sub-Saharan Africa as annual development assistance, but the losses caused by constrained international trade are calculated by UNDP as UNCTAD to be five to six times as much. According to this logic, Africa would gain from decreased aid and more fair trade or, as the saying goes, 'less welfare and more employment'. If this became the case, the political leadership in the West would not have to ask its constituency for budget allocations, as increased cooperation with Africa would be paid by the consumers and not out of taxpayers' money.

Similarities notwithstanding, the ideas behind partnership have some important differences. In the United States it is more a question of how to replace aid with trade and investments. Evidence of diverging interests within the administration and inside the US Congress between different approaches has resurfaced.

In April 1997, the Clinton administration presented policies based on a new 'Partnership for Economic Growth and Opportunity' with Sub-Saharan Africa to Congress for consideration. The policy was a compromise between a broader, more encompassing US Africa policy as aimed at by the administration on the one hand, and strong domestic political forces on the other, wanting to consolidate the subordination of the continent as a more adequate approach compared to the proposed delinking by the more conservative forces. The policy is believed to create certain opportunities for the strongest of the Sub-Saharan countries, but difficulties will remain for the poorest. As the 48 countries constituting Sub-Saharan Africa are quite diverse, with varying capabilities and opportunities, a selective US commitment is on the agenda in Washington DC. Special attention and supportive development assistance will be concentrated on only a few countries with which the USA for various reasons considers increased trade to be of importance.[10]

The new US approach vis-à-vis Africa is clearly shown in the case of Angola. In Angola, oil plays a very important role in the provision of US energy. With exports to the USA corresponding to 7 per cent of imports, Angola is on the way to become one of the most important individual providers to the United States. This figure is expected to be doubled within ten years. Even if the lion's share of Angola's oil production is off-shore, a long-term provision security requires political stability. The oil companies have a long experience of the goodwill of the MPLA government, and its capacity to honour its agreements. This has been increasingly important in today's situation, when oil covering several years of future production has been mortgaged for short-term loans. The oil companies have also paid significant sums in signature bonus, already at the signing of the exploration contracts. Political chaos in Angola would, consequently, be negative for strategic American interests.

With a certain time-lag, the US foreign policy as regards Angola is now beginning to be redirected to coincide with the interests of the oil companies. This changed attitude is visible not least in the heavily increased aid flows, which, during the second half of the 1990s, have gradually made the USA Angola's largest partner in international development cooperation.

In sum, the present US policy towards Angola and the efforts to get it accepted by Congress reminds us very much of the US constructive engagement vis-à-vis Mozambique some ten years earlier under the auspices of Chester Crocker. For the US administration, continued South African destabilisation along with Renamo activities had become counterproductive. This is not to say that internal US consensus on this point was achieved. The experience from Mozambique, where the US military as well as civil intelligence for a time continued to work in the opposite direction, is also valid for the present situation in Angola. In fact, the process of globalisation with its liberalisation and privatisation of security forces has indisputably increased the divergent approaches from different US entities. However, as the case of Mozambique shows, the US national security interest, when defined, will soon get the upper hand. The question to which we now turn is related to the present political configuration in Africa and identification of internal social forces capable of using such an increased room for manoeuvre for a more coherent development strategy.

## Towards legitimate governance in Africa

The changed discourses on aid and the new emphasise on partnership, more fully involving the business sector and the civil society, were soon to have their followers. In late 1990 a number of European governments presented their visions for a new partnership with Africa. Western countries saw the capacity of the new generation of the African elite to seize this opportunity to increase social and political stability on the African continent as decisive if the continent were to find its way out of subordination and misery.

From an objective point of view the interest of the elite exists. As discussed earlier, with the termination of the Cold War, the possibilities for the African leadership to exploit the traditional East–West rivalry in consolidating their political power has ceased. At the same time, the organic crisis that characterises the African continent points to the need to expand the concept of security, based on national conditions according to which ruling elites can rejuvenate their lost economic and political legitimacy. Instead of external support, the leadership has to strive for an internal legitimate power base.

The African leadership was not slow to respond to the new enlightened self-interest at hand in Washington. At the beginning of 2001, South Africa together with Nigeria, Algeria and Senegal presented their views on a New Partnership for Africa's Development (NEPAD). The point of departure for the approach is that Africa must take on responsibility for its own destiny. Through its own efforts to increase economic performance and to strengthen democracy the continent must try to regain the confidence from the international private financial markets. However, in order to reduce poverty and to avoid present trends of marginalisation in the world economy, the African leaders asked not only for increased international development assistance but, above all-market access to increase trade. However, the proposed framework for action presented by these African leaders has met with suspicion from abroad and severe critisism from within. A number of critics in the West have pointed to the fact that the programme is not sufficiently anchored in African civil society, making it another elite project. The critics from within point to the fact that the aim of the programme to regain confidence of the international financial markets will further strengthen external dependency and reinforce the impact of Westernized development strategy with its neo-liberal approach.

There are various circumstances pointing to the fact that the Western paradigm of development in an African context constitutes an obstacle for the ability of the elite to develop an internal legitimate power base. The specific circumstances that characterised the modernisation of Europe no longer exist. The possibilities for resource utilisation in order to replicate European industrialisation on a global scale are exhausted, as was highlighted during the Rio Summit. The nation-state itself, so important for the process of European modernisation, is challenged not only from the outside by globalisation, but also from the inside by unsatisfied basic needs and the fact that the way states are formed and ruled is generally not conducive to cultural pluralism. Endeavours by the African elite to transform the pre-colonial, but still durable, political-administrative structure into a nation-state formation following the same European model that the colonial powers had applied, have been complicated by the fact that the Western world itself has gradually entered a post-Westphalian transition. The West is now searching for alternative nation-state formations to regain political legitimacy and counteract the negative impacts of the process of globalisation. In Africa as in Europe, the need for good governance must be met with an adequate balance among different levels of society, be they local, national or regional.

This implies an alternative mode of development based on the satisfaction of the basic needs of the rural population, the integration of prevalent traditional values with modern aspirations and a legitimate exercise of power. Internal power-sharing is required in order to enable the alternative elites to more fully participate in the policy-making process. This can, in some cases, imply the need for constitutional changes that have another framework for state-formation than the European model offers, one that is fully adapted to the requirements of a multi-ethnic society. A legitimate exercise of power also requires comprehensive poverty alleviation combined with a decentralisation of decision-making power. Eternal poverty creates tensions and social instability. In this sense the importance of local resource mobilisation is not only financial, but above all socially and politically required for rebuilding the legitimacy of the state and the local authorities.

Hence, for a legitimate exercise of power, the elites are primarily in urgent need of a mode of development capable of integrating modern aspirations more fully with the prevalent traditional values. Experiences from Mozambique point to the existence of various social forces that could make such an undertaking possible. However, these experiences also underline the fact that a large proportion of the national elite have sought new external allies to achieve their own private enrichment. New sets of tensions within national elites between those in need of an internal base for accumulation and those in needs of an external base have also been observed by various scholars at a more general level outside Mozambique (Shaw and Inegbedion 1994, p. 395). Some have sought bases of support through adherence to the Washington Consensus while others have tried to find a place in what Susan Strange calls the 'international business civilisation' (Strange 1990).

Meanwhile, it has become increasingly clear that structural adjustment will be unable to reestablish the macro-economic balance at a level compatible with development needs. The possibility of increasing integration into the world economy and the process of globalisation has furthermore been effected by the transformation of traditional industrialised capitalism into some kind of a more network-based capitalism. In order for geographical areas to be attractive for such networks an educated labour force as well as a high-tech IT-based infrastructure are required. Africa lacks these and they can hardly be developed in the near future. Some governments, not the least in southern Africa, have tried to establish specific development corridors in order to create required conditions. However, as the Maputo corridor witnesses, the investments are extremely capital intensive and produce limited linkages to motivate further investments. The job creation needed to increase productivity and purchasing power for the majority of the available labour force has not been accomplished. The part of the elite that defended the reform programme most ardently is the target of bitter domestic criticism. The part of the elite that linked up with international business interests feels that it has been used by these interests, and finds it increasingly difficult to play its role of 'lumpen bourgeoisie'. In addition, political figures wanting to maintain their leadership positions after elections must find ways of reestablishing legitimacy among their own people.

The more inwardly oriented 'organic intellectuals' play a most crucial role here in order to transform the effort for an alternative and the frequently mentioned but rather vague development vision into a coherent strategy capable of defending the interest of a large part of the social strata in the country. The importance that the strategy must give to the identification and satisfaction of local needs must be equal to that given to reducing dependence on international aid. A strategy placing importance on an expanded base for internal accumulation is a prerequisite for the mobilisation of sufficiently strong social and political forces to launch a Gramscian 'war of position', not only within the public administration itself but also, and particularly, in relation to the external financial institutions.

Thus, political forces in southern Africa face two challenges: one is to keep the national project alive and sufficiently active for the emergent social leadership not to be coopted by the donor community or the 'international business civilisation' (becoming 'instrumental intellectuals', splitting the Gramscian organic intellectuals), and the other is to ensure that the national project is really national, in the sense that it takes as its starting point the needs of the peasant population and can respond to some of the demands presented by the emerging movements of social resistance.

## Coinciding interests and counteracting forces

Experiences from Mozambique point to that the real challenges for the African elite consist in their capacity to formulate an alternative development strategy in terms of a 'national project' that can satisfy and thereby unify the various political forces in play. The problem for this undertaking is, however, that at present the social forces in Africa, pushing for an alternative, more rural and inward-looking strategy are dispersed and politically fairly unorganized. So is the alternative political leadership. In fact, probably the greatest harm that the structural adjustment programme with its aid conditionality has implied is severely reduced creative capacity for most political leaders. The aid dependency and inflow of virtually hundreds of different aid organisations has taken the time away from independent thinking and elaboration of strategies and killed the vision-making capacity for the future at all levels. As all strategies at the sectoral levels, along with their budgets, must be approved by the Bretton Woods institutions even before presented to the parliament for internal debate, the national political motivation for such an undertaking has eroded.

The economic liberalisation accompanied with privatisation has simultaneously motivated the leadership to give priority to their personal interest. In this sense the structural adjustment programmes have had a remarkable success. Collective action and strength have been replaced by individualism and neo-Darwinism where only the fittest will survive. The lack of collective vision obviously reduces the possibilities for creating political alliances (in the

Gramscian terms of historic blocs) at the national level able to unify sufficient social carriers and political power needed for an alternative development. For many of the political leaders, there doesn't seem to exist any alternative at all to what is decided upon and financed by the 'Washington consensus'. The lack of vision for the future and of any alternative to the present structural adjustment programmes make the leadership forced to subordinate itself to the predominant Western development paradigm and all kinds of aid conditionalities. The actual and realistic alternative that the leadership face is not a more inward-looking strategy but reduced aid and increased marginalisation from the world economy, i.e. an involuntary delinking.

Mozambique is a good example of the attempts being made to avoid such a situation. Here the leadership of the country tries, together with representatives of the international donors, to convince the international financial markets that the country is on the right track. Although the statistical basis is quite deficient, the economic reform programme is described as a success story. But Mozambique also does show the difficulties, and what happens when trying to hide the problems. In spite of a rapid economic growth in certain areas, the poverty in the countryside is increasing. It is very difficult to mobilise the necessary resources to alleviate the conditions that are keeping the country dangerously close to the trap of low-level security equilibrium. The rural population lacks access to agricultural tools and a working commercial network. The confidence in the government has been further weakened, and serious demands for the partition of the country are voiced. At the same time, the leadership starts to realise the importance of broad political alliances, and a 'smart partnership' between different social groups, to meet the challenges of globalisation. Different initiatives are taken to create this political alliance between the political elite, the enterprises, the civil society and media. Thus attempts are made via partnership to achieve the national consensus around vision and strategy which the Western multiparty system and the parliamentary debate have not been able to reach. However, the problem still remains that the market has never been interested in combating poverty.

In Angola also great efforts are made. The image disseminated in the West that the war is caused by two elite groups struggling for shares of oil and diamonds, while external interests are cheering for their profits, is strongly simplified. Instead of gaining from continuous war, the national elite are becoming more and more dependent on internal legitimacy and a decent base of accumulation. The emergence of a coinciding elite interest in increased political stability is also evident.

On the one hand, the end of the Cold War has removed the possibility of basing governance on external legitimacy. Even if the government's income from oil makes it possible to continue the financing of the war, the rearmament after 1992 has swallowed a huge part of the oil revenues. Periodically, this has created cash-flow problems, which have had to be resolved by short-term and expensive foreign borrowing. According to estimates, the debt service uses 35 to 40 per cent of export revenues. This has forced the government into an agreement with the IMF, which is considered to be a prerequisite for rescheduling both in the Paris and the London Clubs.

On the other hand, the exclusive character of globalisation does not permit the Angolan economic elite to gain a foothold in the global economy. The layers in the Angolan society, who possibly could have built a 'primitive accumulation' out of oil and diamonds, and putting the money in insecure investments in the international financial market, are today confronting a situation where investment within the country may seem to be more secure in the long run. The increasingly fragmented domestic economy has, however, eroded the conditions for production and investment in productive activities. Investments outside the dominating oil and diamond sectors require expanded internal markets and an increased purchasing power. This, in its turn, increases the necessity of political and social stability. Different actors, of which some for various reasons earlier created the structural obstacles to peace and development in the country, now start, for quite other reasons, to challenge these structures, making them visible, and thereby contributing to gradual change. Strategic plans for a transition from war to peace are drawn up in cooperation between the government and the UN system, in which the emergency aid is linked to development cooperation. The need for strengthened local mobilisation of resources and local administration are emphasised, as well as the importance of macro-economic balance. At the regional level, the discussion regards how 'smart partnership' may be able to reinforce conditions for economic development and common security.

The problem in Angola is in the short run dependent on how the government and the international and regional community can reach an agreement on how to handle the post-Savimbi situation.

The risk that the new peace agreement will be followed by an uncontrolled proliferation of small and desperate armed groups should not be underestimated. One must not forget that many of UNITA's generals were born into the war, brought up to a life of war, and constitute a potential raw material for a new generation of warlords. Globalisation has interfered at the local level and created its international networks, making possible a continuous illegal exploitation of diamonds or production of drugs, and individual enrichment. This also applies to generals and higher officers on the government side, which will demand special attention in the ongoing process of demobilisation.

Angola shows clearly how domestic elite groups in need of internal accumulation can, as mentioned before, become active actors in the peace-building process. Hence, whether the historical role of the elites in societal change is conflict prone or inclined to peace building must be contextualized and based on their present situation. Various elite groups can subjectively perceive themselves as deprived of entitlements (conflict-prone). Their own perception of privation makes them strive for social change. Somewhere, however, one finds a limit. At a given point they realise that the difference between their own assets and others is legitimate and something they in the short run have to live with. As best the situation can be changed in the long run. But when they have reached this point, the next question arises. Will the existing structures permit their continued accumulation (and political legitimacy respectively) in order to not only change their situation in the long run but also to maintain and consolidate their present level of needs satisfaction? This reasoning is at hand as well within the transnational elite preoccupied with the survival of the system as within the national African elite concerned with their own survival. As regards the latter, the political as well as economic elites will at a given time experience objective needs for structural change permitting peace and stability to survive as a social category (propensity to peace). It is our argument that the marginalisation of Africa has increased these needs for change of the economic elite in the same way that the end of the Cold War has increased the political elite's interest in change, as they cannot base their legitimacy upon external support any longer.

## Seizing the opportunity

The enlightened self-interest of western elite groups in combating poverty and promoting development in Africa has once again, at least rhetorically, manifested itself through the UN millennium declaration, endorsed by 147 heads of states or governments in early September 2000. World poverty is to be reduced by 50 per cent until year 2015. After September 11th, 2001, the Bush administration articulated these new security interests and reconfirmed the need for poverty reduction in its Millennium Challenge Account presented to Congress in March 2002. International development assistance provided by the United States should increase by 50 per cent during the coming years. Indisputably, there is also a growing awareness that terrorism cannot be dealt with through military means only but, above all, requires strengthened efforts to reduce poverty and deprivation, where often desperate political actions like terrorism are rooted or find fertile grounds for recruitment of adherents.

It is the main argument of this book that the new security interests of important western economic and political elite groups are creating an opportunity for the transformation of some of the world order structures impeding peace and development in Africa.

If this opportunity for structural change is not seized, and if instead a mixture of the trends towards marginalisation and subordination were to become predominant, the room for manoeuvre for national governance in Sub-Saharan Africa will drastically decrease. It is true that there is something in the arguments launched by various western Africanists at the beginning of the 1990s (e.g. Clough 1992) that increased marginalisation could increase room for manoeuvre for an alternative development. In fact, such arguments followed on from the long-standing analysis of the dependency school that strongly advocates delinking (Amin 1990).[11] However, the dilemma is that such marginalisation will be accompanied by a substantial decrease in aid flows. As considerable external resources are required for the envisaged transformation of the colonial structures of production that still predominate, the Sub-Saharan countries will be forced into the 'worldwide race to attract private capital' that Summers earlier advocated (Summers 1997). Apart from the fact that the record is less than impressive, the demands of the financial markets for returns on their investments are not very compatible with the effort for a more inwardly-oriented approach. Accordingly, continued marginalisation will, admittedly somewhat paradoxically, decrease the room for manoeuvre for national governance in Sub-Saharan Africa. However, as earlier discussed, the possibilities of seizing the structural opportunity for change are simultaneously challenged by different actors at various levels.

At the global level, the possibility of taking advantage of the structural opportunity for change is challenged by strong isolationist and parochial forces in the West, which want to withdraw from international involvement. Paradoxically, some of the NGOs questioning current resource allocation through the Bretton Woods institutions are involuntarily aligning with these forces of reaction in opposition to continued international cooperation. This illustrates the dilemma that legitimate questioning of the 'Washington Consensus' can possibly reduce the chances for the social forces fully to utilise the existing structural opportunity.

The possibilities for change are also challenged by that part of the political and economic elite that is reluctant to question the 'Washington Consensus', reorient the reform programmes and agree to debt forgiveness. These forces are not prepared to give up the disciplinary power that the short-term macroeconomic remedies of the IMF still represent. On the contrary, they strive for the continued subordination of the continent in order to maintain the status quo and consolidate short-term Western influence. The aim is to overcome the contradiction created by a universal Western development paradigm in combination with prevailing ecological constraints, namely reduced replicability of the paradigm, without having to fear giving an opening to free-riding from competing civilisations.

As regards the dynamics at the regional level, Hettne conceives the efforts of parts of the political leadership for reinforced regional cooperation as the second phase of a double movement, and as a possibility for counteracting marginalisation and increasing the global leverage of the continent (Hettne 1997). Continued external support encouraging such regional integration can indisputably be expected, not the least from a security point of view, aiming to enable Africans to solve African problems in Africa. As regards southern Africa, the abolition of apartheid implies new patterns of conflict that must be dealt with on a regional level. Migration, access to water and the illegal drug trade are some areas of concern. Developments within South Africa and its relations with neighbouring countries will be crucial to future regional development. The present political instability could increase if the new government is unable to match up to the people's enormous expectations and this, in combination with external rivalry and reluctance for cooperation on more equal terms, could contribute to increased chaos in the region. It is furthermore difficult to imagine strong regional cooperation without strong and legitimate states at the national level. Although a multilevel approach is called for, with more of the conventional as well as new state functions carried out on various levels, the involvement of the local community and increased territorial emphasis is required in order to achieve conflict resolution and more long-term sustainable peace and development.

As discussed, the objective of the emerging coinciding elite interests is not only to facilitate the progressive integration of African countries into the world economy but also to foster the integration of poor populations into the economic, social and political life of their countries. However, such integration can only be carried out on the local level following coordination at the national level to allow the necessary sub-national regional balance in resource allocation.

At the local and national level, Mozambique's experience indicates that the real challenges to the African elite lie in their capacity to formulate an alternative development strategy in terms of a 'national project' that can satisfy, and thereby unify, the various sub-national political forces involved. Such a national 'consensus' is a prerequisite for the political alliances needed between social bearers at different levels in order to implement the strategy. In the next chapter we will elaborate further on some crucial elements that such a national project needs to include.

# 9
## Out of the Trap

The argument of this study is that the uneven process of globalisation, reinforced short-term and long-term contradictions, and a new pattern of conflicts has resulted in a need for the political elites in the Western countries to redefine their national security interests vis-à-vis Sub-Saharan Africa. This need has been accentuated by the end of the Cold War. A consensus has been reached by a more reformistic economic and political elite with enlightened self-interest on the importance of allowing an African bourgeoisie to emerge that can elaborate and implement an inclusive process of accumulation, facilitating increased local participation, purchasing power and rehabilitated social trust. In order to avoid the trap of low-level security equilibrium, there is a need for an alternative development strategy that combines constructive aspects of modernisation with values from the traditional sector.

This study further argues that transnational developmental interests are coinciding with the interests of the African elite, whether the economic activities of the latter are internally or externally oriented. Contradictions within the present structures, both in the world order and in the national and local social relations of production (Cox 1987), have begun to constrain the fulfilment of the national elite's economic and political aspirations and have thereby begun to challenge its survival as a social group. Reduced possibilities for an externally based legitimacy that permits a response (coercive or democratic) to increased popular demands forces the African elite to turn inward, to strengthen its vertical links with civil society and to seek an alternative development strategy.

As highlighted in this study, the implementation of a poorly designed structural adjustment programme has not solved the economic problems created by earlier government failures to establish conditions for development in rural areas. On the contrary, the problem has been aggravated by additional market failure. In the economic vacuum created by the crisis of the state and the lack of institutions enabling the transition from a state-led economy to a more market-oriented economy, new economic zones have emerged, from the interest of the rapidly expanding illegal international network, be it in the production of narcotics, illicit drugs trade, arms trafficking, the unregulated storage of toxic waste or money laundering. The legitimacy of the state has eroded even further and social instability has increased in both rural and urban areas.

Of special concern is how the more individualistic Western development thinking, together with the inability of the state to offer protection and security, is rapidly destroying traditional horizontal linkages in the villages, substituting them with vertical relations and a new social relationship in the form of informal but protective landlordism. Even though this development constitutes a society's defence against the influence of a perverted market economy, this social protection is not necessarily progressive, and history shows how it tends to reinforce social distrust (Polanyi 1957).[1] In a southern Africa context this could mean that organised violence in the countryside becomes permanent. Although there are major differences, there are enough similarities between the development of rural Mafia-dominated capitalism in southern Italy during the 1800s and current developments in the countryside of Angola and Mozambique to cause serious concern.

These circumstances require an analysis of whether or not it is possible, in the short run, to adjust the country's economy through restrictive monetary policies aiming at increased export earnings and decreased budget expenditure. Our findings question the logic behind the design of the structural adjustment programme in poor countries like Mozambique, namely the wisdom that a macro-economic balance is a short-term prerequisite for achieving structural transformation in the long-term. The chronic imbalances during the colonial times point to the need to start the other way around. A comprehensive structural transformation of the countryside, increasing productivity, demand and domestic market expansion, should be carried out before any macro-economic balance can be achieved.

This is not to say that structural transformation should neglect the importance of correct macro-economic policies. The budget must have the long-term possibility of being balanced, the financial gaps closed, the inflation rate acceptable and the foreign exchange rate realistic. However, the problem is not only a question of correct timing and sequencing: the measures so far taken have emphasised macro-economic policies too strongly at the expense of the needed poverty eradication.[2]

## Searching for a way out

In the search for a way out, the pattern of the present economy set in the colonial days of an externally-oriented economy must be transformed through a more inward-looking strategy aimed at satisfying the basic material and non-material needs of the population.

The design of such a development strategy must take into consideration the requirements for enabling the settlement achieved to develop into a more long-term phase of conflict resolution. These requirements involve a complex set of socio-political and socio-economic considerations. The research carried out by Anders Nilsson (1999) has identified some fundamental socio-political cornerstones on which to build bridges from conflict settlement to conflict resolution in a southern Africa context.

Experience gained from the recent development in Angola and Mozambique contributes with four requirements for moving out of the trap of low-level security equilibrium: (1) the need for inclusivity–the sub-regional balance; (2) the need for a rural development strategy; (3) the need for increased local resource mobilisation; and (4) the developmental role of the state and the need to provide the peasantry with continuity, security and public goods.

## Inclusivity – the sub-regional balance

The sub-regional imbalance and marginalisation of large geographical areas within the nation state, which has been the consequence of the colonial borders is a factor behind the feelings of marginalisation and frustration generating rivalry and conflicts between alternative elites and the central power. Thus, a national development strategy has to be as inclusive as possible, and strive for an extensive sub-regional balance. This concerns not only productive investments and access to social infrastructure. It also concerns equal possibilities to participate in economic activities, as well to participate in, and exert influence on, the political decision-making process. The question of language for reinforced identity and self-esteem should again be mentioned. This can raise the question of constitutional changes, allowing for multi-ethnic states with parallel languages within education and public administration. This may contribute to the creation of new historic blocs, and the required national consensus on a development vision and strategy.

## The role of rural development

At the beginning of the 1980s, when structural adjustment programmes were introduced, the need for social equality and reducing the gap in living standards between urban and rural areas was strongly advocated, in accordance with the analysis provided by Lipton (1977).

Since then, strong concern has been expressed over the impact of the structural adjustment programme on the majority of the Mozambicans who live in the countryside. There has been little investment, there are few opportunities for salaried work and the majority of the rural population lacks access to an efficient marketing network by means of which agricultural surpluses can be sold and where, most importantly, agricultural implements such as tools and seeds can be bought to produce a surplus.

One reason for such neglect was the South African destabilisation, which made any investment programme in the rural areas difficult to carry out for security reasons. However, the Country Assistance Strategy papers for Mozambique produced by the World Bank in Washington, indicates other reasons for the neglect. Apart from measures for stimulating the growth of agricultural exports (to facilitate internal resource mobilisation or to repay debts) the documents contemplate little to assist small-scale farming, despite considerably improved security in the countryside and the resettlement of returning refugees.

The documents reflect the fact that the conventional conceptualisation of a non-existent role for farmers in the development process still prevails at the World Bank headquarters in Washington. Consequently, the Bank's internal forecasts expect that, following the economic modernisation, agriculture's contribution of some 25 per cent of GDP will be maintained and the distribution of IDA credits gives very low priority to the agriculture sector. Following the neo-liberal ideology, the sector's development is to be taken care of by private entrepreneurs and market forces, once an enabling environment has been created.

The economic history of Europe is the history of how the peasantry was captured. Surpluses extracted from the peasantry have been crucial for any kind of accumulation in the European process of modernisation, be it capitalism or socialism.[3] Despite frequent affirmations that similar kinds of surplus extraction from the rural areas were possible in post-independence Angola and Mozambique, this was hardly the case. A scattered peasantry, low productivity and limited quantities for sale made the cost of marketing extremely high, and the extractable surplus minimal (Tickner 1992).

However, having said that, rural development still plays an important economic role in the short term as well as in the long term. The conditions for balancing the state budget depend on the state's ability to increase its tax collection base and/or domestic savings. In turn, the conditions for improving the trade balance depend on the possibility of transferring domestic demand for imported goods and services to locally produced goods and services. These two factors are totally dependent on the occupation of the rural population, increasing productivity and having the ability to mobilise local resources. In other words, the peasants' productive potential must be used in order for the macro-economic balance to be established. Furthermore, taking advantage of the rural population's production potential is a prerequisite for long-term sustainable economic development. Improved purchasing power is a necessary condition for expanding the domestic market and for establishing dynamic links between town and countryside and between agriculture and light manufacturing industry. There are obviously a number of other important reasons for giving priority to the rural sector. One is related to the need of poverty eradication. A particular aspect of rural poverty in Mozambique is economic vulnerability. Due to the war, individuals have few assets, whether in the form of human capital or of physical wealth, over which they have security. Hence, measures are needed to stabilise and consolidate the household economy, simultaneously improving the external macro-economic balance by making domestic food production a decisive tool for import substitution. Another important reason relates to the question of scarce resources and the need of the poor to take short-term measures to guarantee their survival that do not take environmental questions fully into consideration. In the case of southern Africa worsening poverty, rapid demographic growth, lack of fertile land and falling water reserves, together with changes in climatic conditions, create the danger of new shortages during the coming decades. At the same time, food supply on the world market is not expected to develop at the same rate as the demand that will result from worldwide population growth. In addition to substantial price rises, there is a great risk of social agitation, new patterns of conflicts and political tensions. With a demographic growth of 3 per cent annually, Mozambique will have a population of 75 million by 2050. The country will then be below what is considered to be the danger limit for the arable land/inhabitant ratio (0.7 hectares per capita). At this point, a dramatic increase in the use of mechanisation, fertilisers and artificial irrigation is necessary to maintain food production, giving rise in turn to increased unemployment among peasants and worsening poverty. A third reason relates to social equality. During recent years social differentiation has increased fairly fast. Female-headed households have been particularly affected, because when, after the war, they returned to their home areas they had neither the material resources nor a sufficiently large family to be able to begin farming for themselves, which meant that they often remain in a state of dependency in relation to better-off neighbours for whom they work on an irregular daily basis, often paid in food (Åkesson 1994). This differentiation is aggravated by traditionally unequal patterns in the local division of land, in which different clans have different access to land in a function of their social status.

## Local resource mobilisation

In discussing the question of local resource mobilisation, I prefer to use the concept 'local development' rather than 'rural development'. To use the term 'rural development' risks limiting analysis to questions that are directly linked to the peasantry, and seeing agricultural production and marketing in an over-narrow perspective. For the peasants increasing production, marketing their surpluses and satisfying consumption needs are all of equal importance. The 'local development concept' is important because it includes urban and semi-urban areas and offers the space for a dynamic economic inter-connection between town and countryside. Demand and purchasing power in the semi-urban areas are important as bases for local markets and for expanding peasant production. As Braudel showed, local markets and their informal credit systems played a major role in European economic development (Braudel 1979).[4]

In discussing the concept of local mobilisation of resources, a distinction between two stages is called for. In the short term the aim is to encourage the general growth of production in order to satisfy basic needs, thus enabling families to save and ensure their food security through a minimum of capital in terms of cattle, goats or chickens that will sustain them in the years of poor harvests. Improved social security networks and investments in domestic goods also form part of these security savings. In the medium term, local mobilisation of resources is linked to attempts to consolidate a surplus production at local community level that can contribute towards financing social needs such as health services, education, road maintenance, etc.

The importance of making better use of the possibilities that actually exist for local mobilisation of resources thus has various dimensions though it is often seen merely as a possibility for obtaining finance that should be tried when there are no other options. The dilemma is that many poor peasants cannot contribute towards local resource mobilisation of this kind in the short term. On the one hand, there is a problem of production methods and access to land; on the other, there is a tendency not to take more from nature than is required to guarantee immediate food needs. However, it is worth emphasising that fieldwork has drawn attention to the fact that the importance of local mobilisation of resources is not only financial, but above all social and political. It is primarily a question of increased local participation for satisfying locally identified needs so that the legitimacy of the state and the local authorities can be rebuilt – and this is why the problems related to poverty must be attacked. This underlines the importance of looking upon development as a process aiming to create conditions that will enable each human being to realise her/his potential for political, social and economic fulfilment in a manner consistent with the common good.[5]

## The developmental role of the state

A legitimate exercise of power requires a comprehensive strategy for poverty eradication combined with a decentralisation of decision-making power. As the experience from Mozambique shows, local resource mobilisation is required not only financially, but above all socially and politically, for rebuilding the legitimacy of the state and the local authority. The traditional silent resistance of the peasantry can only be transformed into local participation in implementing the development vision through increased social trust and increased state credibility as a development agent, concerned with peasant well-being.

The need for social forces and their 'organic intellectuals' to rehabilitate lost political legitimacy and social trust in order to avoid an approaching organic crisis and initiate a process of development raises the question of the validity of the nation-state project as such. In re-launching the discussion on the importance of local identification of needs, resource mobilisation and basic needs satisfaction, the starting point of this study is not the 1980s view that idealised peasants and peasant society's possibilities of using all its inherent potential for development once it was de-linked from the state.[6] Peasant society traditions are often hierarchical and not very democratic, and can even constitute obstacles to development, in the sense that the rural areas can have plenty of resources and potential for increasing resource mobilisation, but using them is unviable for different cultural and structural reasons. Local development will accordingly not be conceived as a way of de-linking from the state. On the contrary, local development and decentralisation are a reciprocal need for the state and the local community, enabling legitimacy and social trust to be reconstituted. Legitimacy and social trust are the most important preconditions for development, and the state at central level indisputably has an important role as catalyst and supporter of the public sector's development efforts at micro-regional and local levels.

As earlier discussed, provided that the constitutional framework permits a decentralised multi-ethnic state, the role of the state will still be important. In fact, it is the national and local levels that shape the political forces and provide space for their articulation. At the present juncture, the state elite play a preponderant role in the creation of the needed historic bloc and for the development process as such. The market forces and national entrepreneurial skill, together with 'civil society', are too weak to relate adequately to the process of globalisation, minimising the effects of the ongoing process of marginalisation. Experiences from Mozambique point furthermore to the fact that the state is presently the only development agent capable of acting as a catalyst for a more territorial, bottom-up development process (Abrahamsson and Nilsson 1996), provided that the need for good governance can be met with an adequate balance between different levels of society, whether local, national or regional. The nation-state level is also where the main interaction with the surrounding world takes place and where the room for manoeuvre of the country's international relations is determined.

## Continuity versus opportunities

The need for a locally based development strategy obviously raises the question of how to transform the prevailing modes of production earlier discussed in terms of an economy of affection. For Hydén the state is incapable of playing any developmental role as it is too penetrated by these relations of affection (Hydén 1983). Furthermore, an economy based on informal rules and social obligations with low market integration and low purchasing power makes it difficult for the market economy to expand.

Consequently, it is thought that measures are needed to initiate a process of social transformation able to break down the economy of affection and replace it with opportunities for a more utilitarian and profit-maximising oriented peasantry to emerge (Hydén 1983).

In the case of Mozambique, as described, the economy of affection emerged in part as a result of the national market never having needed to expand domestically during the colonial period and because salary levels (and consequently purchasing power) had to be kept as low as possible. It also emerged due to the continued need of the political elite and the local population for a network of social protection, even after political independence. This means that neither the market nor the state can break down the economy of affection so long as the need for traditional protection networks continues to be felt by both the population and the elite. Accordingly, and quite contrary to conventional wisdom, neither the state, as advocated by Hydén in the late 1970s (Hydén 1980), nor the market, as advocated by him some three years later (Hydén 1983) can break down the economy of affection as long as peasant propensity to minimise risks remains. Instead, the existing economy of affection must be taken as a starting-point for local development.

Such a statement requires another conceptualisation of the rationality of the peasantry. Instead of trying to implement measures to enable market opportunities for a more utilitarian and profit-maximising attitude to emerge (often through the price mechanism only), efforts must firstly be made to rehabilitate social trust and the peasantry's need for security and continuity. Such efforts are necessary in order to increase local participation and resource mobilisation. For this to occur, strong emphasis must be placed on rehabilitating the commercial network in remote rural areas, but such undertakings cannot be carried out by private traders alone. Many of the scattered peasants are too poor to be either producers or consumers from the market's point of view. The experience from Mozambique points to the need for state intervention to act as a catalyst. An increased role for the state does not mean that the centralised top-down perspective that characterises Frelimo's efforts to come to grips with the rural question should be followed. A more bottom-up perspective based on the local identification of needs is an important requirement.

A continued focus on inflation and short-term stabilisation will however impede government efforts to provide resources for the rural trade and food security needed to enable the peasantry to participate more fully in surplus production and local resource mobilisation. Hence, a more expansive monetary and financial policy with increased budget allocations and access to credits is called for. This does not necessarily mean that it has to be financed through monetarising parts of the deficit (i.e. expanding domestic credit to government). An increase in the state budget could be financed through reorientating current aid, to channel a large portion as decentralised budget support instead of general balance of payments support. Preferably, however, it should be financed through an immediate cancellation of the debt, which would immediately reduce the prevailing budget constraints and ease possible inflationary pressures.

This raises the issues of the room for manoeuvre for change and the possibility of alternative development, to which we now turn. A rural-based development strategy with increased local resource mobilisation would contribute to creation of such room for manoeuvre.

## Provision of public goods

The literature has devoted much space to the question of how the inherited colonial state could be restructured to attain a good developmental state, with regained legitimacy and a popular belief in the capacity of the political system to make decisions about resource distribution.

During recent years the Bretton Woods institutions have realised the significance of a strong and effective state, which can provide the legislative framework, the institutions and the public goods that a well-functioning market economy requires. In this context the cultural and socio-economic pattern of the economy of affection is seen as a strong obstacle. Its low productivity does not allow for the needed tax base. The peasants live dispersed in large areas. They are following a risk-minimising strategy, search for continuity and security, and are reluctant to change the basic mode of production just to seize the temporary opportunities of the market. The strategies formulated for rural development continue to build upon forms of functional modernisation. Often it is only a question of concentrating scarce resources to help foreign owners maintain the mechanised cash-crop farms, which were established during the colonial era. There is still a lack of active systems for marketing peasant surplus production, and also of agricultural inputs and consumer goods. Worse, family farmers in many areas even lack access to agricultural tools. Any discussion about how to relegitimate the political system is firstly about how to supply necessary public goods.

The lack of legitimacy for the state is to a great extent due to the fact that legitimacy for peoples' aspirations for a better life after political independence has not been achieved. The state has never had the administrative capacity required to undertake a regional distribution of the benefits that the functional strategy of modernisation has occasionally created. This capacity has not increased with globalisation and the political requirements for downsizing. In large parts of the countries the state is simply not present. In such areas, evidently, other local forms of political decision-making logically take over legitimacy. That is why traditional patterns of life and culture, as well as praxis of justice, are continuously living in parallel with the new formal legislation. The problem is that legal procedures not always are legitimate – and vice versa.

Simultaneously, the role of the state still embraces the contribution to a growth of civilness, i.e. the civil society. The civil society is needed to improve the capacity to articulate the needs and interests of the peasantry, to bridge contradictory needs of different sub-national identities, and to create the necessary bases for dialogue in order to prevent conflicts developing into violence. In order for this reinforced 'social cohesion' be allowed to develop, a protective framework of rules is needed. Until new, still not known, institutions have been able to emerge at different levels, the *de facto* existing state must find a way to take on this task.

As discussed, this is not easily achieved via a functional development strategy. The required legitimacy can only be achieved through a more territorially-directed strategy. Decentralisation of the political decision-making and establishing a meeting-point between the customs within the economy of affection and society's judicial praxis may increase the participation of the local communities. The way is to take as the point of departure the 'really existing economy' of affection, and complement traditional customs with modern methods. Instead of which the attempt is usually to complement and locally anchor modernisation through inviting traditional leaders, whose popular base and legitimacy are often questionable, to participate.

Improved legitimacy of the state can furthermore only be achieved through improved social trust. The most important public goods that the state can provide are those which facilitate the emergence of this social trust. First and foremost there is food security. We will come back to the question of how food security can be improved, for example through a reinforced commercial network. But improved food security presupposes individual security. In too many African countries people have to enter partly mined fields in order to produce food. The question of security is thus probably the most important factor for legitimacy creation. This brings us into the question of violence and the role of the defence forces.

Regarding defence, the society must find forms to move from private to legitimate public use of organised violence. The state's lack of resources has meant that it has lost its monopoly of legitimate use of violence. Protection and security services have been privatised, and national armies have lost control of the escalated spontaneous violence, and sometimes also participate in violent looting in order to survive. Instead of a legal and administrated payment of taxes, new mechanisms have appeared for extracting resources through organised violence. In the current situation, we must reformulate the 'Hobbesian dilemma' to find a solution. The dilemma does not any longer consist of state abuse of the source of protection, but in the absence of the state, and the lack of means for protection of the population. The provision of security by the state is, thus, the most important condition for all local development and poverty eradication. The state must be enabled to resume its monopoly on legitimate violence. For this to take place, two issues must be tackled.

The first is the demobilisation of soldiers, who have previously been at war. The demobilisation must be understood as a process which is not completed until the soldiers are reintegrated into civil society. Financial means for this reintegration must be made available. Unsuccessful reintegration and inability to sustain themselves and their families lead demobilised soldiers to dig up their guns, which have temporarily been stowed away, or accept recruitment into private armies. Especially noteworthy is the situation of demobilised middle-rank officers. They have often spent a long period within the defence forces, together with their families, and lost many important civil connections.

The second issue is the proper concept of security, and the relation between the armed forces and the civil society. Since the war of liberation the armed forces have been associated with national independence, have won a considerable respect among the liberated population and acquired an important role in the creation of a national identity. After independence, the armed forces often wanted to build further on this legitimacy, in taking a position as both symbol and condition for the national project's wanted modernisation. The post-independence new objective of protecting the country from, mainly, external enemies, came, at the same time, gradually to distance the armed forces from society at large. This implied a growing impotence in providing the population with security against internal violence, something that gradually came to erode the legitimacy of the defence forces as such. This reduced capacity to provide internal security, together with a lack of available jobs and projects for the demobilised, as well as poor conditions for those still in the army, encouraging the creation of private armies. Hereby, the state's monopoly on legitimate violence gradually evaporated. The new, internal security threat that has resulted from intensified globalisation also demands a new and expanded concept of security. This could lead to a new role for the armed forces, and new interfaces with the civil society. Providing the defence forces with resources so that the forces can provide public goods in the form of individual protection and security would reinforce the legitimacy of the defence, and enable the state to regain its monopoly of legitimate violence.

# 10
# The Role of International Development Cooperation

In order to allow an African national elite to emerge, capable of elaborating and implementing a development strategy aimed at increased local participation, purchasing power and rehabilitated social trust, an encompassing transformation of some of the prevailing world order structures will be required. In this chapter we primarily focus on the role of international development cooperation. The main argument is that aid, if properly designed, could make an important contribution ending frustrations at local level and thereby contribute to peace and development.

However, if the West expects Africans to solve African problems in Africa, the West must also allow Africans to decide how to develop Africa. Such an affirmation raises the legitimate question whether increased space for African values will be compatible with continued international aid. So far international development assistance has been used for the diffusion of a Western development paradigm that can hardly be implemented in an African context.

Back in the early 1960s, the first development decade of the UN, radical forces in the West criticised the use of aid for diffusion of Western values, which would consolidate dependency and unequal development. More conservative forces, often for the same reasons, strongly supported aid. At the time, the radical elite in Africa supported the views from the left, at least rhetorically. Amilcar Cabral recommended that the Swedish solidarity movement, which sought advice on how to channel its support, should first concentrate on political change in their own country. At the same time the dependency school urged for a delinking from the world economy.

During the 1970s, the positions changed. Radical liberation movements in Africa and the American defeat in Vietnam constituted factors indicating that the requirement for a global structural change originated in the attempt to achieve human dignity by developing countries. At the same time, conservative forces became more parochial and reduced their support for continued assistance.

During the 1980s the bilateral aid flows stagnated and became simultaneously more short-term oriented. Balance of payment support and relief aid were given priority over more ambitious long-term development goals. This tendency continued during the early 1990s.

Notwithstanding the failure of aid to contribute to peace and development in Sub-Saharan Africa, international development assistance is nevertheless considered a prerequisite for the alternative development advocated by this study. Lack of social trust and political legitimacy at present makes the necessary local resource mobilisation difficult. Provided that international development assistance is reoriented and channelled into rural areas with the objective of acting as a catalyst for increased local participation, aid could contribute in transforming vicious circles into their opposites and thereby promote peace and development. I have argued that such a design would be in line with emerging interests amongst the political and economic elite in the West as well as in Sub-Saharan Africa. One effort on the part of well-known US 'Reaganites' to contribute to such a reorientation of foreign aid can be found in Crocker (1995):

> Our goal should be to strengthen, not further weaken, African governments so that they become capable of carrying out the basic functions of government anywhere. ... On the other hand, there is every reason for a reassessment of current assistance. Too much flows to assorted US contractors, consultants and insider constituencies. Too little of it goes directly to nurture African capabilities to build the kinds of societies and institutions that can stand on their own.

Accordingly, new national security interest has drastically changed the role of international development cooperation. In order to fully understand the driving forces behind and the dimension of such development, a further elaboration of our analytical model is called for.

## The geopolitics of aid

Aid efficiency is usually measured in relation to the impact of aid in the recipient country (impact-related efficiency). However, it is also important to evaluate aid efficiency in relation to the underlying motives of aid in the donor country (motive-related efficiency). Such an undertaking facilitates a fuller understanding of why aid at times is inefficient, or worse, does harm from the recipient's point of view.

These underlying motives reflect the dominant opinion and patterns of thought prevailing in the donor country (the discourse of the historic bloc). Hence, the dominant (hegemonic) discourse related to aid is constituted by different discourses in interaction, each one related to one of the justifying motives. The following analytical model departs from the components of

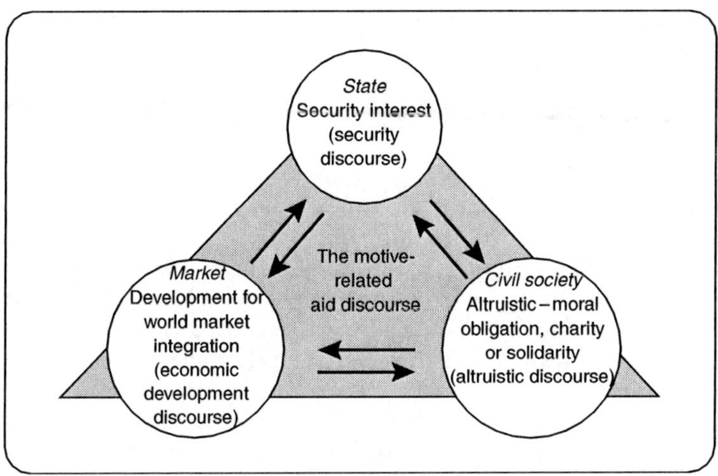


*Figure 10.1*   The composition of the motive related aid discourse

the historic bloc and their respective discourses and aims, in identifying the underlying motives for aid, to form an aid discourse.

The model given in Figure 10.1 identifies three motives, each with its peculiar discourse. In civil society, the altruistic motive is frequently articulated by public opinion. Moral obligation, charity or solidarity provides the justification for short-term humanitarian assistance. The motive for the economic elite (in this sense the market is here treated as an actor) to provide international development assistance is to create conditions and an enabling environment for a more comprehensive integration of the recipient country into the world market. Such understanding has become dominant in the economic development discourse. While the political elite is believed to share the altruistic concern of civil society and the developmental perspectives of the market, their perception of national security interests, and hence the geopolitical considerations, frequently gets the upper hand in their policy decision-making.

The model emphasises the importance of interaction between discourses as well as the impact of possible time lags. While the altruistic discourse, with its roots in values and belief system, is more static and therefore not easily transformed, the security discourse (based upon its perception of threat and identity) is somewhat more dynamic and adaptable to circumstances. The economic development discourse is even more so and displays a strong flexibility over time. However, it is the triangular relationship between these discourses that shape the motive related aid discourse. In reality the aid discourse is squeezed between the more static altruistic discourse on the one hand and the more dynamic security and development discourses on the other. Reality changes and discourses are transformed accordingly, although with a certain time lag. Furthermore, the policy level may be influenced by changed discourses quite fast. It takes more time to get the new security thinking to influence the implementation level, be it the military or economic sector. Such time lag is important to observe because it is in this time lag between changed reality, transformed discourses and their influence on the implementation level that opportunities emerge and room for manoeuvre for proposals and alternative thinking increases.

The reason why it is important to understand aid and its justifications as the outcome of the dominant discourses is the fact that these discourses are not always congruent. At times they are contradictory. When they are congruent, motive-related efficiency is high. Aid can be implemented with a more coherent force.

Since its inception a strong motive for international aid has been moral and altruistic. That also explains why descendants of the victims of abuse now try to remind us of colonial obligations and seek reparations as entitlement, be it for the slave trade or for more recent failure to prevent genocide, in order to counteract the increasing aid fatigue. As discussed in the first chapter, such moral duty also manifested itself in Western exceptionalism, i.e. the need to defend and spread Western values (of modernity, individualism, private property, democracy and human rights), claimed to be universal. Development was assumed to be a replica of the European model, with the market as the driving force (cf. Wilsonian version of manifest destiny). In the long run, international commercial interest and actors would replace aid. The main objective was to create the conditions for market expansion and foreign investments. (i.e. an enabling environment).

However, it is also true that aid always has had significant geopolitical motives. This became evident in what has become known as the founding speech of international aid, delivered by President Truman in the late 1940s. During the 1950s, US aid was called 'mutual security assistance'. In general terms, the security discourse and the development discourse moved more closely hand in hand. The altruistic discourse added a touch of rhetoric. This was hardly surprising, as development was seen as a means to security and vice versa.

During the 1960s and 1970s, Western national security interests vis-à-vis the south continued to be dominated by the policy of containment. Satisfaction of basic needs and decreased poverty was on the agenda. The security discourse harmonised with a Keynesian development discourse. Still, however, the altruistic dimension was present. One of the important aims of the development-oriented state was to eradicate poverty through radical income redistribution. In reality, however, this noble goal was subordinated to the requirements of the market. Achievement of economic growth and macro-economic balances would create conditions for foreign investment and creditworthiness in international financial markets. Consequently the development discourse started to shift, albeit gradually. With the Berg report in 1981 the neo-liberal thinking reached hegemony. Keynesianism and the belief in the developmental state were replaced by adherence to the market. This shift in development thinking coincided with (and was facilitated by) a remarkable shift in the security discourse. The Reagan administration entered into the second Cold War and the need to 'roll back communism' shaped political decision-making. International development cooperation became decisive in order to spread Western values and to facilitate the development and extension of the Polanyian 'first movement'.

## Peace and development as a global public good

After the end of the Cold War, the concept of security has been broadened and deepened. Inherent contradictions in the process of globalisation, earlier overshadowed by the preoccupations of the Cold War, have put non-military issues on the agenda. Possible connections between poverty and conflict have been brought into focus.

This has resulted not only in a change of the security discourses but also in a gradual change of the economic development discourse. Global poverty is to be decreased by 50 per cent before 2015. Such a global undertaking increases the room for manoeuvre for international development cooperation to deal with local poverty and conflicts. Over time, the combined and interlinked efforts to reduce poverty and increase political stability will make the security discourse and the economic development discourse converge with the more altruistic discourse behind international development cooperation. This will not only increase motive-related efficiency but enable increased impact-related efficiency of aid. Decreased efficiency gaps are important prerequisites for coming to terms with the aid fatigue evidenced by public opinion.

Having said this, one should not underestimate the constraints that international political economy and its world order structures impose on the impact-related efficiency. It is however, believed that decreased aid fatigue could increase the room for manoeuvre for a more radical change of the framework within which international development cooperation takes place. In fact international development cooperation by itself could contribute considerably to the creation of a more enabling international environment for sustainable development. The role of aid is foremost in contributing to the conditions required for sustainable national development, fair international commercial relations and smart global partnerships with scope for win–win solutions for all actors and partners involved. In the course of such an undertaking, international aid will constantly confront the prevailing structures, global or local, that impede development and make them visible. By so doing, international aid will constitute a first-class source of empirical evidence for identifying necessary measures to be taken globally to create the regulatory framework for global trade and finance that will facilitate a more inclusive process of globalisation.

Hence, instead of facilitating the development and extension of the first Polanyian movement, experience from international development cooperation can provide guidelines for the second movement and thereby facilitate the achievement of a new 'great compromise'. With the renewed geopolitical role of aid, the coherence between the different discourses shaping the aid discourse increases, but to reduce the impact-related efficiency gap, different policy-making authorities in donor countries need to increase internal coherence. The positive contribution that development assistance could give to local development in rural areas will obviously be offset by continuous protection and international food subsidies given to food producers in rich countries. This, in combination with demands for liberalisation of trade in the developing world, will drive local peasantry out of the market in countries with lower productivity and without financial means for the payment of corresponding subsidies. In the same way, strong adherence to the implementation of economic reform programmes aiming to increase exports will be counterproductive if the international trade regime does not permit increased market access and outlets for such exports. These are some examples of demands that an emerging transnational civil society presents at various global summits, be it in Seattle, Prague or Seoul. Empirical findings from international development cooperation will contribute to legitimise and justify such demands.

Indisputably, the political organisation at global level following the new security thinking and its related regimes and regulatory frameworks may take different forms. However, it is the argument of this chapter that international assistance properly designed and contextualised can play an important role in poverty eradication and conflict resolution. Hypothetically, aid may influence the relation between poverty and conflict in two ways; reduced poverty might reduce conflicts and reduced conflicts might reduce poverty. Preconditions for the fulfilment of this role are that different local contexts for poverty eradication are taken into account and that the different phases in a conflict are understood, rather than in separate terms, in terms of an integrated process. This requires a more holistic approach and a reconsideration of the fundamentals of aid (i.e. target groups, contents and channels).

## The need for a holistic and a more coherent approach

In discussing the role and impact of international development assistance, aid is frequently separated into four different kinds. The main justification behind such categorisation is the different underlying motives and their time perspectives.

(1) Development cooperation is based upon long-term cooperation, mostly but not necessarily between governments aiming to come to terms with more structural constraints to development.

(2) Humanitarian assistance is more short-term, aiming to contribute to the resolution of more acute economic crisis. Frequently, this kind of assistance is channelled through non-governmental organisations.

(3) Relief intervention deals with intervention based upon external requirements. The state is weak (in terms of political legitimacy) and the economic crisis (with its human suffering) has been coupled with a political crisis and violent human right abuses. This situation is often referred to as a complex emergency.

(4) Recently, the specific requirements of war-torn societies have raised demands for aid to be designed for post-conflict reconstruction. Here attention is drawn not only to destroyed physical infrastructure but foremost to lost legitimacy and the destruction of the social fabric.

For various reasons I am extremely sceptical of this kind of categorisation of aid. The reason behind this scepticism is that development cooperation tends to neglect the existence of the trap of low-level security equilibrium with its inclination to violent conflicts, whereas relief interventions in so-called complex emergencies only address the symptoms and not the underlying causes behind this trap. I will elaborate on this further in what follows.

The combination of aid-fatigue and the increased need for various relief interventions to combat human suffering has resulted in the importance of long-term development being somewhat downplayed during the past decades. Aid allocated for local resource mobilisation and rural development has, in fact, drastically diminished. An increasing portion of aid money has been allocated for economic reform programme and debt relief – measures on macro level, to create an enabling environment and sufficient credit rating on the international financial markets to attract private foreign investment. The hope is that commercial actors will take care of long-term development and modernisation through trade and partnership. Accordingly, conventional aid has been redirected for short-term humanitarian assistance and immediate poverty alleviation.

There are two problems with this faith in the capacity of the market to initiate development and modernisation. The first is empirical. Private foreign investment depends on infrastructures permitting secure water and energy supply, skilled labour and domestic market outlets. Aid in the form of balance of payment support will not provide what is required, neither will the foreign commercial actors. The second is related to the fact that the market and its requirements do not take political or social aspects into consideration, be there a question of redistribution of income or regional balance. Thus market-related development does not address the earlier discussed gaps of frustration. On the contrary, through its functional approach to development, the gaps will rather become increased and so will the trap of low-level security equilibrium. This is why I am concerned about the emerging division of labour between international trade and development aid.

The risk of increasing the trap of low-level security equilibrium frequently also accompanies relief aid channelled through donors or through autonomous NGOs for complex emergencies. I find this concept extremely problematic. At the local level, the efficiency of social institutions for political decision-making are reduced by the prevailing lack of social trust. It should however not be taken for granted that such lack of legitimacy and social trust is caused by the actual conflict. It is frequently a consequence of a deep-rooted historic structure with its origins in the trap of low-level security equilibrium previously discussed. Short-term intervention to ease human suffering through external provision of relief aid will not address these structural problems. Instead, the crisis of legitimacy and social distrust is in danger of becoming aggravated as existing local institutions for political decision-making are frequently by-passed and existing possibilities for local resource mobilisation not explored. Hence, from a peace and development perspective the challenge is to find ways of including a more long-term development perspective ('provention') in order to avoid development degenerating into a situation where short-term humanitarian assistance or relief intervention are called for.[1] Even if development has already reached such a stage it is nevertheless important to include a more long-term development perspective in assistance and interventions to rehabilitate lost legitimacy and the social trust required for a sustainable conflict resolution. This development and legitimacy-creating perspective is not only something that should be considered and included in a post-conflict programme for reconstruction. It must characterise all kinds of international development assistance, making the above categorisation of reduced relevance.

The need for a more holistic approach to development also concerns international development assistance aiming to contribute to and facilitate conflict resolution. As discussed, previously conflict resolution must be understood from a more holistic perspective and not only as a process with several distinct phases. The measures aiming to achieve settlement of the conflict as well as the measures aiming to consolidate the cease-fire must constitute integrated parts of the measures aiming to permit a sustainable resolution and reconciliation. Accordingly, the question of satisfying human needs must be addressed in the peace agreement. This applies to both *material* needs linked to local resource mobilisation and the regional balance of investments, and to *immaterial* needs, like political and social participation. In this context topics such as the multi-ethnic state and military demobilisation with subsequent civil reintegration of the armed forces are pertinent. The need to approach conflict resolution and development in this holistic and integrated way is equally important regardless of where in the social hierarchy of the population these needs prevail. To feel needed – to be able to develop – politically, socially and economically does not only apply to ordinary people, it also applies to political and economic elites. Experience shows clearly that peace agreements not addressing these issues have been extremely short-lived. Here we find the difference between what the Norwegian researcher Johan Galtung once called 'positive and negative peace' (Galtung 1996). This is the reason why I emphasise the need to address these issues in terms of being included or being excluded. Such a holistic and synchronous approach will increase aid efficiency from the recipient point of view but it requires a reconsideration of the orientation, channels and target groups of aid. We will now turn to the dimension and scope for such a reconsideration of these fundamentals.

## The context of poverty and conflict: the Angolan trap of low-level security equilibrium

The aid discourse has gradually changed its conceptualisation of poverty from a question merely of low income to a question of deprivation of basic needs. However, the poverty-oriented aid is in practice squeezed between its altruistic motives to combat poverty in a broader sense and a development discourse in which the understanding of poverty is shaped by the Western project of modernisation. In this view, poverty is measured not in social assets but in money. African subsistence farmers are by definition poor. In order to get less poor their incomes must increase in monetary terms – something requiring expansion of markets and economic growth.

However, poverty is contextually determined and cannot universally be approached by westernised modernist thinking. In Africa, poverty is foremost measured not in money but in access to food. Food security is the prerequisite to seizing any opportunities provided by the market. Furthermore, poverty reduction through economic growth requires expansive monetary policies and income redistribution. In contrast, neo-liberal thinking pushes for restrictive policies and achievement of budget balances. However, weak institutions create few trickle-down effects, and domestic entrepreneurial skills are not developed as conditions do not permit poor people to participate in local production and trade. As low productivity and subsequent low purchasing power will maintain the economic trap of low-level equilibrium, the approach will neither reduce poverty nor create conditions for a sustainable expansion of the market.

Experience of the situation in Mozambique clearly shows how reduced monetary supply and credit ceilings together with the privatisation of the state banking system constrain the government action that is required to gain the participation of the private sector. This is especially so in rural areas in a war-torn society where the need for rehabilitation of physical, social and commercial infrastructure (so called 'crowding-in' measures) is immense.

International development assistance must be designed to address such rural needs. If not, the legitimacy of warlordism will be increased even further. The Angolan experience and the tendencies by the donor community to, in awaiting a termination of the war, concentrate their aid on the provision of humanitarian assistance only is illuminating in this regard.

Although sufficient research at local level in Angola is not available, anecdotal evidence points to the emergence of new pattern of conflicts, to which literature on warlords (Kaldor 1999; Reno 1998) is relevant. The understanding of the conflict in terms of an emerging New Political Economy resulting from the exclusive character of globalisation is also illuminating. As discussed earlier, our main analytical problem is linked to the lack of adequate tools to assess the importance and relative weight we should give to this new phenomenon, and how much we can generalise.

However, regardless of the level of generalisation, the transformative character of the emerging New Political Economy does not automatically imply that the process needs no external intervention. It is nevertheless true that the view that proclaimed grievances, if at hand, are only deliberately generated in order to stress the justice of the struggle, neglects the fact that the activities of the warlords often are considered legitimate and therefore obtain considerable and weighty local support. As discussed in earlier chapters, the people who gather to the cause (i.e. become politicised) often perceive the reason for this legitimacy to be injustice and/or exclusion. Such a social phenomenon is known as relative deprivation. But even if the observation of the local legitimacy of the warlords is most probably correct, the concomitant violence and human abuses could never be legitimate and are seldom understood as such by the population.

Following ongoing discussions within the UN system, peace and development are starting to be considered as human rights and public goods. At stake is the political stability required for envisaged worldwide expansion of the market economy. We need a more inclusive process of globalisation which permits access to legal sources of accumulation for the deprived elite in the Third World. That is why new global security interests are repoliticising aid in terms of promoting stability and security. Hence, it is my argument that the subsequent increased room for manoeuvre for aid intervention, that its new role as a facilitator for the second movement implies, is not observed by the post-modern thinking with its apolitical conclusions (Duffield 2001)

These omissions in the literature are important because they imply a simplified diagnosis with subsequent ineffective policy solutions. The fact that this subjective feeling (of injustice, indignity or of being excluded) often is manufactured by the stakeholders in the war does not change the necessity of coming to terms with the grievance in order to change the perceptions which fuel the conflict. Indeed, as the World Bank itself concludes, even if objective grievances do not necessarily generate violent conflict, violent conflicts generate subjective grievances.

If a similar kind of pattern is at hand in Angola, as seems likely, then our challenge is not merely a question of solving the problem of the UNITA military leadership not adhering to the Lusaka agreement. The peace agreement must include the measures in order to escape from low-level security equilibrium trap, characterised by continued warlordism (durable disorder) and not permitting the creation of the social trust and horizontal and vertical links that are required for sustainable economic and social development. Accordingly, sustainable peace can only be achieved if long-term socio-economic development issues are addressed. Possible social bases for warlordism must be eradicated. International development cooperation can play an important role in this regard, provided a more holistic and multilevel approach could be applied. Humanitarian assistance should include a long-term development perspective more fully supporting domestic resource mobilisation. Poverty in the broad sense of deprivation of capabilities could only be eradicated through enhanced local production and trade. Capacity-building must be supported at both the central and local level so that international aid and credits can be negotiated, coordinated and monitored accordingly. Agreed conditions on macro-economic performance, to restore international credit ratings, should not be allowed to endanger national restructuring of the armed forces, access to local credits and micro-economic development in rural areas.

Indeed, in the case of Angola, an extraordinary financial, human and social capital injection is needed to avoid the low-level security equilibrium trap. Such aid should be implemented as 'proventive' action aiming to create conditions for a positive peace (Galtung 1969; Burton 1990). I'll now elaborate further on these points.

## Towards a social cohesion support

Development should be understood as social change driven by conflicting interests. The challenge is to avoid these conflicts escalating into violent ones. 'Provention' measures are constantly required to reduce gaps of frustration and gaps of legitimacy and thereby move out of the trap of low-level security equilibrium.

This is the reason we have to avoid the continuum thinking where relief aid is designed differently from development cooperation. In this sense, there are no contextual differences to take into consideration when designing international cooperation for countries in violent conflict, countries with long experiences of peace, or war-torn countries in process of reconstruction. In what follows I will discuss the role of international development cooperation based on the perspective that the development aspect must constitute the point of departure for all situations. Although it should be admitted, and emphasised, that countries in conflict or war-torn countries first need to identify islands of civility from which base measures can be taken in order to normalise the situation, the common challenge that characterises all countries involved is how to leave the trap of low-level security equilibrium to permit conditions for a sustainable development.

The first condition of escape is a significant injection of capital (financial, human or social) to reduce the gaps of frustration and legitimacy. The objective of the injection is to make the emergence of an historic bloc possible. i.e. a functioning market, a strong state and a vibrant civil society.

Indisputably, the main part of this injection must be mobilised internally although increased international development assistance is considered a prerequisite. Experience from the early 1950s and the role the Marshall Plan played as a catalyst for the reconstruction and development of Europe tells us about the impact international development cooperation may have, if properly designed. Before further elaboration of the design of such support, it should be noted that such an approach requires the radical reorientation of present aid. The concentration of support to achieve macro-economic balances must be scaled down and complemented by increased focus and importance to micro-level support for local development. Two important arguments for such a reorientation prevail. Firstly, the importance of local development in the creation of social and political stability and hereby its role for sustainable development motivates a high priority. Secondly, such stability is probably as important as macro-economic balances to avoid the classification of being a high-risk investment country.

Thus international development cooperation should contribute to increased (a) vertical legitimacy and (b) horizontal social trust, and hence to (c) the social cohesion that is required for the anchorage of the dialogue in society. The need of *legitimacy creation support* and *social trust enforcement support* obviously increases the need to *contextualise* aid, i.e. to design it case by case according to prevailing economic, political and social realities. However, despite such strong need for contextualisation, some general remarks on the design of social cohesion support should be made.

## Orientation and target groups

The linkage between food security and social trust referred to in Chapter 9 provides a useful illustration. As argued, food security is not only a prerequisite for a normalisation of living conditions in the process of conflict resolution. It is also a requirement for any sustainable local development. Lack of food security reduces individual predictability and security. For a risk-minimising peasant this does not only increase vulnerability to social change, hence to development as such, but it also reduces propensity to participate in communitarian work (school building, maintenance of roads), collective self-help system or in other reciprocal activities (field clearing, harvest). Instead of reinforced horizontal links increasing reciprocity and social trust, a tendency towards adopting individual solutions, using any existing vertical links could be observed. This tendency obviously decreases social trust and the social cohesiveness necessary for sustainable peace and development.

The provision of food security also brings us to the question of legitimacy creation support. As I have described, it is not certain that the question of food security is really addressed by relief aid to the absolute poor. Instead, support to dispersed peasants as regards agricultural inputs (tools, seeds) or access to a rural commercial network or micro credits to local traders might have a far more sustainable impact. Such support will not only address physical but also social and political requirements of food security. Resumed agricultural production, and investments in physical and commercial infrastructure are necessary for the normalisation of living conditions. Hereby, the legitimacy of the political system will be strengthened. It is in this sense I prefer to talk about local development instead of only rural development linking semi-urban areas more fully to rural areas. The normalisation of life required for increased social cohesion and political stability requires support to various elite groups in order to create the possibility of political influence and affirmation. Not only demobilised soldiers but also demobilised middle rank officers must be socially reintegrated.

If relief aid is required, local purchase must have priority even if local costs of production are exceeding subsidised prices on international markets. Furthermore, relief aid should be understood as a means to reestablish social trust and not as an objective as such. Food for work is one example how food aid can constitute such a mean and thereby decrease the gaps of legitimacy.

## The channels of aid

This brings us finally to the question of channels. When discussing local development, we are led to the question of civil society. This association is reinforced by the fact that the decreased legitimacy of the state and the imperfections of the markets lately have inclined donors to channel more and more aid directly to target groups through non-governmental organisations.

A weak state, as earlier discussed, is one administratively unable to provide the public goods required by the population, thus reducing its legitimacy at central as well as local level. But is it possible and desirable to create the 'good' state? We should not preclude the possibility that new, hitherto unknown institutions will be necessary for political decision-making at different levels in order to come to grips with the gap of legitimacy. Since the state is too small to deal with global problems and too big to understand local preoccupations (Hettne 1995), the functions of the state presently to be found at the national level might have to be centralised to global or regional level, while other functions are decentralised to the local level. What we know is that public institutions are required to provide the administrative, legal and financial framework necessary in the development process. There is a great need to create physical and legal conditions permitting civil society, commerce and private entrepreneurs to act and develop. The market and non-governmental organisations cannot provide the resources required. Accordingly, the donors' attempt to reach local target groups through decentralising aid to reinforce empowerment and dialogue ought to be carried out within state structures and those systems for communication between the central and the local level that authorities have created. Paradoxically, local development seldom emerges in a bottom-up fashion in countries where civil society is weak at the local level. In such a situation civil society is still in need of the protection of the state until any feasible alternative protective regime can be identified.

If not properly contextualized, aid can do harm. As discussed earlier, the decreased civilness caused by decreased legitimacy of the state has strengthened sub-national, i.e. ethnic and regional identities. Reduced space for dialogue has in turn led to increased rivalry and propensity for violence between different identity groups. Accordingly, many of these groups have started to create NGOs of their own to strengthen their sub-national identity. An urban elite, trying to increase its social power and base of affirmation not merely supported this development, but took over the leadership of these NGOs, creating new problems of legitimacy and democracy. At the same time, many of these primary groups have become globalised. International non-governmental organisations (INGOs) looking for partners and sub-national groups looking for financing found coinciding interests for partnership. Paradoxically, the efforts of the international donor community have supported this development, for in their attempt to reach local target groups through NGOs, donors have given these organisations tasks and influence over the development that widely exceed their political mandates, and often their capacity. One should not forget the fact that these non-governmental organisations are not subject to parliamentary scrutiny or corresponding demands for transparency that are placed upon the state.

However, the problem is not only a problem of legitimacy but one of social cohesion. NGOs do not operate throughout civil society, so their operations could sometimes have a divisive effect increasing rivalry between different groups rather than reducing propensity to conflict. Thus the support of the international community, if not properly designed, can further decrease the prospect of achieving social cohesion and national identity based upon a multicultural society.


## Conditions for aid

The lack of legitimacy of state bureaucracy has implied an increasing fear by civil society and non-governmental organisations that aid channelled through the state, no matter how good the objectives and purpose might be, will never reach the intended target groups but will be deviated to satisfy other needs. This brings us to the concluding remark: the question of conditions. Empirical evidence indicates various problems raised by imposed conditions linked to macro-economic reform programmes. Lack of national ownership has not only implied lack of implementation but has also constrained the room of manoeuvre for the government to take needed action. The lack of ownership is explained by the fact that the conditions were designed in Washington based upon a country strategy (CAS) also elaborated in Washington. It is the intention of the Bretton Woods institutions to reverse this situation in the elaboration of the Poverty Reduction Strategy Paper by increasing the involvement of the civil society in economic planning.

This is a first step. Obviously, international development assistance should be linked to the condition that the agreement forming the basis for cooperation will be respected at the time of implementation. This is perhaps even more important for supporting social cohesion, being channelled to a large extent through existing state structures. In the same way as the provision of international credits, debt relief and balance of payment support, requires agreement on conditions I argue strongly for the need to include a similar kind of conditional thinking when providing aid for local development. The great difference is that such conditions must be identified and elaborated by the partners together with the intended target groups at local level. These locally identified conditions, determining how the decentralised social cohesive support should be designed and implemented, must be agreed upon before the development cooperation starts. If such conditions are not identified, agreed upon and implemented, the efficiency of aid, be it donor motive-related or recipient impact-related, will be considerably reduced.


## Summary

The orientation and dimension of aid is the result of three interacting discourses: security, development and altruistic. When these discourses converge the efficiency of aid is at best, be it from the donors' point of view (motive-related efficiency) or from the recipient countries' point of view (impact-related efficiency). When the discourses diverge a troublesome efficiency gap is developed, gradually provoking measures to change either the discourse(s) or their internal relationship, in order to obtain a new coherence.

During the first one and a half development decades of the UN (i.e. during the 1960s and early 1970s) the congruence between the different discourses was strong. As accounted for earlier, poverty was seen first as backwardness, and later as exploitation. The remedy in both cases was a rapid modernisation, to catch up with the industrialised world. Such an approach was in line, not only with the development discourse and the altruistic discourse, but also with the security discourse in the West. The attempt to modernise would create a need of technology, finance and access to markets, all areas where the Western countries had the upper hand vis-à-vis the threatening communist world.

The demand for a New International Economic Order, and the radicalisation of the non-aligned movement during the second half of the 1970s gradually started to transform the security discourse. The efforts to contain communism were conceived as a failure. At the same time the Keynesian developmental approach based upon a strong intervening state had started to be questioned. Gradually the emphasis shifted to a more neo-liberal approach in which the role of the state would be substituted with the role of the market. With the arrival of the Reagan administration in the beginning of the 1980s the new security discourse guided the design of US foreign policy. For national security, communism had to be rolled back. The main policy for this undertaking to integrate 'vulnerable' Third World countries into the international market, and most notably its financial markets on terms decided by the west. The changed security discourse not only occurred simultaneously with the change in the economic development discourse, but the two discourses changed in the same direction at the same time, reinforcing their coherence. Both, however, diverged from the altruistic discourse, which was still emphasising poverty reduction through an intervening state. This created significant efficiency gap. This was demonstrated by reduced economic growth and increased poverty during the 1980s and the 1990s, and increasing aid fatigue.

With the end of the Cold War in the early 1990s the traditional Western national security interests towards Africa to contain (or roll back) communism became outdated. Subsequently, reduced geopolitical motives, combined with aid fatigue, also brought the level of aid to its historically lowest point in 1998. However, the reinforced and uneven process of globalisation soon made new national security interests emerge as far as the Western countries' relations with Sub-Saharan Africa are concerned. The increased interdependence could make the African problems spill over and affect other parts of the world. Reducing conflicts and establishing political stability moved up the international agenda to facilitate an African renaissance, and enable African states to integrate more successfully into the world market. The different discourses gradually started to converge again. The international development cooperation started to regain its geopolitical motives. The need to contain the 'African danger' brought the security discourse into line with the altruistic discourse, swiftly followed by the development discourse, on the needs for poverty eradication and debt cancellation. Increased understanding of the relation between poverty and conflict gives the international development cooperation its opportunity for a renaissance. This new coherence can reduce the efficiency gaps, provided two preconditions are met: Firstly, aid must be used in order to confront the existing structures that impede development on different levels in order to make such structures visible. Secondly, aid must scale-down its ambitions to solve macro-economic imbalances in the short run. Instead, aid should be oriented towards increasing social cohesion in society. By linking the orientation and the design of aid more fully to a credible development vision and strategy, the impact related efficiency can increase sufficiently to come to terms with aid fatigue, thereby motivating the massive transfer of resources required to remove poor countries from the low level security equilibrium trap permanently.

Until new, as yet unknown, political institutions have emerged which can provide a protective regime for increased civilness, the role of the state is fundamental. In fact the horizontal social trust required for a reinforced dialogue within society can only be created if supported by the vertical legitimate structures of the state. The achievement of state legitimacy requires, too, a new approach to development. The process of globalisation makes it unlikely for a state to be properly equipped to redistribute any benefits from such a strategy. Instead the legitimacy of the state must be created through a more territorial approach to development, enabling a stronger participation at local level in the identification of needs and mobilisation of resources. For such a development to take place a decentralisation, within the state structures, and a democratisation of the political decision-making process, using existing social institutions at the local level, are two prerequisites. From this it follows that the main role of the future international development cooperation is to support legitimacy creation and social trust reinforcement. This is what I understand with the term 'social cohesion support'.

By more fully linking the orientation and the design of aid to the impact related efficiency can increase sufficiently to come to terms with the aid fatigue and motivate the massive transfer of resources required for getting the poor countries once and for all out of the trap of low-level security equilibrium.

# 11
# Conclusion

This book is about structural change. The main argument is that the new, and contradictory, circumstances emerging after World War II have started to change national security interests in the western hemisphere and gradually increased the room for manoeuvre for structural change, to make the process of globalisation more equal, democratic and hence sustainable.

The prevailing political situation and balance of power shaped by the logic of the Cold War, which created conditions for the Great Compromise and the implementation of the framework of rules of the Bretton Woods Conference soon came to erode the pillars on which the Great Compromise rested. The problem was not only that the 'open door policy' and free trade gave rise to a dynamic which gradually came to reduce the economic and political room for manoeuvre of the nation-state, and thereby erode the preconditions for embedded liberalism. The serious paradox emerged through the needs of finding other means of financing the US leadership than by traditional taxes. A so-called 'bastard Keynesianism' resulted when this financing came to be done through an excessive monetary expansion combined with a budget deficit that was never repaid. This is how the forces emerged which soon were to give birth to increasing international oil prices, recycling of the petrodollar, expansion of the eurodollar market, the debt burden and its need of economic reform programmes.

The international inflation caused Keynesianism to be abandoned. Neo-liberal deregulation allowed for a deepened market expansion. The world went from international cooperation between states and companies to a transnational cooperation between different networks – which created a *dis*embedded liberalism. The national and redistributive state was down-graded. The state monopoly on legitimate violence was gradually weak-ened, in parallel with privatisation of security and protection. Through the decreased legitimacy for the nation-state, the base on which the Great Compromise rested was dissolved. The result came to be a deep-ened uneven development, increased poverty, and new patterns of conflicts and war.

In the last phase of the existence of the national historic blocs there were some efforts by elite groups with enlightened self-interest to save the stability of the system through a new Great Compromise at the global level, in order to control the prevailing contradictions and to increase room for manoeuvre for national governance. The aim behind the demands for a New International Economic Order (NIEO) and Massive Transfers of Resources (MTR) in the middle of the 1970s was to eradicate poverty and increase purchasing power to create markets in the South and thereby new opportunities for employment in the North. Through increased interdependence, common security was expected to increase. But this global social policy did not find a sufficient political momentum to be implemented. The conditions for transnational historic blocs were not yet in existence. Interests of economic and political elites did not coincide sufficiently. On contrary, the approaching second Cold War increased the realist influence at the expense of more liberal thinking. Consequently, new security threats allowed the USA to continue its deficit budget policy. Attempts to create a global second movement came at the wrong moment. One will not get a sufficiently strong second movement before the moment when the contradictions created by the first movement have reached their limits of extension. The room for manoeuvre could be used by the forces in the first movement to continue their global expansion (roll back communism). Thus, the exclusionary character of globalisation was initiated.

As a consequence of non-regulated globalisation the contradictions have worsened further. Even if the contradictions display national differences, not least according to the strength of the states, the increased global interdependence have made them increasingly non-manageable. Especially serious are the poverty-related environmental problems, which have further limited people's ability to safeguard livelihood in traditional homesteads. This has made it impossible for the international community to contain poverty. It has also made the poverty-related environmental problems intervene in, and aggravate the more slow-flowing and long-term ecological processes. Taken together, the development ecological problems have come to intervene also in the more short-term economic and political problems, making it even more difficult to maintain the required political stability needed for the market economy to function. Poverty has become a problem for the global elite. Hence, poverty reduction in order to re-establish political stability is sought for. Debt cancellation, changed rules for international trade, and regulation of capital flows have gained priority on the political agenda.

At the same time elites in the poor areas are demanding fair trade. They demand improved access to the markets of the rich countries, and certain rights to protect part of their own agricultural production and vulnerable industry from international competition, during a period of consolidation (the infant industry argument). Today, as we know, the contrary situation is at hand. While the Bretton Woods institutions demand liberalisation and reduction of trade barriers, and increased export by the countries of the South, the rich countries are protecting their own domestic market against external competition. Recently, the Bretton Woods institutions were forced to drop their demand that the sugar market in Mozambique should be liberalised and that trade barriers on sugar should be lifted, in order for new loans to be disbursed. Mozambique has, rightly, demanded corresponding measures also in Europe – something which turned out to be more difficult to implement.

The enlightened self-interest of Western elites in poverty reduction is nothing new. Their self-interest in political stability and fear of communist expansion lay behind the creation of the welfare state in Europe after World War II. They realised that the system could not regain its balance short of structural changes. However, the question today is if there is a political momentum already to seize the emerged structural opportunity for change. The international negotiations on reforming globalisation to make it less exclusive show clearly that the elite with such enlightened self-interest (the so-called global reformists) are far from having the upper hand. Extensive resistance comes from more nationalist and isolationist groups in the US Congress, and is also showing itself all too clearly in the European political debate.

## The African scene

The conflicts in Sub-Saharan Africa are coming to be seen as resource wars leading to complex humanitarian emergencies. The assumed driving force behind this new political economy is to be found in the African precolonial traditions earlier contained by the Cold War but now released and reinforced by the process of globalisation and the subsequent increased marginalisation of Africa in the formal world economy.

Consequently the literature draws on four conclusions from its understanding of such 'new wars'. Firstly, the relation between poverty and conflict is questioned. The driving force behind the conflicts is a greedy elite and not popular grievances. Secondly, the elite, whether it is external or internal, is thought to fuel the wars so long as it benefits from them. As the goals of elites in rivalry are incompatible their changed power relations will lead to some kind of Durable Disorder (Duffield 2001). Hence, instead of regression into complex political emergencies, the conflicts should be understood in terms of transformation of their economic and political relations, leading to emerging political complexes. Thirdly, this makes the efforts to solve the conflicts via outside intervention extremely problematic. To be resolved, conflict must reach a mutually 'hurting' stalemate (Zartman 1989), enabling the transformation of incompatible goals into compatible ones, at which point the involved elites would consider the conflict ripe for settlement. Fourthly, before such a ripe moment is reached international development cooperation, with the exception of humanitarian assistance, is probably counterproductive.

This so-called Renoland, named after the studies of William Reno in Sierra Leone, indisputably exists (Reno 1998). It surfaced clearly at the start of the 1990s and contributed, especially through Robert Kaplan's description of the Coming Anarchy (Kaplan 1994) to the spread of Afro-pessimism. Admittedly I, together with my colleague Anders Nilsson, joined the alarmist forces based upon the development of the political economy of Mozambique, with its tendencies towards criminalisation and its hibernating war lords.

The problem with such an actor-oriented and somewhat ahistoristic analysis is, however, that it generalises from some imperfectly understood synchronic phenomena. We lack sufficiently sophisticated socio-psychological analytical tools for an analysis of the driving forces behind such phenomena as warlords who, with a certain popular legitimacy, gradually transform parts of the formal bureaucratic state structure into informal private structures for individual enrichment. Consequently, we also lack analytical tools for understanding what importance and weight that we should give these tendencies in relation to the importance of various measures that attempt to counteract the very same tendencies.

Based upon our continued action-oriented research in Mozambique and Angola, it has over time become clear that the lack of adequate analytical tools and subsequent methodological constraints could lead us to indulge in excessive generalisation, where the particular is insufficiently recognised. A more structural, holistic and historicist approach would provide empirical evidence capable of question and to provide modifications of all four conclusions just referred to.

Firstly, taking a broader perspective of poverty, empirical evidence points to the existence of links between relative deprivation and conflict. Due to pre-colonial and colonial 'borders' and subsequent political and economic fragmentation, different elite groups have always conceived themselves as excluded from central power. This relative deprivation increases from time to time their need for a social base for affirmation. They try, consequently, through what Nilsson describe as instrumentalisation of politics from above, to exploit any tendencies of politicisation of identity from below (Nilsson 1999). As discussed, such politicisation of identity is facilitated by the low productivity of the economy of affection in combination with the incapacity of the state to provide required public goods. Hence ordinary citizens will often be vulnerable to being politicised. Frustrated, mostly urban, elite groups may accordingly under certain circumstances be able to mobilise the population to organised violence. Through this triangular relationship between alternative elite groups, the economy of affection and the state, the trap of low-level equilibrium (to which Keynesian economists have drawn attention) has been complemented with a political and social dynamic. For many countries in Africa this has involved something that we refer to as the 'trap of low-level security equilibrium'.

Secondly, for reasons given in this study, national as well as transnational elite groups have begun to want peace and political stability in Africa. The former can after the Cold War no longer base their governance on external legitimacy, at the same time as their subordinated role in globalisation is constraining their external accumulation. As regards the transnational political elite, new national security interests mean that they wish to keep the African dangers in Africa. Aid fatigue, however, means that the necessary measures for this can scarcely be financed via taxes. There is a need for cooperation with the business sector. Clinton travelled to Africa to attract attention from foreign private investors. But the envisaged partnership needs political stability, which places poverty reduction and cancellation of debts high on the political agenda. So the end of the Cold War, together with globalisation, with its marginalisation of the African continent, have created new, and reinforced old, contradictions. These factors have also contributed to coinciding interest between national and transnational elite groups who wish to change the conditions that render the continent a high-risk zone for private investment.

Thirdly, in order to seize this structural opportunity for peace we must understand the conflict resolution process as indivisible. Conditions for political stability can only be achieved if a perspective of development is integrated into the peace agreements, i.e. are included as early as possible in the peace process. This is what should be understood by the concept of 'provention' (Burton 1990). In other words, it is counterproductive first to talk about peace and then about development. In fact, it is the other way around – something that is clearly visible, both in the war-torn Angola and the seemingly successful Mozambique (where both the real situation and the election results point to an explosive situation). The factors behind our triangular trap of low-level security equilibrium must be addressed, i.e. questions of inclusive power sharing/multi-ethnic society, hoes/seeds/credit to the peasants in economy of affection, and the rehabilitation by the state of physical, commercial and social infrastructure. Success in these areas cannot be achieved within a functional development strategy. Decreased redistributive capacity of the state, linked to increased needs of local mobilisation of resources, show that a more territorially directed development strategy is needed.

Fourthly, the role of international development cooperation must be understood against the background of its geopolitical importance for the donor country. New security interests after the Cold War do not only intensify the motives for aid, but will also make it possible for aid to be more effective, and thus decrease aid fatigue, which is hampering today's development cooperation. To seize the opportunity for peace a substantial injection of financial, human, and social capital is required, and it is here aid has a role. Given that the critical mass for development depends on internal resource mobilisation, yet aid can work as catalyst. Instead of looking only at how conflicts influence aid, we must start to look at how aid influences conflicts (negatively and positively). In order for aid to function positively for peace and development in Africa, its macro-economic focus on balance-achieving measures must be complemented with efforts to create legitimacy and social trust. Accordingly, it is our opinion that the great future challenge for aid lies in a gradual reformulation of the balance of payment support to a more peace-directed social cohesion support. This could constitute an aid renaissance. To contribute to a sustainable peace would, in this perspective, be an explicit objective of international development cooperation.

## Restructuring the mandates of the Bretton Woods institutions

However, for such a progressive role of aid to be possible, the Bretton Woods conference needs to be revisited and the global structures within which international aid operates transformed. A more conflict-preventive and conflict-resolving focus of the international aid flow to Africa will require a reformulation of the current structural adjustment programmes. The acute need for the African countries to achieve a macro-economic balance, regarding both state budgets and current accounts, has to be viewed as a long-term goal, capable of achievement only after the satisfying of the basic needs of the population and after the expansion and rehabilitation of the internal productive structures. Current demands for debt repayment in the short term have turned out to be counterproductive, since the prevailing emphasis on promoting export-oriented growth is gradually destroying the domestic basis for long-term economic development.

In this regard, the present mandates given by the member countries of the Bretton Woods institutions should be reconsidered. Short-term conflict resolution, as well as long-term economic growth and development, require, in the case of Africa, immediate bilateral and multilateral debt forgiveness.

The International Monetary Fund, should after writing off Africa's debt, withdraw from the continent. The World Bank should not be dismantled or privatised but reconstructed as a multilateral aid agency. Through transformation of its debts and future credits to receiving countries, the World Bank's experience of assisting Third World governments in 'good governance and getting the fundamentals right' could be useful in a move towards sustainable economic development in Africa. The financing of such an exercise could be internally mobilised by the Bretton Woods system, either through the issue of Special Drawing Rights, a reduction of gold reserves, the utilisation of accumulated profits, or slightly increased interest rates vis-à-vis the industrialised countries. Such a restructuring of the mandates of the Bretton Woods institutions should also be accompanied by a shift in their policies towards a much more expansionary approach, and a broadening of 'conditionality' to include indicators of social and economic development process at the local level as well as investment and sectoral productivity rather than a narrow monetary focus. Ecological sustainability must become one of the central features of future economic development. The original mandates given to

Bretton Woods (to promote economic growth and the expansion of world output) were all derived from an economic analysis which not only ignored social aspects and human development, but also the prevailing ecological constraints.

We are at the crossroads, with reinforced risk of endemic strife. Either sincere joint global efforts are made in order to permit the African continent to find its way out of subordination and misery, or the continent will continue to be further marginalised in the world economy. The present tendencies for the latter point to a further paradox: when the development of the African continent was in geopolitical Western interests, it little mattered whether the African regimes were corrupt or repressive, and there was a scramble *for* Africa. Now, in the post-Cold War era, when the African continent, at last, is allowed to be free from a world system creating so much suffering for its population, and when there seem to be real prospects for democratic development, there is a scramble *from* Africa. This study argues that a disengagement from and de-linking of the African continent effectively consolidates misery and social instability, counter to recent Western requirements for the establishment of democracy and human rights, and threatens international stability.

Instead, in order for legitimate African governments to achieve conflict prevention and democratic socioeconomic development, thereby keeping African problems in Africa, extensive Western support is required. It must however, be clearly stated that the debt forgiveness called for is only a partial, albeit necessary, measure. Above all, international trading policies must change in favour of Africa. The present composition of export/import merchandise makes the continent a loser in the World Trade Organisation and maintains external aid dependency even after debt forgiveness.[1]

These efforts require, however, an international order with some kind of hegemonic leadership in a Gramscian or Kindlebergian sense.[2] The recent literature highlights the extremely limited scope for such hegemony to arise.[3] As illustrated in the literature, the hegemon is relatively benign. Affiliation with the hegemonic system is not coerced but invited on the basis of the benefits that the hegemon offers the member nations. However, the available analysis suggests that the embedded contradictions characterising the Bretton Woods system have undermined the capacity of any nation to take on a hegemonic international leadership because there are simply too few benefits to offer. In the post-Cold War era, development has also gradually reduced the political will for such undertakings unless multilateral burden-sharing can be obtained, as there are simply few benefits to gain. The problem is further aggravated by the fact that the capacity and will to be led has eroded on the national level following decreased scope for social contracts and legitimacy of the state as a consequence of the incapacity to provide for the basic material, social, and cultural needs of its population.

Political leaders are trying to counteract these tendencies of fragmentation and disintegration through various means of regional cooperation and integration aimed at controlling the invisible market, albeit on a supranational level. Doubts can be raised as to the successful outcome of such endeavours, particularly so for Africa, which, to a large degree, is dependent on international regimes for the future finance required for the rehabilitation of the economy as well as for political legitimacy. It is difficult to imagine necessary action on debt forgiveness and changed conditionalities without proper initiatives being taken on the international level, no matter how successful regional efforts might be. Hence there is a danger that the process of regionalisation in the North will marginalize the African continent even further, thereby aggravating the severe difficulties the continent is presently facing in trying to restore a minimum of social order and stability. It is in this regard that the geopolitical realities permitting a reassessment of the mandates of the Bretton Woods institutions represent a real danger. In its need to go beyond the Cold War in identifying its national security interests and formulating its foreign policy, the US Congress could be motivated to terminate its financial support of the Bretton Woods institutions and argue for the abolition of the entire system. This danger does not decrease when the US domestic financial problems that the American leadership is presently facing are taken into consideration. Recent elections have not only totally changed the political context in United States with regards to Africa, but they have also reinforced the socio-political transformation behind US isolationism, which almost surely points to future divergent strategic interests between the United States and Europe. Efforts to strengthen cooperation after September 11th turned out to be illusive in connection with the Iraq war. Such increased parochialism of the United States could reactivate the European interest in cooperation with Africa. The danger in such a scenario lies, of course, in the incapacity of Europe to either contain or resolve the African problem.

Such a situation would drastically increase international instability. As a consequence of continued disorder at the international level, the vacuum created by a withdrawing hegemon, limited market forces, and a still-embryonic civil society at the national level there is a great risk of exposure to various organised, but illegal, activities orchestrated by the increasingly influential international mafia-network. Such a development reduces the scope for socio-economic development and conflict provention on the continent even further and prevents the legitimate African governments from managing their own conflicts and keeping their problems in Africa. Such a development could also force the North to take parochial actions to isolate itself from African disorder. The dilemma with such an approach is that such actions will only provoke an escalation of the problems. The roots and nature of migration, illicit drug trafficking, money laundering or environmental destruction, among others, are global in character and can be insulated neither on the national or regional level. This underlines the need for an international regime to be reestablished.

It is against this background, paradoxically enough, that the question could be raised as to whether the moment is ripe to revisit the Bretton Woods conference with its original goal of embedded liberalism. In the post-Cold War era, the embedded contradiction could disappear, making it possible to transform the IMF into the World Central Bank that was originally intended, being responsible to and subordinated to the UN Security Council. In the same way, the World Bank could be transformed into a much-needed central aid agency, undertaking development cooperation based on grants instead of soft loans. Foremost the present World Trade Organisation could be replaced by the International Trade Organisation (ITO) as originally proposed by Keynes with special funds for stabilising world market prices and to assist countries with temporary balance of payment problems. Such a restructuring of the Bretton Woods institutions according to keynesian original proposals seems to have the greatest capacity of all the endeavours to create an international regime capable of coping with future challenges.[4]

I am aware of the fact that the concept of 're-embedded liberalism' is ambiguous. The process of globalisation makes regulation for full employment and social welfare on a national level incompatible with open (deregulated) markets on the international level.[5] I am not advocating any reestablishment of state capacity in a Westphalian sense as a remedy to the problem. For many scholars, the process of globalisation has made the nation-state concept obsolete.

However, as argued in this study, the fact that the process of globalisation has reduced the capacity of the state to intervene in the economic and political process does not mean that the role of the state is less important. It has indisputably changed, but the state still remains the most important actor in the international system.

What I am anticipating, and very much advocating, is open markets in a true Alfred Marshall sense at the local/national level (i.e. free competition and full access to information) but with some kind of regulation of trade and money flows on the international level agreed upon and implemented by sovereign states. Such an undertaking should thus be seen as the *inverted* way of embedding liberalism in comparison with what was originally attempted at during the Bretton Woods Conference.

For countries like Mozambique, this would allow for more correct and honest diagnoses of their macro-economic problems, producing proper remedies. After World War II it was fully recognised that, before reconstruction could be achieved in Europe, any effort to create macro-economic balance would be in vain and the European currencies would not be strong enough to be convertible. Hence Europe was not allowed to receive loans from either the IMF or the World Bank until 1958, when rehabilitation was considered sufficiently complete to enable Europe to enter its final phase of development. This exercise was financed through a massive transfer of resources under the Marshall Plan and was cast against the backdrop of the inter-war Depression and World War II. This financing was considered a prerequisite for international security and national stability. The same situation holds today, in Africa even if it is Africa and not Europe that is the main focus for our concern.

## The future of Peace and Development Studies

The empirical findings of this project have shown that the envisaged structural opportunity for change could be at hand, provided two inter-linked conditions exist. Firstly, the contradictions in the system should be perceived as non-manageable by important elite strata and by civil society. Secondly, a sufficiently strong coinciding interest for change should develop between different elite groups. This means in no way that the elite is considered to be the main subject of history. On the contrary, whether the structural opportunity for change will be seized or not depends ultimately on the involvement of the civil society. The crucial point is its links to and interaction with the elite and whether these are sufficiently strong to activate the historic bloc of which civil society constitutes an important part.

By asking how structures have been socially constructed we are able better to understand how change can be achieved. The structures themselves are not visible. However, though they are analytical constructions, the constraints they create make them visible when confronted by the actions of the actors. One of the main conclusions to be drawn from this book is that reinforced and strengthened interaction between different actors is required to identify the room for manoeuvre and the entry points, making it possible to more fully enter the political process and the ongoing war of position at the right moment and with the proper issues. In order to facilitate such a reinforced interaction in the more asymmetric relations between the more powerful and the powerless, the confrontative dialogue has been pointed to as one possible method to be used. In order to initiate such a dynamic and to seize the presented structural opportunity, an alternative development strategy is called for which is capable of challenging and extending the limits of the politically possible.

Another conclusion to be drawn from this book is the fact that the future *raison d'être* for Peace and Development Studies depends on its capacity to contribute to such an achievement. One prerequisite highlighted by this study is its capacity more fully to merge Conflict Resolution theory with Development Studies. World society conflicts cannot be dealt with without bringing in vital developmental issues. As argued by Nilsson (1999) this in turn requires a paradigmatic shift within Development Studies, capable of transcending its modernist functional approach and of instead focusing on top-down/bottom-up as well as vertical/horizontal interaction. Another, connected, prerequisite relevant to the focus of this study relates to the content of International Relations theory and its meeting point with Development Studies. The argument put forward is not only that a synthesis of the dominant theoretical schools within the field of International Relations theory is required. A more full integration of Development Studies into the research area is called for.

As regards the needed synthesis of various International Relations theories, the more traditional approaches within the field have never devoted much attention to structural change. One obvious reason is the realist dominance within the discipline and its proclaimed ambition to describe the world as it is, leaving on the more idealist and normative discussion on how the world ought to be to Development Studies. Through its separation of politics and economics, the concentration of International Relations theory on the former made the latter become foremost a question of how to navigate internationally and domestically manage the dynamics put in motion by the market forces. Consequently, the discipline never got equipped to understand conditions for structural change, let alone contribute to bringing such a change about. Its inability to provide guidance for seizing opportunities for structural change could also be explained by the discipline's concentration on 'high politics'. The virtual exclusion of the Third World and the process of development from the study of International Relations has, however, become extremely problematic in the present stage of globality where the weakest parts of the system also create the strongest pressure for change.

However, recent development has caught up with theory. The strong coinciding interests between different elite groups to emancipate the system from inherited limits to continued globalisation requires enlarged political constituencies for transnational historic blocs to emerge capable of achieving new Great Compromises on the global level. Simultaneously, the new information technology has enabled global networking between local civil societies. Guidance is needed as regards the role of civil society for high politics and how the pressure for change from above could be linked with and benefit from similar pressure from below. Thus, to assess the future prospects for transcending the problem-solving measures within existing structures, historical and contemporary contradictory circumstances must be identified that constitute entry points for social forces, enabling them to reinforce the dynamics already in motion and to bring a structural change about.

Some promising efforts in this regard have recently been conducted within the field of International Political Economy. The old realism, focusing upon state actions and international power relations, has started to be complemented by historical materialism. Thus the material framework within which historical social actions took place (i.e. social relations and forces of production as well as the international division of labour) has been brought in to the analysis. This Coxian 'new-realism' broadened the range of determining forces beyond state power and shifted the focus towards the state/society complex and the interaction between the local level and the national level (Cox 1997). Furthermore, the realist conceptualisation of the international balance of power has further been linked to the liberal notion of international interdependence, looking more to cooperation than to conflict.

Consequently, the international political institutions have been included in the notion of the neo-realist structures (Keohane 1984).

Following the integration of these different perspectives, the time has now come for the Coxian new-realist state/society/world complex to be enlarged with the Keohanian more institutionalist approach striving to bring the agent–structure interaction on the international level more fully into the analysis. The question of how the structures came about (the realist focus on power) could thereby be complemented by the question of how they were maintained (the liberal focus on interdependence) and what could bring about their change (historical materialist focus on social change). In fact, it is an important argument of this book that it is where a more materialistic approach and a more liberal elite approach meet that the driving forces of structural change can be found.

Now, turning to the need for more fully integrating Development Studies in the area of International Relations, one of the main arguments of this book is the fact that the prevailing world order structures can be changed by the actors' pattern of actions and thoughts provided that a consensual and coherent development vision is at hand. By bringing in Development Studies, the elaboration of coherent strategies capable of challenging the structures could become possible. In this way the problematic contradiction between problem-solving measures, supposed to consolidate a given structure, and more critical approaches aimed at changing the structures, could be transformed into a progressive dynamic.

However, the problem for Development Studies is that the internationalisation of the state coupled with the liberalisation of market forces has made the very core of Development Studies obsolete. Simply speaking, there are no traditional developmental actors at the national level capable of bringing a functionalist redistributive development strategy about. Hence, despite possible growth and modernisation the mainstream strategies are no longer capable of delivering basic needs satisfaction for important strata of the population. That is why the development gap between the haves and the have-nots is increasing along with relative deprivation, frustration and at times intensified conflicts endangering political stability and peace (Nilsson 1999).

Furthermore, and somewhat paradoxically bearing in mind its normative ambitions, its focus on the local and national level has never enabled Development Studies to analyse the contradictions on the international level, let alone contribute with guidance to how they could be utilised. Development Studies has never had the ambition to challenge the world order structures by confronting them with conflictive development strategies making the structures visible. Accordingly, it has never devoted much attention to the strength and role of the existing coinciding elite interest for structural change. Thus the discipline is missing the crucial point, namely that the existence of such coinciding interests on the international level increases the room for manoeuvre for national governance, independently of whether the opportunities for change are seized or not. Such neglect constitutes the main reason why development during the 1990s increasingly has been understood as an immanent process not easily influenced through policy measures, let alone changed.

Hence, the challenge ahead is twofold. Firstly, it is a question of understanding existing correlation of political forces and identifying the room for manoeuvre it provides. Secondly, it is a question of elaborating a strategy that can use the present room for manoeuvre and simultaneously increase it by making the constraining structures visible and objects for change. Accordingly, it is not a question of development studies identifying a development strategy that can facilitate the progressive integration of the poor countries into the world economy through economic adjustment, as required to attract private foreign capital flows. It is more a question of *how* to identify a development strategy capable of fostering the integration of poor populations into the economic, social and political life of their own countries. The increased penetration of the local level resulting from the process of globalisation during the 1980s has meant that an increasing number of people are being excluded from access to sufficient private and public resources, and thereby from opportunities for living a decent life. As discussed, the mainstream Western development paradigm with its claims for universality is the problem of development rather than being part of the solution. Thus, an alternative development strategy is called for to come to grips with the alarming poverty and growing global inequalities.

This brings the 'basic' back into consideration, namely the question of surplus creation and its allocation. Tensions between accumulation and mobilisation must be decreased in order to reduce the role of force in development (Hettne 1984). The alternative approach within the discipline of Development Studies is considered especially important for contributing with increased sensitivity to the role of more territorial and bottom-up perspectives in the local mobilisation of resources, permitting due attention to the specificity of different societies and cultures (Hettne 1995). Thus, through a more fully integration of Development Studies into the research area, the more structural and deterministic theories, whether realist or Marxist, could be complemented with existing room for manoeuvre not only for top-down actions by concerned elite but also for bottom-up actions by social forces. It is in this bottom-up–top-down interaction that the main forces for social change can be identified.

Sustainable resolution of world society conflicts requires new approaches to development. This fact provides an opportunity for a renaissance of Development Studies. Prevailing contradictory circumstances create coinciding interests and opportunities to restore the role politics and to change some of the most important world order structures. In order for such a structural opportunity to be seized by various actors, entry points need to be identified that make it possible to enter the political process at the right time and with timely issues. This in turn requires a coherent development strategy based upon a vision of future development as articulated by the historic bloc of a given society, however, with due attention to the requirements for sustainable societies in northern and southern countries alike. Such requirements could rehabilitate the *raison d'être* of Peace and Development Studies, provided that the following conditions can be met.

Firstly, the opportunity for structural change must be able to be seized in such a way that the process of globalisation could face its isolationist and nationalist opponents. Consequently, the research area much be able to contribute to a global village with what Hettne calls 'world order values' expressed in three preferred outcomes: peace, development and ecological sustainability. The need to achieve these values by attacking the corresponding problems – war, starvation and environmental degradation (Hettne 1999, p. xxiv) – constitutes an imperative for the future of Peace and Development Studies.

Secondly, such normative strength (Nilsson 1999) requires, however, theoretical elaboration and synthesis. The process of globalisation has made visible the present conceptual blind spots within International Relations theory and Development Studies respectively. An important argument outlined in this book is that an elaborated and synthesised International Relations theory, with its structural focus, complemented by Development Studies, with its interest in change, could provide an adequate multilevel analytical framework for a more fully understanding of structural change and conditions for a sustainable global development.

Such a provision will indeed be an important academic contribution to structural change in which social forces not only seize the opportunity for change but also seize it in a way that is compatible with global justice and human dignity.

# Notes

## 1 Conceptual framework

1. Timothy Shaw draws our attention to the danger of the dichotomy between 'the now-fashionable democratic development' and the new threat of 'corporatism or other forms of authoritarianism' (Shaw 1995, p. 89). Shaw shares the preoccupation of John Saul (Saul 1995) that 'globalization is leading towards corporatism in which only a few established group interests will be incorporated'. According to Shaw, structural adjustment programmes as such stimulate the emergence of corporatism through their support of the rise of a national bourgeoisie at a time when available resources for individual enrichment are reduced. However, the fear of *corporatism* is ambiguous not least with regard to its impact on development. As Cox noted, tripartism was the form corporatism took in the evolved industrial states of western Europe (Cox 1987, p. 161). Cox describes how 'the increased complexities of national economic management after World War I required greater state intervention. Governments were no longer prepared to leave wages and employment questions entirely to the interaction of employers and unions' (Cox 1987, p. 74). Hence increased state intervention transformed the earlier bipartite relations in the direction of tripartism. In fact 'Corporatism in its origins was a challenge to the ideologies of both liberal self-regulating market and Marxist class struggle' (Cox 1987, p. 171). The question is what kind of corporatism we are talking about and what kind of constraints it imposes on the legitimacy of the *historic bloc* (Cox 1996, pp. 131–2). We shall revert to this Gramscian concept as the political and social configuration referred to permits an alliance between the national elite and various national forces within society that are considered most crucial for the future development of the nation-state building in Sub-Saharan Africa.

2. Economic efficiency is the key phrase behind requirements for adjustment and austerity. Along with downsizing and outsourcing of state activities, these constitute the main pillar of the adjustment programme imposed by international creditors. Cox concludes that 'the state is tributary to something greater than the state' (Cox 1996, p. 154) and 'governments' accountability to foreign creditors came to outweigh accountability to their own citizens' (p. 195).

3. A fact that was constantly stressed in the interviews conducted between 1994 and 1997. This affirmation is also supported by various scholars. Shaw expresses it as follows: 'After a decade of ideological and institutional decline, the state is set for renaissance, albeit in revised format. The lessons of both NICs and Structural Adjustment Programmes (SAPs) point to a necessary role for a "new" state in terms of economic direction, infrastructural development and welfare provision. The new consciousness of the unacceptable human and financial costs of un or under employment, vulnerable groups, infrastructural decay and rising levels of crime and insecurity, especially for women and the elderly, point to the imperative of a "strong" rather than a weak or shrunken state' (Shaw 1995, p. 260).

4. The Gramscian notion of civil society differs widely from the neo-liberal understanding of the concept. In the neo-liberal tradition, the state and civil society constitute opposite poles, in the sense that a strong civil society can only exist alongside a weak state, and consequently never alongside a strong state. One of

the reasons behind the different interpretations of the concept is ideological and linked to different traditions with regard to views on the nature of the state. In the neo-liberal view, the state has its own interests, which potentially place it in opposition to the interests of citizens. In defending the citizen neo-liberal politicians are arguing strongly in favour of the minimalist state referred to earlier, whereas Gramsci stressed the question of legitimacy and thereby the redistributive functions of the state.

5. In Mozambique, the peasantry is probably more dependent on the markets than the peasantry in the rest of Sub-Saharan Africa due to the colonial heritage with its pattern of migrant labour. Most subsistence farmers gradually became dependent on the purchase of food to complement the production within the family. This necessity did not stem only from fluctuations in production for climatic reasons, storage scarcity or social obligations but primarily emanated from the fact that one important factor of production, the males, were frequently absent and their labour force substituted with money remittances. As will be discussed later, this did not mean that the Mozambican peasantry was captured by the markets. It is true that the peasants needed the market to exchange their production into consumer goods. However, they approached it more as consumers and adapted their production of surpluses for sale according to their own consumption needs. This, in its turn, implied that the peasants could temporarily withdraw from the market, as they were not dependent on it for their immediate survival. They were, however, dependent on it for their well-being in the long run. The different time horizons are important here, since these short-run possibilities of withdrawing from the market if social networks so permitted made the peasantry keep and maintain such networks. The rationality, security and continuity of these social networks is far more important than the possibilities of taking advantage of any opportunities offered by unreliable market forces. In that sense the peasants were more risk minimisers than profit maximisers. The unreliability of the market stood in sharp contrast to the peasants' need for continuity and implied a lack of the social trust that was required to enable the market as a social system to develop. In other words, the market did not reach out to the peasantry to the degree required to establishing it as a social system that could gradually transform the traditional society into a civil society.

6. I limit my use of the concept 'civilisation' to a set of collectively shared, and hereby predominant, values and belief systems in a given society, sustained by common concerns. In essence, this is how I understand the Coxian 'realm of intersubjective meanings', a concept elaborated later in the chapter. Such a broad definition allows for the concept 'business civilisation' coined by Strange (Strange 1988), and this will be used in discussing the emerging transnational elite.

7. According to modern world system theory, world capitalism has an interactive nature in the sense that the capitalist mode of production is expanding successively throughout the world and thus coming to incorporate an increasingly large part of it (Wallerstein 1974).

8. Although this development paradigm is Western in the sense that it encompasses important values in the belief system of the Western civilisation, I would argue that it is going beyond the concept of Western civilisation by bringing in elites and influences from other civilisations and values. The social upheaval in Algeria, for example, should not automatically be understood as a 'clash of civilisations' in the Huntington sense. It could also be a question of frustrated alternative elites and various social groupings being 'excluded' from the benefits of modernisation,

mobilising a violent reaction towards the symbols of the exclusive development strategy applied by the government. More research is needed in order for more definite conclusions to be drawn.

9. An influential think tank, the Council on Foreign Relations, claims to have taken the initiative in publishing Huntington; *Clash of Civilizations* and to have organised some 100 seminars across America to counteract more parochial forces within American civil society. According to the Council, these efforts did not result in the anticipated reactions (Interview no. 112, New York, 28 June 1972).

10. Though there are strong similarities, I prefer to use the term 'world order' rather than 'world system'. The latter might become connoted with world system theory (Wallerstein 1974) and its more durable structures over time (*longue durée*).

11. The concept 'Westphalian' has been introduced to the discipline of international relations by Richard Falk and Robert Cox, among others. According to Hettne, by this term Cox refers to 'the concept of an interstate system derived from the principles that scholars have attributed to the peace of Westphalia that concluded the Thirty Years' War in 1648: the sovereign independence of states; each state being motivated in its international behaviour by a consistent national interest; the interstate system regulated by a balance of power among the principal powers' (Hettne 1995b, p. 12).

12. Stephen Gill provides us with an illustration of these efforts through his study on the Trilateral Commission. The task of the commission was not only to defend the values of a liberal international economic order internally, but also to persuade the inward-looking Japanese elites of the merits of the more outward-looking Western belief system and values (Gill 1990, pp. 143–202).

13. The content and impact of disciplinary power and the power of socialisation are illustrated by the Mozambican case. Economic policy is formulated by the Washington Consensus and imposed upon Mozambique. The government is committed and makes impressive efforts to implement the programme. In parliament its ministers defend the measures taken, accept devastating criticism and insist that the programme is theirs and that they are in the driver's seat. In private, they confess that they do not want to lose face or international credits. They feel strongly that there are no alternatives.

14. His article entitled 'Dominance and Leadership in the International Economy', published in *International Studies Quarterly* in the beginning of the 1980s, contributed to the further development of so-called 'public choice theory' and the conditions under which individuals could get their interests satisfied through collective actions (Kindleberger 1981).

15. Talking about the need for reassessing egoism, Keohane confessed that 'I do not switch to an assumption of pure altruism, but I do entertain the possibility that governments will define their self-interest in such a way as to make their own well-being dependent on the welfare of others. Under these conditions, international regimes will be easier to construct' (Keohane 1984, pp. 110–11). An example of how the elite can articulate self-interest is provided by Gill in his study on American hegemony and the Trilateral Commission (Gill 1990).

16. The concept of interdependence is particularly important when trying to understand the asymmetric relationship between Mozambique and South Africa (Blumenfeld 1991). The dependence of the former on the latter has been fairly well documented. At the time of independence migrant labour and transit traffic from South Africa contributed to half of Mozambique's foreign revenue (Abrahamsson and Nilsson 1995b). South Africa's dependence on Mozambique has been less

understood. Not only did it become a buffer of protection against international sanctions (the boomerang effect was often used as an argument by South African officials) but first and foremost South Africa depended heavily on Mozambique for cheap access to energy (Cahora Bassa complex), for cheap access to the Indian Ocean from the Transvaal area and for cheap access to migrant workers (not only for the mines but, much more important, some 500,000 illegal workers in the agricultural sector). The importance of this point was stressed during an interview with the former South African Minister of Foreign Affairs, Pik Botha, in Pretoria, 12 March 1997. This kind of interdependence illustrates how the weaker partner can use its weakness against the stronger, and change the asymmetry on specific issues. Likewise the power relations between Mozambique and South Africa explain the different military approaches that the latter pursued towards Angola and Mozambique (Abrahamsson and Nilsson 1995b).

17. The United States' misuse of its hegemonic power has been an area of constant review by critics from all strands within the academic field, be they realists (Gilpin 1987), neorealists (Ruggie 1983), liberals (Keohane 1986) or more independent scholars (Strange 1988).

18. In this study, levels are conceived as arenas where actors and structures interact. Cox discusses structures on three different levels, modes of social relations of production, forms of state, and structures of world order (Cox 1987, p. 394). For Cox each particular society comprises several connected types of production relations. Production provides the material basis for any form of state. Accordingly, the principal structures of production have been encouraged and sustained by the state. The structure of production in a particular society gives the basis for its class structure, in turn defining the nature of the state (Cox 1987, p. 6) Cox furthermore draws our attention to the fact that the structures at the different levels interact: 'changes in the organization of production generate new social forces which in turn, bring about changes in the structures of states; and the generalisation of changes in the structure of states alters the problematic of world order' (Cox and Sinclair 1996, p. 100).


## 2  Bretton Woods Revisited

1. At the time, Lord Keynes had been appointed assistant to the UK Chancellor of the Exchequer and acted as Britain's chief negotiator in the economic dealings with the Americans. His own perceptions of the preparation of the conference done by the Americans illustrate the influence and bargaining position of the latter. One month before the conference he commented on the proposed scheme prepared by the American chief negotiator and assistant of the US Secretary of Treasury, Mr H.D. White, as follows: 'Dr White's conception of all this seems to get "curiouser and curiouser". 42 nations, making 43 in all, have been invited for 1 July. They are to have no power of commitment or final decision and everything is to be ad referendum. Nevertheless it now appears that they are not even to have the semblance of doing any work, since that is to be done before they meet. I had been supposing that after meeting they would appoint two or more committees, which would then do the work which it is now contemplated to do beforehand, reporting back to a larger body whenever necessary. The American newspapers have indicated that 'The Conference beginning on July 1 may last for several weeks'. Unless this is a misprint for several days, it is not easy to see how the main monkey-house is going

to occupy itself. It would seem probable that acute alcoholic poisoning would set in before the end' (Keynes 1944, p. 41). In general, Third World countries, still in a colonial state, were not invited to participate in the conference at Bretton Woods. Some thirty years later they raised demands for a new international economic order based on their development needs. However the possible leverage of many of the countries invited to the Bretton Woods Conference is presumably well reflected in the following comments made by Keynes 'Twenty-one countries have been invited which clearly have nothing to contribute and will merely encumber the ground, namely, Colombia, Costa Rica, Dominica, Ecuador, Salvador, Guatemala, Haiti, Honduras, Liberia, Nicaragua, Panama, Paraguay, Philippines, Venezuela, Peru, Uruguay, Ethiopia, Iceland, Iran, Iraq, Luxemburg. The most monstrous monkey-house assembled for years. To these might perhaps be added: Egypt, Chile and (in present circumstances) Yugo-Slavia' (Keynes 1944, p. 42).

2. In five years, between 1940 and 1944, some 350 meetings were held and more than 650 documents were produced and sent to the Planning Committee within the State Department, cf. *The War and Peace Studies of the Council on Foreign Relations, 1932–1945*, Harold Pratt House, New York, 1946.

3. In his classic *Sterling–Dollar Diplomacy*, Richard Gardner presents a detailed account of the origin and contents of the White and the Keynes plans together with Anglo-American opinion at the time (Gardner 1969). Hans Singer, presently Professor Emeritus at the Institute of Development Studies, Sussex, provides us with a brilliant analysis of the emergence and content of the Bretton Woods system in *Third World Economics*, 16–31 August 1993, entitled 'The Bretton Woods System: Historical Perspectives'.

4. Gardner comments upon this in the following manner: 'In the hearings before the Senate Foreign Relations Committee on the Bretton Woods agreements in 1945, Secretary of the Treasury Henry Morgenthau insisted that the Fund and the Bank "are to be financial institutions run by financial people, financial experts, and the needs in a financial way of a country are to be taken care of wholly independent of the political connection". When Senator Fulbright questioned whether economics could be so easily divorced from politics, the chairman of the committee, Sen. Robert F. Wagner of New York, interjected: "I have just checked with Senator Tobey, and neither one of us heard any politics at all at Bretton Woods" ' (Gardner 1969, p. xxi).

5. For a more detailed description, see Mason and Asher (1973).

6. The Keynes plan emphasised as an important principle that any post-war international currency arrangements should depart markedly from the laissez-faire practices of 1920–33 in their acceptance of exchange controls, particularly over capital movements, and their minimisation of possible monetary dislocations affecting the multilateral exchange of goods. Keynes further argued that international measures to provide protection against wide fluctuations in employment, prices and markets would be necessary, within a framework that maximised national autonomy in economic management (Keynes 1941).

7. John Ruggie has elaborated on the historical circumstances behind the achievement of the compromise of embedded liberalism during the first half of the 1940s. See Ruggie (1983).

8. In assessing US foreign policy-making, it is important to note that the USA is not a monolithic actor speaking with one voice. 'Washington' rather comprises various executive and legislative actors capable of pushing policy-making in a particular field in different directions. This situation makes policy-making difficult

to grasp. Apparent confusion and disorder provoked Keynes to burst out on a visit to Washington in 1940, 'But you do not have a government in the ordinary sense of the word' (Vernon 1996, p. 57). Some forty-five years later the president of Mozambique, Samora Machel, joined the doubts, having every reason to question 'whether Washington could remain engaged as a serious and steady African player in the face of these strident and contradictory domestic voices fighting over policy' (Crocker 1992, p. 247). However, examining the various policy papers from the National Security Council issued since World War II, one is surprised to find a strong continuity between various administrations and congressional delegates in setting parameters that limit significantly new directions. The continuation of vital aspects of the policy of a former administration into the policy of the present is partly explained by the fact that values and perceptions creating the dominant culture behind foreign policy-making are embedded in the institutions as such and are not possible to replace from one day to another. The continuity of US foreign policy will be illustrated in the next chapter, focusing on US foreign policy towards southern Africa.

9. This somewhat ambiguous concept reflects some kind of common base for permitting a collective understanding of goals to be attained, although differences can persist on actions to be taken in order to attain these goals. Richard Melanson, provides an interesting account of American foreign policy in this regard (Melanson 1996).

10. The start of the Cold War is generally dated back to the period immediately after the World War II. The National Security Council policy paper, NSC 68, of 14 April 1950 is a good reflection of the understanding of the driving forces behind the Cold War that has been identified as that of the Traditional School (Marte 1994). The Soviet Union was considered expansionist and totalitarian which, unlike regarding relations with previous aspirants to hegemony, made conflict endemic. Unlike the traditionalists, who picture the United States as a world leader with a broad mandate from its allies to 'contain communism', the revisionist approach also holds American interests responsible for creating the Cold War. This school emphasises the decisive role of economics in American foreign policy-making. In fact, some revisionists argue that it was the United States that triggered the Cold War through its aggressive open-door policy and need to expand its economic activities overseas (William 1962, pp. 233–9). My own understanding is that both economic needs (outlets and raw material supply) and political concerns (perceived threat from the Soviet Union) were the main pillars of US national security interests. Indisputably, the logic of the military–industrial complexes also had a strong impact.

11. During the Truman administration, the Roosevelt vision of One World was replaced by the concept of a Free World. The eastern bloc of socialist countries came to be labelled the Second World, and during the 1950s the term Third World became widely used as a concept for the newly independent former colonies, who did not want to align themself with either the 'Free' or the 'Second' World.

12. This kind of exceptionalism is not unique to the USA. It is a dominant feature in many self-images of different populations and particularly their leaders. Galtung calls this exceptionalism 'chosenness' and identifies several different spheres or regions in the present world order with such aspirations (Galtung 1996).

13. The architect behind the 'policy of containment' is considered to be George Kennan, author of the well-known long telegram and at the time US chargé d'affaires in Moscow. In a famous article in *Foreign Affairs*, June 1947, he followed

up on his telegram and launched the thesis that the Soviet Union carried the seed of its own destruction. Instead of wasting resources on a direct confrontation, the western hemisphere should concentrate on containing the diffusion of Soviet ideology (Kennan 1967, pp. 354–67). Hence 'the containment of Soviet power was not the containment by military means of a military threat, but the political containment of a political threat' (p. 358). In fact, the policy of containment was opposed to the Truman Doctrine in the sense that US efforts to contain communism were proposed to be much more selective than the Doctrine would lead people to believe. Instead of placing US aid to Greece in its specific context, aiming to address a specific set of circumstances, the Doctrine put the aid to Greece in the framework of a more universal US policy which, according to Kennan, was not on the cards (Kennan 1967, p. 320).

14. In 1947, Secretary of State Marshall presented before the US Congress an extensive aid programme for the recovery of Europe, later to be called the Marshall Plan.

15. President Truman stated that 'we must embark on a bold new program for making the benefits of our scientific advances and industrial progress available for the improvement and growth of undeveloped areas ... their poverty is a handicap, a threat to both of them and to more prosperous areas' (Truman 1949, pp. 1–9).

16. Obviously the Council on Foreign Relations should not be confused with the US government. However, the work of both Shoup and Minter (1977) and Gill (1990) points to the very strong influence the Council had on post-World War II planning and the subsequent formulation of US foreign policy. Their interpretations correspond to my findings, based on work in the archive of the Council on Foreign Relations in New York. Most of the relevant documents have recently been made available following the classified time span of fifty years, as per the statutes of the Council.

17. Michael Clough, senior fellow at the Council on Foreign Relations, argued in *Foreign Affairs* (1994), that US foreign policy during the Cold War was separate from domestically oriented influences. According to Clough, the US internationalised business community was the most influential social grouping in the foreign policy establishment during the 1940s. Prompted by fear and prosperity, it succeeded in turning the nation of 'no entangling alliances into both the world's policeman and its bankers'. Undoubtedly, Atlanticism and its Grand Area relied on the perceived communist threat for its full implementation. (Historians might, in the future, be able to tell if the threat was exaggerated beyond reality.) The internationalised US business community's need at the end of World War II for a foreign trade policy that would give them access to markets abroad and help secure the supply of raw materials is well documented. In addition, it is evident that the Cold War contributed to what Wall Street considered important for injecting new strength into the entire economy. However, the question to be asked is whether or not the foreign policy of the United States could have mobilised the necessary domestic popular support for its implementation if it was not directly in accordance with United States national strategic interest. In fact, one could argue that the appearance of the Cold War created a base for such a fusion of domestic and foreign policies, albeit insufficient for proper US financing. This analysis could explain why in the post-Cold War era, with new national strategic interests, it has been difficult for the internationalised US business community to maintain popular support for continued US world leadership.

18. The role of the establishment in the design of US foreign policy was first documented by Hodgson (1973).

19. The motivation and design of the Grand Area can be found in Economic and Financial Memorandum E-B34 'Methods of Economic Collaboration: Introductory – the Role of the Grand Area in American Economic Policy' (24 July, 1941), printed in *The War and Peace Studies of the Council on Foreign Relations, 1939–1945*, Harold Pratt House, New York, 1946. A detailed account is given in Shoup and Minter (1977).

20. Using the terminology of the French historian Fernand Braudel, the exceptionalism and the aim to universalise Western values that constituted the overall objective of US foreign policy-making was more *'longue durée'*. This also goes for the need for raw material supply and market outlets. The Cold War political needs, however, are of a more 'conjuncturelle' character. The importance of this distinction will be highlighted in the next section of the study analysing the US foreign policy and southern Africa.

21. This analysis became extremely important, not only for US foreign policy-making but also for theoretical development within the field of International Relations and Conflict Resolution, as the internal causes of revolutionary upheaval were totally downplayed in favour of the communist bloc's ability to export revolution. Consequently, there was no need to develop analytical tools for identifying internal roots of social unrest, and the understanding of sub-national patterns of conflict remained limited. While the State Department became aware over time of the internal forces, especially perhaps during the Carter administration, the total neglect of these factors was a characteristic for the approaches within CIA and the Department of Defence up until the end of the 1980s, when the sudden end of the Cold War made such approaches obsolete (interview no. 118, Washington, 1 July 1996 and No 135, Washington, 29 August 1996, respectively)

22. By imposing rules on the borrowing country as regards the allocation and application of money lent by the Bretton Woods institutions, risk-taking for the commercial bankers is reduced. Hence a lower interest rate on commercial loans than would have been possible to obtain through direct lending could be achieved (Driscoll 1994). Furthermore, both institutions provide loans with various conditions attached that are subsidised through aid money. Following the debt crisis, agreement with the IMF on domestic financial policy became a prerequisite for further commercial borrowing during the 1980s. As regards the World Bank, it promptly shifted its focus to the developing countries, initially through project lending but gradually moving into programme lending with attached conditions of macro-economic performance.

23. For a further elaboration of this point, see Gardner (1969), Gwin (1994), Keynes (1944), Kojo (1992), Kirshner (ed. 1996), Mason and Asher (1973) and Payer (1982).

24. The British and American debates on the outcome of the Bretton Woods Conference are described in Gardner (1969), see also Kuttner (1991).

25. As was said in Washington: if their allies in Europe expected the USA to act as the policeman of the world, they also had to accept the US conditionality of acting as the banker of the world.

26. According to Gramsci, and as discussed in Chapter 1, the difference between dominance and hegemony lies in the legitimacy of the latter. The leader should not only have the capacity to lead but there must also be someone willing to be led. According to my understanding, however, this concept of Gramsci needs to be complemented by the fact that the leader should not only have the (theoretical) capacity to lead but also the political will for such an undertaking. Likewise, the

one willing to be led must also have the capacity to be led, i.e. a mutual inter-action of hegemonic relations must prevail on all levels. This logic is shared by Robert Cox; 'A world hegemonic order can be founded only by a country in which social hegemony has been or is being achieved. The expansive energies released by a social hegemony-in-formation move outward onto the world scale at the same time as they consolidate their strength at home' (Cox 1987, p. 149).

27. In the meantime the original objective behind US bilateral aid, as formulated in the Point Four Program, gradually changed. The programme was based on the balance between what was needed for US security and what could be jus-tified morally for altruistic reasons. The lack of domestic consensus on how to finance US leadership and the defence of Atlanticism meant that national security was progressively emphasised as motivating US development assistance, and the altruistic priorities were increasingly downplayed. The financial con-straints referred to in NSD 68 were soon to become acute as the gap between domestic production and domestic demand narrowed and US surplus production thus decreased. Following the passage of the NSD 68, Congress terminated the Marshall Plan (in 1952) and transferred its functions to the new Mutual Security Administration (MSA, Mutual Security Act of 1951). This act provided for mil-itary aid, defence support, and economic and food aid assistance (Zimmerman 1993, p. 8).

28. This study emphasises the financial aspects of US leadership as driving force behind the expansionary policy. According to this logic, one could argue that the main reason behind the monetary policy was Europe's need to be protected by Pax Americana and to solve the problem of international liquidity (the dollar gap). This conceptualisation of US monetary policies during the 1960s and 1970s could of course be questioned. Bearing in mind the need for a communist threat in order to implement its Grand Area strategy, and hence to guarantee the continuation of Atlanticism, an alternative reading would argue that the main objective for the United States was to establish sufficient financial power to implement the foreign policy needs of its business community, which were formulated by influential think tanks such as the Council on Foreign Relations.

29. Triffin (1967) points to the fact that dependence on the US dollar made the Bretton Woods system contain the seeds of its own destruction. In order for the USA to provide the required international liquidity, the US balance of payments deficit had to increase. In the long run such deficits would undermine confidence in the dollar.

30. The former chairman of the US Federal Reserve Bank, Paul Volcker, expressed this in the following way:

> Only later did it come to be clearly recognised that the special role of the dollar implied both privileges and burdens incompatible with the long-term opera-tion of the system as spelled out at Bretton Woods. Specifically, the use of the dollar as a reserve currency meant that the United States, unlike other coun-tries, could run a balance of payments deficit without giving up its own reserves of gold or without borrowing foreign currencies for as long as other countries were willing to add to the dollars they already held in their reserves. In effect, increased foreign dollar holdings financed the American deficits at relatively low US interest rates in the 1950s and 1960s, and without exchange rate risk to the United States. At the same time, those increased dollar holdings provided an important source for new reserves and liquidity for other countries. (Volcker and Goyhten 1992, pp. 14–15)

31. In the short run, the oil crisis, which tripled the prices for crude oil from the Middle East in the mid-1970s severely affected the US economy. In 1973, the country's oil imports cost some $7.6 billion. By 1977, they approached $45 billion. As a consequence the current account deteriorated. In 1973 the United States enjoyed a $9 billion trade surplus; whereas the trade deficit was estimated at some $25 billion in 1977. However, in reality the USA gained economically from the oil crisis, as the deficit in the current account was fully compensated for in the balance of payments with a huge part of the recycled petrodollars going back to the USA. This situation made the actual US Executive Director in the IMF express concern at the time of the fact that 'the petrodollars are being recycled in such a way that the countries with the strongest economies and external financial positions are receiving the biggest share of petrodollars and on the most favourable terms while the LDC's have access to these funds only through the intermediary of the commercial banks, which naturally charge high rates of interest and management fees' (Lissakers 1977, pp. 3–4).

32. I am indebted to Professor Noam Chomsky for drawing my attention to the fact that the Reagan administration itself pursued a strong protectionist national trade policy, while at the same time imposing neo-liberal concepts upon its trading partners (personal communication, 20 May 1997).

33. The interpretation that the overliquidity created by perverted militarist Keynesianism, reinforced by the Vietnam war, paved the way for this ideological shift towards neo-liberalism in the West during the late 1970s, is supported by Paul Volcker. In his self-criticism, he raised the question whether concerns over the international monetary system should not 'have been brought to bear more powerfully on decisions about the financing of the Vietnam war? That was the period when inflation really gained momentum in the United States and threatened to spread to Europe too, and if we weren't willing to finance the war properly, then maybe we shouldn't have fought it at all' (Volcker and Gyohten 1992, p. 62). Apart from the role of the Vietnam war in the breakdown of the international monetary system, the war implied a turning point in US history from a strategic military point of view as well. The more non-interventionist forces and the so-called Trilateralist understanding became predominant in US policy during the Carter administration. Despite the difficulties for Carter's détente policy and the subsequent revival of the interventionists, public reluctance towards US military involvement in the Third World remained. Since the days of Carter the use of low intensity warfare through support to local allies has thus been an important ingredient in US policy. This strategy obviously increased the room for manoeuvre of the CIA with intensified covert actions. CIA involvement in southern Africa and the Iran/Contras affair are clear cutcases in point during the Reagan administration (Klare 1981).

34. These events do not unreservedly support the various scholars who refuse to accept the thesis of US hegemony in decline (Huntington 1988; Strange 1988). The use of structural power may support hegemonic capacity, but it simultaneously implies a certain consideration of the interests of other actors. Despite being the main shareholder in the multilateral institutions (and the consequent trade-off between using bilateral or multilateral channels for leadership) the extent to which structural power can substitute direct power is not unilinear. Multilateral undertakings open up a certain bargaining space for other actors the dynamics of which should not be underestimated.

35. The former US National Security Adviser during the Carter administration, Zbigniew Brzezinski, was in the early 1960s a strong advocate of the need for the West to support the goal of Third World modernisation: 'it makes little difference how the African leaders act now, whether they are friendly or hostile to the West; what is considered decisive is that their societies reach the stage of "take-off" in the processes of modernisation, with the expectation that subsequently many of the tensions and hostilities to the West will inevitably subside' (Brzezinski 1963, p. 208).

36. At times, the use of structural power can give rise to internal contradictions between more long-term values on the one hand and pragmatic realpolitik on the other. The USA and the UK during the mid-1970 are cases in point. In 1976, the UK applied for a new loan from IMF at the same time as it strived to obtain fresh credits from the international financial markets. The private banks 'instead of trying to impose adjustment policies on the British directly, held back their $1.5 billion loan until the IMF credit and the $3 billion BIS swap line were in place. The IMF loan conditions thereby provided a kind of "umbrella" for the private banks. The Fund demanded that the Labour Government make large cuts in public expenditures to reduce the budget deficit, cut taxes, hold down the money supply, and improve conditions for private investments. These demands led to a cabinet crisis, as the left wing of the governing Labour Party threatened to walk out if the IMF's conditions were accepted' (Lissakers 1977, p. 63). Though the requirements imposed by the IMF were reflecting long-term US values, a cabinet crisis in the UK was not at the time in the interest of the Carter administration. Accordingly, the US government persuaded the IMF to modify its position, thereby averting a cabinet crisis and postponing for a while the fall of Callaghan government. However, long-term values had the upper hand and two years later the neo-liberal Thatcher government took over the cabinet.

37. Margaret Thatcher comments upon the reasons for her support to the US on this issue: 'I said that there was no way in which I was going to put British deposits into a bank which was totally run by those on overdraft' (Thatcher 1993, p. 169).

38. The New York bankers, supported by the Federal Reserve Bank, exercised strong pressure on the administration at the time. The chairman of the Federal Reserve Bank, Paul Volcker, personally played a very active role in getting support from the new administration and changing its hostility towards the Bretton Woods institutions. These efforts were observed by the mass media and described in the *Guardian*, London, 1 September 1982 as well as by the *Washington Post*, Washington, 8 December 1982.

39. The US 'ownership' of the Bretton Woods institutions notwithstanding, its influence over the institutions varied over time. Strong US influence over the World Bank during the 1960s was considerably reduced during the McNamara presidency in the 1970s, when the Bank managed to pursue a relatively independent policy. During the first part of the 1980s the World Bank became revitalised as a tool for US foreign policy. Catherine Gwin, Vice-President of the Overseas Development Council in Washington, made the following observation in her contribution to the documentation of the fifty-year history of the institutions 'Ironically, the Reagan and Bush administrations, which had wanted to cut back on US participation in the World Bank and other international financial institutions, wound up relying heavily on those institutions to handle problems that the United States could not (for budgetary and other reasons) manage bilaterally' (Gwin 1994, p. 53).

40. In fact, during the later half of the 1980s it became normal for a group of donors to be asked to assist the Bretton Woods institutions to ensure that their multilateral loans were repaid, by permitting the recipients to use the donors' balance of payment support. The argument behind this was that the loans were so-called 'preferred' and could not be rescheduled. The IMF was able to neutralise initial resistance from some of the donors towards this idea and achieve homogenisation of aid by working directly with the Ministries of Finance in concerned countries. These Ministries appeared to be both much more conscious of the interdependence of the international financial markets and sensitive to the importance of maintaining the stabilisation of these markets through proper macro-economic policies and debt repayment than were the Ministries of Foreign Affairs.

41. The possible threat to US national security of the Third World debt burden and consequent instability in the international monetary system, is illustrated by NSSD 3-83 issued by the President, 14 March 1983. The reluctance of the US Congress towards the Bretton Woods institutions, and the crucial role the latter came to play for New York bankers, made the former chairman of the Federal Reserve Bank, Mr Paul Volcker, participate in creating a permanent representation in Washington in order to lobby for the benefits of the institutions. (Mr Paul Volcker is currently chairman of James D. Wolfensohn, Inc, from which financial corporation the present World Bank president, James D. Wolfensohn was recruited.) The lobby group is called the Bretton Woods Committee and is a non-profit American non-governmental organisation. Inspired by the experience of similar work carried out by the Trilateral Commission (which is chaired by Volcker), in 1993 the Bretton Woods Committee decided to create a private Commission looking into the future role of the institutions. The Commission included a number of important international official and commercial banking personalities and presented an extensive report in July 1994 (Bretton Woods Commission 1994). The report contained several important suggestions for change that will be further commented upon in the final chapter of this study.

42. At the time, the influence of the neo-liberal philosophy and renewed interest in the financial aspects of the economy at the expense of investment, production and employment began to affect Mozambique. It was argued, not only by the international creditors but also by a new generation of Mozambican economists, that it was not South African destabilisation as such that brought the country to the verge of ruin, but rather the socialist inflationary monetary policy. As argued in this study, such an analysis is totally erroneous. However, this kind of conceptualisation became a key element in the design of the structural adjustment programme (SAP). A good example of this thinking can be found in Abreu and Baltazar (1992). The authors are economists working at Banco de Moçambique and the Faculty of Economics, University of Eduardo Mondlane, respectively.

43. However, in a staff report prepared for the use of the Subcommittee on Foreign Economic Policy of the Committee on Foreign Relations, United States Senate, August 1977, Karen Lissakers drew the attention of the Carter administration to possible political consequences of the political reform programmes. As mentioned earlier, Lissakers was some twenty years later designated US Executive Director in the International Monetary Fund. It is therefore of interest to quote her concerned report to the Senate at some length: 'The difficulty with these policies is that while they may be the most effective way of rapidly bringing a deficit country's external account into balance, they may also lead to higher unemployment, cuts in social welfare programs, and a generally lower standard of living for the people, at

least over the short term. And in desperately poor countries, where the majority of the population may already be living at a bare subsistence level, a decision by the government to impose a program of stiff economic austerity can create social and political turmoil. The requirements that government spending be reduced and the private sector expanded may also conflict with the long-term social and economic goals of a government or of certain political fractions within a country. If the IMF and the other creditors are not sufficiently responsive to these internal constraints, they may push a government into a position of having to choose between acceptancy of the foreign creditors terms – and perhaps having to use political repression to carry them through – or repudiation of the IMF, the banks, and possibly its debts and resorting instead to trade protectionism and go-it-alone policy. ... The Carter administration may therefore have to choose between pressing its international human rights effort, and supporting creditor's demands for drastic economic austerity programs that can only be achieved at the expense of civil liberties in the countries that undertake them' (Lissakers 1977, p. 60).

44. In order to persuade a reluctant Congress of the American national interest in allocating funds to the multilateral development banks in the beginning of the 1980s, the US Treasury Department carried out an internal evaluation of US influence over the Bretton Woods institutions. According to the evaluation, of the 70 cases identified with clear US political goals during the 1970s, roughly 80 per cent were achievable. The failure of the remaining 20 per cent was due to internal contradictions and lack of US coherence. See: Department of the Treasury 1982, 'United States Participation in the Multilateral Development Banks in the 1980s', Washington, DC. In fact, according to this internal report, one of the aims of financially supporting the MDBs was based on the fact that 'In the short term, the MDBs, especially the World Bank, can provide fast disbursing assistance, such as programs or structural adjustment loans (SALs), to US "friends" (although the loan processing, especially for SALs, can sometimes take as long as project loans)'. The World Bank helped Peru in this manner in 1979 and Turkey in 1980–81.

45. *Treasury News*, RR-108, 1995, Statement of the Treasury Secretary, Robert E. Rubin – Subcommittee on foreign operations export financing and related programs – House committee on appropriations, 28 February 1995, Washington, DC.

46. As regards the World Bank, the US efforts to influence decision-making met increased resistance during the second part of the 1980s, due to the increased autonomy of upper-level management staff. The monopolisation of information by top-ranking officials hampered the insight of the US-selected president and the board members. Private interviews carried out in Washington in April 1995. See also George and Sabelli (1994), Gwin (1994) and Krueger (1993).

47. The new approach was labelled 'coaching' and implied extensive training of both functionaries within the recipient countries and, when needed, functionaries within the institutions themselves. The training consisted of different techniques of argument and calculation in order to get the boards of directors of the IMF and the World Bank to approve the various proposals. The method was confirmed during several interviews conducted by the author with the 'coached' as well as with the 'coachers' during 1994 and 1995. The case of Zaire is often quoted as an illuminating example. See Schatzberg (1991).

48. The battle between the IMF and the Tanzanian government, commencing in the late 1970s, is illuminating in this regard. As long as he remained head of state, Nyerere continued to insist 'that Tanzania's economic woes were not of its own making but caused by an unfair international economic system'. Its main actors,

therefore had a moral responsibility to help Tanzania – as well as other countries in a similar predicament – out of its crisis, without first insisting on conditions that were viewed as politically impossible to fulfil (Hydén and Karlström 1991, p. 51). However, the bilateral donors gradually lined up behind the IMF. Tanzania's largest donor, Sweden, contributing some 15 per cent of total aid to the country, was a strong supporter of the Nyerere politics. 'In 1982, however, explicit concern was expressed at different levels, from the Prime Minister via the Minister for Foreign Affairs to the Director General of Sida. The urgency of reaching an agreement on an IMF-supported adjustment programme was underlined, as were the prospective positive effects of such an agreement on the Swedish country frame' (Lundström 1988, p. 113). In July 1989, the Swedish government decided to make a review of the Swedish Development Assistance through the multilateral institutions. The former Deputy of the Swedish Central Bank, Hans Lundström, was appointed chairman of the committee. The committee presented its findings and conclusions in June 1991 (Collicial report no 48, 1991). It strongly recommended continued support to the Bretton Woods institutions and encouraged continued implementation of the structural adjustment programmes. The US influence over the institutions was not commented upon. Before the assignment, Mr Hans Lundström served as the Nordic Executive Director in the International Monetary Fund. Ms Birgitta Hambraeus, the Swedish member of Parliament and a member of the committee presented a strong reservation against the conclusions of the committee.

49. As earlier discussed, Robert Cox describes the structural impact on national governments of the ongoing global centralisation of influence over policy as a process of internationalisation of the state. He rightly observes that the common feature of this process 'is to convert the state into an agency for adjusting national economic practices and policies to the perceived exigencies of the global economy. The state becomes a transmission belt from the global to the national economy, where heretofore it had acted as the bulwark defending domestic welfare from external disturbances.' He further concludes that 'power within the state becomes concentrated in those agencies in closest touch with the global economy – the offices of presidents and prime ministers, treasuries, central banks. The agencies that are more closely identified with domestic clients – ministries of industries, labour ministries, etc. – become subordinated' (Cox 1992).

# 3  Pax Americana and Southern Africa: Coinciding Interests and Change

1. I am indebted to Professor Noam Chomsky for drawing my attention to the recommendation of George Kennan at the time (in PPS 23, 1948) 'that Africa be handed over to the Europeans to "exploit" for their reconstruction (and psychological welfare), because the US wasn't much interested in it' (personal communication from Professor Chomsky, dated 6 September 1995). This attitude is clearly reflected in NSC No 68, 1950-04-14. According to its Appendix 2, p. 6, US aid activities aimed at facilitating the African contribution to European welfare 'have been scheduled at a rate of US$10 million per annum. Further grant aid has been scheduled for the expansion and new development of strategic materials and associated transportation facilities, as well as for the expansion of indigenous food, fibre and other

    essential raw material production *to increase and maintain the contribution of the African territories to the Western European economies'* (italics added).

2.    This awareness is articulated in the following manner. 'To a considerable extent, the African is still immature and unsophisticated with respect to his attitudes towards the issues that divide the world today. The African's mind is not made up and he is being subjected to a number of contradictory forces. This pressure will increase in the future. The African is a target for the advocacy of Communism, old-fashioned colonialism, xenophobic nationalism, and Egyptian "Islamic" propaganda, as well as for the proponents of an orderly development of the various political entities in the area in question, closely tied to the West.' At the same time, however, the Directives conclude by underlining that 'The eventual political orientation of the emerging African states will probably be determined by what the leaders and peoples conceive best serves their own interests, measured primarily in terms of "independence" and of "equality" with the white man. Our policies therefore must be designed to convince the African that the United States wants to help him achieve his economic, political and cultural goals without insisting that he align himself in the East–West power struggle' (NSC 5818, 1958/08/26, p. 4).

3.    The effort to diffuse Western development values and US-style capitalism globally was ambiguous. Strikingly little attention was paid to the apparent contradiction between available and required resources for such an endeavour. The figures presented at the time by the various US post-war study groups, aiming to define the US national security interest (cf. Chapter 2), had indicated that the prosperity of a US-style economy covering 5 per cent of the world's population required access to some 45 per cent of the world's resources and markets. Obviously, it would be difficult for other countries to replicate this. The reason for playing down this paradox, highlighted only some thirty years later during the Rio summit meeting in 1992, is difficult to understand. One explanation might be that the countries in the western hemisphere were acutely concerned to create conditions, through the diffusion of their values, for establishing an open market economy on the global level, permitting a secure supply of strategic minerals and access to market outlets for their surplus production.

4.    The electoral victory of the Afrikaner National Party in 1948, and the subsequent introduction of apartheid legislation in 1950, created a dilemma for the hitherto relatively unquestioned nature of USA–South African ties. The dilemma related to the relative merits of anti-communism and anti-racism as guidelines for USA–South Africa relations. As Schraeder points out, the important asset of the Afrikaner government's anti-communism was counteracted by the possible liability of Washington's association with apartheid. Although the area was still without strategic importance for the USA, the Cold War atmosphere soon gave anti-communism priority over possible misgivings about the racial policies of the Afrikaner government (Schraeder 1994, p. 194).

5.    A detailed account of the nuclear collaboration between the United States and South Africa is given by Mokoena (1993, pp. 115–77).

6.    The dominant view since the times of President Truman, sometimes also called the globalist view, conceived all external Soviet activities as a part of their global geopolitical strategy for world domination (cf. Chapter 5). Accordingly, at the time the globalists also considered Africa to be an unavoidable part of USA–Soviet rivalry (Marte 1994, p. 67). Such an approach was reinforced by the superpowers' neglect of the continent during the 1950s. Ignorance about African realities resulted in a tendency to view all regional crises in terms of East–West conflict. The

developments in Guinea and Congo during the 1960s were taken as proof. Another view, put forward at times by more liberal scholars, the so-called regionalist view, underlines the continent's own historical framework and political agenda, and the economic goals underlying the possible hostility of African countries towards the western hemisphere. Instead of military action to defend US interests, this approach emphasised the need for African solutions to African problems through increased support for economic progress and social reforms.

7. The fear of a so-called resource war between the USA and the USSR was spread by some of the US leaders. Nixon himself referred to a statement said to have been made to the Somali President Siad Barre by Soviet President Leonid I. Brezhnev, indicating that the aim of the USSR was 'to gain control of the two great treasure houses on which the West depends – the energy treasure house of the Persian Gulf and the mineral treasure house of central and southern Africa [and that] [w]hile the United States is partially dependent on imported oil and strategic minerals, Europe and Japan are absolutely dependent on overseas sources' (Nixon 1980, p. 23). Nixon pointed to US dependency on imported chrome as one of many examples. He said that the US National Research Council had concluded that long term US vulnerability in chrome was greater than in petroleum: '92 per cent of our chrome must be imported ... of the world's known reserves of chromium, 96 per cent are in South Africa and Zimbabwe/Rhodesia' (Nixon 1980, p. 30). The same concern characterised the Reagan administration. Crocker drew attention to the danger that if southern Africa's resources came under Soviet control it would mean that the Soviets had their hands on 90 per cent of world platinum resources, 80 per cent of gold and 75 per cent of manganese (Bissell and Crocker 1979). These fears were publicly shared by Alexander Haig while he was acting President of the United Technologies Corporation before joining the Reagan administration (AC 1980, 29 October). This perception obviously had an important impact on US policy and explains its reluctance to impose sanctions against South Africa. However, the fear was not shared by the international economic elite (e.g. the Rockefeller group) nor by the Foreign Office in London. The former launched the so-called 'Zaire argument', advocating that social and political stability allowing the raw materials to be extracted was more important than who holds power in a country, an argument supported by the continued supply of raw materials following the independence of both Angola and Zimbabwe (personal interview no 148, New York 4.9.96). The latter pointed to the 'Angolan government's offer to Moscow to extract the country's minerals, an offer the communists rejected, telling the Angolans to deal with De Beers for diamonds and Gulf Oil for their petroleum since the Russians had a surplus of diamonds, oil and uranium' (Bower 1993, p. 364).

8. The network also benefited the USA: South Africa security supplied Contras in Nicaragua with weaponry on behalf of the CIA (confirmed by the Pentagon, interview no. 127, Washington, 8 July 1996).

9. This unexpected gesture was confirmed during various interviews in the USA carried out 1994–96. However, this was one year before the III Congress of Frelimo when the movement transformed itself into a Marxist–Leninist vanguard party, and four years before ZANU leader Robert Mugabe unexpectedly won an overwhelming election victory in Zimbabwe, following the Lancaster House agreement.

10. British writer Tom Bower describes the Rhodesian separation from British rule in the following way: 'Ian Smith's Unilateral Declaration of Independence was

announced on 11 November 1965. In his lunchtime radio broadcast, bringing the country to a halt, Smith spoke of striking "a blow for the preservation of justice, civilisation and Christianity". Black majority rule, said the leader of the new rebel regime, was to be deferred for one thousand years. Harold Wilson portrayed UDI as "the greatest moral issue which Britain has had to face in the post-war world", and announced limited sanctions which did not include oil' (Bower 1993, p. 92).

11. The Rhodesian issue was very sensitive for the Commonwealth, whose members exercised strong pressure on the British to act. This was clearly manifested when Nigeria decided to nationalise part of British Petroleum's investments there, as a consequence of its dissatisfaction with British policy (Thatcher 1993, p. 74). In London, therefore, concessions on the Rhodesian issue were considered cheaper than imposing sanctions against South Africa. Hence the former became a means of postponing the latter.

12. At the time of independence, close to half a million Portuguese returned to Portugal from Angola and Mozambique, provoking strong political and economic pressures there. Some 15 per cent were estimated to have been born in Africa (Pires *et al.* 1984).

13. The perceived threat in Pretoria was reinforced by the creation of Marxist–Leninist parties in Luanda and Maputo and their subsequent Treaties of Friendship with Moscow. Notwithstanding the long tradition behind this radicalisation, Mozambique's political orientation was more practical than ideological. It stemmed from a combination of influential external and internal events. Western support to Portugal during the war of liberation, combined with the South African invasion of Angola following independence, produced a conducive political environment. The analysis of Portugal's colonial role and the need to opt for an armed independence struggle, experiences from the liberated zones and the decision by China to provide support to UNITA and FNLA in Angola, were also part of these events. The latter led Frelimo finally to choose sides in the Sino-Soviet conflict, with a subsequent need to show Moscow its new loyalty (interview no. 151, Maputo, 2 October 1996).

14. The Southern Africa Development Coordination Conference (SADCC) was officially founded on 1 April 1980 in Lusaka by the Front Line states of Angola, Botswana, Mozambique, Tanzania, Zambia and Zimbabwe, plus Lesotho, Malawi and Swaziland.

15. The newly installed State Security Council in Pretoria, intended to coordinate all aspects of South Africa's foreign and domestic policy under the total strategy, never became a monolithic power centre. Most Western analysis of the South African Scene seriously underestimated the infighting among different interest groups inside the white South African elite. Foreign Affairs and Finance were among the ministerial departments that strongly opposed the policy of military destabilisation, instead wanting to use the country's hegemonic and structural power. However, the location of the anti-apartheid struggle in the region served to provoke the more racist and reactionary forces within the area still further. For the time being these forces within the South African Defence Force and the Portuguese 'hibernating' colony in South Africa got the upper hand in regional foreign policy-making.

16. During the 1980s dependency on South Africa increased, not only as a consequence of South African destabilisation but also due to the European interest lying primarily in reestablishing outward oriented linkages, and downplaying intraregional trade. As a consequence, trade among the SADCC partners during the 1980s

remained at around 4–5 per cent of total foreign trade (Harlov 1997). As far as Mozambique is concerned, it is fair to argue that the negative economic and political consequences that stemmed from creating the SADCC at a time when the apartheid regime still was in power in Pretoria far outweighed any positive gains. The short-term costs for Mozambique of South African destabilisation were dramatic, and are well documented. Both the transport infrastructure and the social infrastructure in the countryside were wiped out in a war described by the US Deputy Assistant Secretary of State for African Affairs US 'as one of the most brutal holocausts against ordinary human beings since World War II ... a systematic and brutal war of terror against innocent Mozambican civilians through forced labour, starvation, physical abuse and wanton killing' (Roy Stacey, quoted in Hanlon 1991, p. 47). Reduced capacity for food production, coupled with drought, created famine and more than one third of the population had to seek refuge (Abrahamsson and Nilsson 1995b). Estimates indicate that over 1 million people were indirectly or directly killed, of whom nearly 500,000 were children under the age of five (Economic Commission for Africa 1989a, p. 3). Less documented is the difficulty in reducing transport dependency on South Africa and the unlikelihood that the objectives in this regard could have been achieved without strong interest and support from the South African transport industry itself. The latter controlled much of the regional cargo flow by providing the know-how and the international network required for efficient international transport, and constituted a clearcut example of what Susan Strange describes as structural power in the international transport sector (Strange 1988). In that sense, the whole endeavour of the SATCC (the special commission within SADCC created for Transport and Communications) to reduce transport dependency on South Africa, could be expressed as technocratic naiveté (Abrahamsson 1989). The impressive investments in hardware made in the corridors could not be used efficiently without access to the software in the hands of South Africa (Abrahamsson 1989).

17. The Constellation of States (CONSAS) concept represented the economic and commercial tool of the total strategy. It had its roots in Vorster's détente policy aimed at increasing South African dominance over the continent through increased economic cooperation (Murray 1987).

18. A perception frequently underlined by high-ranking military officials in Maputo during informal conversations with the author.

19. The civilian and more reformist component of the Soviet political leadership preferred to give priority to domestic economic problems in order to increase the Party's internal legitimacy than to external activities in Africa with very doubtful cost efficiency. At the beginning of the 1980s, the refusal to let Ghana and Mozambique into CMEA was a clear signal that the Soviets were not prepared to reinforce their political and economic support, unless there was a strong political reason. During the 26th Party Congress in 1981 Brezhnev talked about developments, under complicated circumstances in the socialist-oriented countries (Valkenier 1986).

20. The Soviet involvement in southern Africa at the time should also be understood as a result of strong pressure from the Non-Aligned Movement to increase its African support during the meeting in Alger 1973; as well as in Colombo 1975. The American Soviet analyst Campbell concludes that 'The Soviet Union's interest, influence and involvement in southern Africa was dramatically and uncharacteristically high in the period from 1975 to 1980. However, in the period since, southern Africa has decreased in importance to the USSR' (Campbell 1986).

21. An account of the Nkomati accord, its background and intended objectives for different actors is given in Ohlsson and Stedman 1994 (pp. 99–101).

22. The term 'Constructive Engagement' was used for the first time by Chester Crocker in his article entitled 'South Africa: Strategy for Change'. The article was published in *Foreign Affairs*, Winter 1980/81, before the inauguration of President Reagan and Crocker's recruitment onto his staff.

23. The Cold War could be defined 'as a pattern of hostile interactions expressed in a global rivalry – which is, in nature, ideological, political, economic, technological, and military – between two powers or power blocs that stops short of a hot war due to the reciprocally deterring effects produced by the devastatingly destructive armaments both sides possessed' (Marte 1994, p. 2). Although the conflict in southern Africa did not provoke the involvement of fighting troops from the superpowers, the term 'Cold War' is ambiguous. From an international perspective the term Cold War is applicable in order to describe the context of the conflict. For the peasantry, falling victim to appalling terror, the logistic and material support given by the superpowers to the different sides made the conflict Hot. In some instances the conflict has therefore been described as a low-intensity warfare (Klare 1981). More frequently the term destabilisation has been used. I will characterise the conflict as an armed struggle involving actors at different levels and with different motives, where the predominant motives were racist and ideological at the regional and international levels respectively.

24. The more regional approach is normally ascribed to the Carter administration, whilst the Reagan administration approach is characterised as 'fairly extreme globalist', reinforcing the East–West conflict. According to this analysis the Carter regime would have brought Namibian independence closer, whilst the Reagan administration is accused of having delayed the settlement and hence peace and development in southern Africa. Obviously, such an understanding underestimates the strong continuity in US foreign policy, which also framed the content of 'constructive engagement'. It is true that the foreign policy of the Carter administration, supported by Cyrus Vance and opposed by Brzezinski, initially strove for détente and the containment of communism through defence of human rights and democracy. In this sense we can talk about a more regionalist and liberal approach, as the defence of US values was considered the best way to increase US legitimacy and thereby its power. However, the détente policy's difficulties in responding to the perceived expansion of Soviet power in the late 1970s, exemplified by the Soviet invasion of Afghanistan, made Carter return to a more globalist view during his last year in the presidency. Increased power became a prerequisite for pursuing the policy of human rights and no longer the other way around. In fact, according to National Security Adviser Brzezinski, the détente policy's difficulties created 'an arc of crisis in Africa' which laid the foundations for a more Cold War-oriented policy during the Reagan administration (Marte 1994, p. 98). Hence, it is true that the US reaction to the perceived Soviet expansion came fully to light during the subsequent Reagan administration. However, those who failed to understand the importance of the continuity of US foreign policy were certainly taken by surprise by the fact that the Reagan administration in practice came to increase aid to Zimbabwe, maintain restrictions in its relations with South Africa and try hard, with assistance from London and later Maputo, to reinforce its dialogue with Angola (Martin 1989, pp. 23–46).

25. The question of the South African nuclear threat was raised by Crocker in Crocker 1981b, and has later been substantiated through various declassified documents,

see Mokoena (ed.) 1993, pp. 115–16 and Simpson 1993, pp. 740–1. The use of the threat was confirmed by former CIA officials during the interviews conducted in Washington (interview 136, 29 August 1996). The main target was Luanda Harbour, in order to stop the arrival of Cuban troops.

26. Confirmed during various interviews carried out in Washington 1994–6 (*inter alia*, interview no. 78, 4 April 1995).

27. The support that Mozambique obtained from the international capital interests– Rockefeller, Oppenheimer, Balsemão and various members of the Trilateral commission – was of particular importance in getting parts of the conservative wing of the Reagan administration to accept the intended policy. The Trilateralists considered apartheid obsolete and were afraid that the system would hinder the development of a market economy and thereby endanger the secure supply of essential raw materials. For this economic elite the danger of political instability was far more important than the 'Resource War' with the Soviets, which was widely debated at the time. With the Nkomati agreement, both Rockefeller and Oppenheimer began to consider Machel as a person with whom they shared common interests, i.e. someone understanding the need to abolish the apartheid system through negotiation and not through confrontation with the white minority regime in Pretoria (confirmed in interview no. 43, New York, 28 July 1994). Another very influential lobbyist was the former Rhodesian-based British businessman Tiny Rowland, the main shareholder of the Lonrho group, with important assets all over black Africa. Of special concern for Lonrho was to stop South African destabilisation endangering revenue from the pipeline bringing oil from Beira to Zimbabwe, and its European trade of tobacco and tea from Malawi and Zimbabwe. Although his success in influencing UK foreign policy was limited, Tiny Rowland created close relations with the US State Department and played an important role as an intermediary during the Reagan and Bush administrations, something that over time became appreciated not only in Washington but also in Maputo and Harare (Bower 1993). The commercial group's interest in abolishing apartheid which had some influence on the various Foreign Offices was poorly understood by the Western solidarity movements. Instead of analysing the dynamics created by the interaction of the twin goal of the economic elites, namely to abolish apartheid and to increase South Africa's integration into the world economy in order to establish a market economy, they frequently focused their analysis on the latter aspect (see, for example, Hanlon 1986, p. 52).

28. This analysis underlines the importance of understanding the policy of the Reagan administration towards apartheid in light of the overall US national strategic interest formulated during and immediately after World War II. The perception of the Soviet threat decided whether the more short-term political interests or more long-term economic ones had the upper hand in US foreign policy-making during the 1980s. Hence, those interested in abolishing apartheid logically strove to scale down the destabilisation of Mozambique, provided that the country abandoned its socialist-oriented policy and supposed support for cross-border actions by the ANC. According to this logic, continued infrastructural destruction would be counterproductive from both an economic and a political point of view. Economically, because of the subsequent costs of rehabilitation required for a transition to the market economy. Politically, because Mozambique might be forced to turn to Cuba for support and the conflict would escalate. This analysis does not dispute the probability that the State Department could have been forced to use another strategy if the Soviet threat had been conceived as real. In that case a US policy aimed at

reinforcing the apartheid system in order to satisfy its raw material supply needs could not have been excluded. Such a policy would not necessarily have been conducted through direct military intervention, but most probably through some kind of low-intensity warfare with logistic support to Renamo, and if necessary the involvement of US Rapid Deployment Forces (a strategy elaborated under the Carter administration for this purpose; see Klare 1981).

29. *Washington Post*, 10 July 1989, confirmed during various interviews with US officials conducted by the author 1994–6.

30. The controversy created by the loan is well reflected in the *Washington Post*, early November 1982, and was confirmed during various interviews with US officials conducted by the author 1994–6. The US effort for fresh credits to South Africa reflected another, and important, dimension of its policy towards South Africa, namely the prevailing interdependence between the countries not only as regards global covert action (cf. South African covert support to Contras) but also in the economic sphere. The economic setback in South Africa in the early 1980s was related to the increased purchase of dollars by the US Treasury in order to keep the dollar value up at the time. Consequently the value of gold decreased from $613 an ounce in 1980 to $350 an ounce in mid-1982. The Pretoria government was able to compensate through the IMF credits, as the US commercial banks followed swiftly to provide more credits (Minter 1986, p. 319).

31. The Nkomati Accord was an achievement of extreme importance for Crocker and his team, as it made it possible for them to remain in charge of US Africa policy during the second term of the Reagan administration, a fact confirmed in Washington (interview no. 26, 7 July 1994) and perceived by the Pretoria regime as one important reason for the strong US pressure on the parties to sign the agreement (interview no. 18, Maputo, June 1994).

32. According to the agreement, the ANC would only be allowed to keep a minor diplomatic representation in Mozambique, something that was considered by the apartheid regime, the Front Line states and the ANC to imply a weakening of the anti-apartheid opposition in South Africa (Mokoena 1993, p. 282). Consequently, most of the ANC leadership, Front Line states leaders and international apartheid movements reacted negatively to the signing.

33. In view of the infighting between various executive agencies, it is of no surprise that the logic behind 'Constructive Engagement' did not win consensus in Washington. The Defence Intelligence Agency (DIA) continued to strive for recognition of and support to Renamo until the late 1980s, and factions within the Central Intelligence Agency (CIA) wanted to weaken the Frelimo government in order to obtain further political concessions. Both parties actively obstructed the implementation of 'Constructive Engagement'. Evidence of this has been provided by Crocker (1992): 'In my eight and a half years at the helm of the Africa bureau, no policy battle was more bitter. Few presidential-approved policies were more shamelessly undercut by people in the President's own party, his own administration and, even, his own White House staff'. The State Department did not even manage to get US intelligence to provide it with proofs of South African violation of the agreement to make it possible to start pressurising Pretoria. 'Despite our requests, it somehow was never possible for US intelligence to document Renamo's barbaric *modus operandi* or pattern of continuing South African support. We had to track the story down ourselves' (Crocker 1992, p. 284). Secretary of State Shultz shared this opinion: 'Our policies of support for Savimbi's UNITA guerrillas and opposition to Renamo's guerrilla effort were under constant domestic political

attack alternately from the right and the left wings in Congress. Bill Casey's pursuit of different foreign policy goals, using the CIA as his platform and his source of influence, was also a continuing problem for Crocker and me as we pursued what had been approved as administration policy' (Shultz 1993, p. 1113). The affirmations have been confirmed in interviews with various US officials representing the Pentagon and the CIA carried out by the author in Washington in 1994–6. The complexity increased as infighting inside the CIA itself (between the Deputy Directorate of Intelligence providing the National Security Council with analyses of gathered intelligence, and the Deputy Directorate of Operations, responsible for covert actions around the globe) was frequent, a phenomenon referred to during these interviews. A written account of the role of CIA in the design and implementation of US foreign policy is provided by Robert Gates, Deputy Director of Central Intelligence during the Reagan administration, in Foreign Affairs, winter 1987/88. An excellent account of US private intervention in the war in Mozambique is provided by Kathi Austin (Austin 1994). Similar infighting in the Pretoria government was also illustrative of ignorance and arrogance among its officials: 'So deeply did they disagree about Mozambique, that Botha excluded Van der Westhuizen (head of Pretoria's military intelligence) from our restricted discussion on that topic' (Crocker 1992, p. 216). According to Crocker, Van der Westhuizen reacted strongly to this: 'You're wasting your time talking to them – I run Mozambique' (Crocker 1992). Documents captured by the Mozambican government at Renamo's headquarters in Gorongosa underline this infighting and illustrate how the South African Defence Force considered Foreign Minister Pik Botha as a traitor (NSA 01919 1985/10/03)

34. Ironically, as Howard Wolpe, the chairman of the House Subcommittee on African Affairs of the US Congress pointed out, the Cuban factor that shaped 'Constructive Engagement' and made it so controversial became one of the major factors in achieving the peace agreement in the region. 'It was above all else, the Cubans, after increasing their forces from about twenty thousand to in the neighbourhood of fifty thousand and delivering several significant military defeats to the South Africans, who facilitated the negotiations that Crocker wanted to implement and the agreement that Crocker wanted to achieve much earlier' (Schraeder 1994).

35. The limited sanctions imposed in September 1985 (Executive Order 12532) followed by the Comprehensive Anti-Apartheid Act of 1986 (Executive Order 12571) undoubtedly came to have an important impact on developments. In retrospect this is also confirmed by their strong opponents (interviews 117 and 145, Washington July–August 1996). Since the inception of constructive engagement Crocker had strongly objected to sanctions, arguing that they would take one important stick away from the mediators and furthermore possibly imply a South African withdrawal from the negotiations. The issue of sanctions accordingly became extremely controversial, and was used by the opponents of constructive engagement as an explanation for the policy's difficulties in delivering. The concern was raised that the USA was contributing to increased suffering of the people in the region (Mugabe 1987). The intensive debate became somewhat academic, since the geopolitical realities combined with strong economic interests made it impossible to impose any sanctions before the mid-1980s. What we know in retrospect is that over time a trade-off took place in the US Congress, which puts a large question mark over the political gains of sanctions if they had been imposed earlier. The right wing in Congress accepted sanctions in exchange for the repeal of the Clark Amendment (August 1985) and the US support for

Unita (October 1985). Assisted by its own research into Renamo outrages, the Gersony report, the State Department only just succeeded in getting Congress to refrain from giving Renamo support in 1987. As anticipated, Pretoria immediately withdrew from negotiations. So did the government in Angola following the US decision to reactivate its support to Unita. The peace process thus lost momentum over the next one and a half years (confirmed interview 155, Pretoria October 1996).

36. Anecdotal evidence in Maputo claims that the preparation for the Reykjavik summit meeting between the USA and the Soviet Union (October 1986), and Gorbachev's effort to reach a general agreement on disarmament, motivated Moscow to downplay its regional commitments during the second half of the 1980s. This understanding is shared by Marte who, quoting the South African Afrikaans journal *International Spectator* 41/7 (July 1987), p. 376, states that 'although the Soviet Union did support South Africa's African National Congress (ANC), it was reluctant to provide massive military aid, and, during the second Soviet–African conference for peace and social progress, in 1986, the Soviets advocated a political solution for the South African problem' (Marte 1994, p. 63). Such interpretations are further supported by the fact that during the 27th Congress of the Party in March 1986, Gorbachev did not even mention the socialist-oriented countries in his speech. However, he concluded by emphasising the need for the developing countries to implement the rules of the market economy, as Moscow lacked the resources to finance any alternative approach to economic growth and prosperity in the Third World. This further scaling down of Soviet commitment towards Africa was in fact an important message from Gorbachev to Washington. Preparing for the Reykjavik summit, the Reagan administration had made it clear that its four-point agenda should apply (NSDD 245, 1986/10/07): 'we were determined not to allow the Soviets to focus our negotiations simply on matters of arms control. So we continuously adhered to a broad agenda: human rights, regional issues, arms control, and bilateral issues. ... Engaging with Moscow on key regional issues, particularly Afghanistan and southern Africa, put us in a position to sustain diplomatic pressure and exploit whatever opportunities might emerge' (Shultz 1993, p. 266). In the aftermath of Reykjavik (October 1986), where the four-part agenda was strictly followed, Shultz took Crocker with him to the next Moscow summit (May 1988) 'in an effort to highlight the negotiations for Namibian independence and to enlist Soviet support for our efforts' (Shultz 1993, p. 1101).

37. This study's findings of strong continuity in US foreign policy towards southern Africa are supported by various US scholars and established Africanists. The former President of the African Studies Association, Crawford Young, had come to the conclusion that despite the fact that the Kennedy, Carter and Reagan administrations each 'entered office with an African policy project that diverged sharply from that of its predecessor', in every case 'the actual change was far less than what appeared in prospect from the blueprints' (quoted in Schraeder 1994, p. 7).

38. The research found substantial differences between different administrations as regards the means to be used for achieving the foreign policy goals. These are mostly explained by the constant effort to balance the USA's own strategic interests and the demands for independence, sovereignty and majority rule in Africa. As the former seemed to carry more importance than the latter, a certain double standard could be noted from time to time, reflected in the policy of the Kennedy administration towards the liberation movements in southern Africa. Strong support

in the UN for the decolonisation of Africa did not prevent the USA in practice giving priority to its NATO connection with Portugal (Marte 1994). Continued access for US defence forces to the Azores air and naval bases and in the Atlantic Ocean obviously played an important role in US support to its Nato ally in Lisbon (Minter 1994, p. 144). The frequency of such double standards depended on different interpretations of the Soviet threat and the capacity of Moscow to exploit the racial question for its own benefit. Furthermore, as observed by the former Assistant Secretary of State for African Affairs, Herman Cohen, from time to time 'the public commitment against racism and colonialism and the governmental fear of revolution and majority rule led to a "speak loudly but carry a small stick" policy' (quoted in Ohlson and Stedman 1994, p. 50).

39. The heavy infighting between different US executive agencies described in this study is a logical consequence of such contradictions between short- and long-term interests. Hence, emphasising the importance of long-term coinciding interests does not imply that the importance of short-term interests should be downplayed. In fact, one important factor in the US contribution to conflict settlement in southern Africa was the Iran/Contras incident. Most of the CIA officials within the National Security Council at the White House during the first Reagan administration who had a strong influence on design and implementation of US foreign policy, including for southern Africa, had to be removed on the discovery of the CIA involvement in Nicaragua. This increased the decision-making capacity of the State Department considerably during the second Reagan administration, and the African Bureau under the leadership of Chester Crocker gained strengthened autonomy to implement its policy of 'Constructive Engagement'. This fact, commented upon by *Africa Confidential* (*AC* 1987, 7 January), has been empirically substantiated throughout the research whether during interviews or through analysis of declassified documents. However, it is the argument of this study that existing conspiracy and diverging short-term interests can at most delay, or temporarily divert, the long-term interests from getting the upper hand in policy design and implementation.

# 4  Mozambique and the Washington Consensus

1. The request was made by the Minister of Foreign Affairs, Joaquim Chissano, in connection with the first visit of Chester Crocker to the region, April 1981.
2. The diplomatic clash between the countries in the early 1980s occurred when some US diplomats were expelled from Mozambique accused of being US intelligence agents. As a consequence Congress blocked further food aid to the country. In practice that also meant strong pressure from US officials to reduce multilateral food aid as well, especially from those agencies where the USA had strong leverage.
3. The review of different 'Hearings before a subcommittee of the committee on appropriations', United States Senate, during the second Reagan administration 1985–8, carried out by the author, clearly verifies this assertion.
4. The administration frequently gave practical reasons for using the institutions: 'Some of the newly emerging nations are understandably sensitive about accepting technical conditions for assistance from one of the great powers ... This sensitivity is eliminated or greatly reduced when aid is furnished through an international organisation of which they are members and from which they are willing to accept conditions for aid ... The same advantage of working through international organisations also carries into some kind of pre-investment activities where a single

nation might be suspected of seeking to shape another's development programme for selfish ends. In short, in some of the politically sensitive countries an international agency can lay down stricter conditions for aid than a single country' (Assistant Secretary of State Harlan Cleveland, Hearings, Subcommittee of the Committee on Appropriations, House of Representatives, 16 August 1961). In Payer (1974), a similar statement is attributed to former Assistant Secretary of State Douglas Dillon during hearings with the same subcommittee in March 1959 (Payer 1974, p. 43).

5.  There is quite a comprehensive literature looking into the geopolitics of food and how the USA uses food as a political tool. An analysis of the politics of US food aid policy is provided in Ruttan (1993). The analysis on the use of US-paid food aid as a power tool corresponds to observations made by the author in the field, when preparing relief assistance in Mozambique in 1983–4. These observations were further confirmed in various interviews conducted by the author at the UN in New York and with former officials in the Reagan administration in Washington. The sequencing of the events has been partially documented by Hanlon (1991) and Abrahamsson and Nilsson (1995b).

6.  There is no doubt that the severe drought in combination with increased South African destabilisation were the main factors. However, the underlying factors are much more structural, with roots in the colonial heritage. Forced migration of male labour reduced the capacity for preparing new land as required by the subsistence agricultural system. Subsequent overexploitation of land increased vulnerability. However, in colonial times this vulnerability was counteracted by access to local trade, and the cash transfers from migrant labour made it possible to purchase food as a complement to decreasing production. This rural trade system broke down at the time of independence, and access to food security vanished. The peasantry entered into a kind of economy of affection, where the social network created on a risk-minimising approach reduced the role of the market still further. In order to increase purchasing power and the standard of living of the peasantry, since independence the state has tried to rehabilitate the rural trade network, especially in remote areas where the peasants neither produced nor consumed enough to attract private traders.

7.  Confirmed by involved Mozambican, US and Bretton Woods officials during interviews conducted in Maputo and in the United States in 1994–6 (for example, interviews no. 14, May 1994; no. 69, April 1995; no. 82, April 1995; no. 117, July 1996).

8.  A perfectly clear understanding of this was reflected by all of the involved officials during the conducted interviews (see note 7). The US use of the Bretton Woods institutions as foreign policy tools is also frequently discussed in various US governmental reports. Besides the documents referred to earlier (US Treasury 1982; Gwin 1994) the US General Accounting Office 1996 report underlined the national interest of the USA in continuing support to the Bretton Woods institutions. Simpson's review of the National Security directives of the Reagan and Bush administrations gives several examples of US intention to use the IMF as a principal foreign policy tool in different parts of the world (Simpson 1993): NSDD 101, 2 September 1983 dealing with US strategy towards Liberia, has as an objective to 'actively encourage the World Bank with other foreign donors to increase their constructive involvement in and support for Liberia' (p. 319); NSDD 54, 2 September 1982, dealing with US policy towards eastern Europe 'offered rewards – such as ... membership in the International Monetary Fund – for

countries that cooperated with US initiatives or resisted those of the USSR' (p. 75); and NSDD 163, 20 February 1985 on US policy towards the Philippines talks of up to US$615 million support to the government of Ferdinand Marcos in International Monetary Fund 'standby' assistance to face the indigenous Communist-nationalist New People's Army (NPA) (p. 445). It is of interest to note that all the security directives give greater importance to use of the IMF than to the World Bank, although it is the latter that has more frequently been the object of academic scrutiny (e.g. by Sanford 1983). The obvious reason is that the activities of the IMF are considered more secret and access to information about its activities is consequently more restricted.

9. May the frequent US Treasury claim that the Bretton Woods institutions are their cost-effective tools for implementing US foreign policy be wishful thinking? The statements could be rhetorical, aimed at motivating a reluctant Congress to continue with required budget allocations. Furthermore, it is one thing to have a tool, quite another to be able to use it. Although the USA is the largest shareholder in the institutions, its decision-making capacity depends on various interests and contradictory forces, not the least within the US administration. There are though, some well documented cases when the USA has succeeded in using the institutions as tools for foreign policy implementation. One frequently quoted example is the Philippines, another is Zaire. As regards southern Africa, Mason and Asher 1973, pp. 586–91 refer to World Bank lending in the mid-1960s to Portugal and South Africa.

10. The extensive studies carried out by the Overseas Development Institute under the auspices of Tony Killick suggest that our findings from Mozambique on how the USA succeeded in using the Bretton Woods institutions as tools for its foreign policy-making, are also applicable on a more general level. On the impact of the IMF in specific countries, Killick concludes that 'the standing of the Fund in these countries is threatened by political lobbying of major shareholders in favour of (or against) particular borrowing countries, in promotion of their own foreign policy objectives' (Killick 1995, p. 121). During the interviews conducted in Washington by the author in 1994–6, the means used by the USA for such lobbying was described as a two-leg strategy: firstly, the Treasury and thereby the US Executive on the board of the IMF had to be persuaded of the political benefit, and secondly the concerned country has to be coached on how to present and argue for its application (see, for example, interview no. 78, April 1995). Following post-Cold War difficulties in the 1990s in maintaining its leading role in the institutions, with the increased influence of Germany and Japan, the USA had to extend its own power base within the boards of the institutions. According to NSD 34 from January 1990 regarding partnership with Panama, the Action Plan to Foster Economic Recovery states that: 'The Secretary of the Treasury shall establish a Support Group of friendly donor countries to help clear Panama's arrears to the IFIs. Treasury will ask the IDB to play a special role in the Support Group.'

11. Whereas the IMF focused on the short-term goal of stabilisation and the need to achieve balances in the state budget and current account mainly through restrictive monetary policies and devaluations, the World Bank concentrated on more long-term structural adjustment. However, through cross-conditionalities, achievements of the 'bench-marks' of the IMF are normally prerequisites for structural adjustment loans from the World Bank. In the case of Mozambique, for the political reasons referred to, the World Bank proceeded with its first credit in 1985

without the country as yet having an agreed stabilisation programme with the Fund. Such an agreement with the IMF was only reached in 1987.

12. The political necessity of this proceeding has been confirmed in various interviews with concerned Mozambican as well as US government officials conducted by the author during 1994–6. The initial prognosis provided by the Fund on how to close the country's financial gap (cf. for example, *IMF 1991*, Report EBS/91/136) was based on the low-level scenario of a future export volume of coal in the range of 3,000,000 tons per year, which is almost thirteen times higher than the current capacity of production facilities. The report did not foresee any investments required for upgrading the country's production units or for transporting the coal to the nearest harbour 500 km away. The attention of the fund officials having been drawn to this fact, the forecasts presented one year later did not include any revenues from coal exports in the low-level scenario at all; instead, the outlook was mainly based on the export of prawns and the so-called 'non traditional commodities'. No analysis whatsoever was presented as regards the production capacity or possible markets outlets for these kinds of commodities.

13. As the importance of these external factors is crucial for an understanding of the country's present economic difficulties some elucidatory facts regarding the extreme international dependency are called for. In the case of Mozambique, the economy has never in modern times shown a macro-economic balance. The current account showed a chronic deficit. The deficit was covered by Lisbon, which in turn covered it through the gold transfers from South Africa in payment for cheap Mozambican labour recruited for the South African mines. The modernisation strategy chosen at the time of independence reinforced the pressure on the trade balance. Furthermore, through its propensity to import the vulnerability to price fluctuations on the world market increased. Hence, the international increases in oil prices had an immediate and enormous impact. From having represented 6 per cent of total imports in 1973, oil imports rose to 20 per cent in 1981. In relation to Mozambique's exports the change was even more dramatic. From having corresponded to 13 per cent of export revenues in 1973, oil imports took a total of 60 per cent of export revenue in 1981 (Abrahamsson and Nilsson 1995b, p. 104). The reason for the increased ratio was a consequence of regional political dynamics, which drastically reduced Mozambique's service revenue. The sanctions implemented against Rhodesia had an estimated cost of US$150 million per year. South African economic destabilisation implied a reduction of Mozambican employment in South African mines, from some 120,000 to 40,000 from 1975 to 1981. To that should be added the diversion of South African transit traffic from Mozambique to its own ports, and South Africa's unilateral change of the gold agreement. The reduced service revenue was counteracted as international cheap credits from the Eurodollar market became available in 1977 following the need of the US bankers to recycle the petrodollar. The debt burden increased accordingly and approached some US$1400 million by the end of the 1970s implying a debt service ratio of 32 per cent (World Bank 1987). A combination of events made the situation unsustainable in the years to follow. Firstly, the second oil price increase in 1981 coincided with a sharp decrease in export revenues. Due to extensive drought and the South African targeted destruction of key production units for export and infrastructure to market outlets, severely affecting traditional export of cashew nuts, sugar, cotton and tea, export revenues declined by 20 per cent in 1982 and another 40 per cent in 1983, from $280 million to $130 million (IMF 1987). Consequently oil imports took some 90 per cent of export revenue

in 1982 and exceeded exports by 60 per cent in 1983 (Abrahamsson and Nilsson 1995b). Secondly, the increase in international interest rates affected not only the total debt servicing, which increased from 32 per cent in 1980 to 130 per cent in 1983 (World Bank 1987; IMF 1987) but above all the terms for obtaining new credits. Strong limits on foreign exchange allocations had to be implemented, the severe impact on import-dependent industrial and agricultural production notwithstanding. For obvious reasons the labour force could not be adjusted to an actual operating capacity of, at times, no more than 20–40 per cent of installed capacity, with consequent mounting losses and increased dependence on easy bank credit. Furthermore, declining production undermined the tax base of the government. Reduced revenue with increased expenditure for defense eroded any attempt at a balanced budget.

14. Such commitment contradicts the prevailing wisdom within the World Bank since the early 1980s following the Berg report (World Bank 1981), which identifies the African state as the principal obstruction to the rational and complete introduction of adjustment. The logic behind such thinking is that structural adjustment is normally perceived as a threat to rent-seeking patronage and hence the political survival of the elite.

15. In fact this is an important characteristic of the Frelimo leadership since the struggle for independence. It stems from the watchword of Samora Machel 'do what must be done – if you lose the initiative you are lost' and frequently, though sometimes implicitly, came up during conversations between Mozambican decision-makers and the author.

16. Emphasising the external factors does not mean neglecting the internal political constraints. The research carried out by Anders Nilsson, described in Abrahamsson and Nilsson (1995b), clearly shows social unrest in the countryside caused by Frelimo's modernisation development strategy. In the same way as this social unrest was to have a major political impact in the long run, the external factors referred to came to have a major economic impact in the short run, linking up to and reinforcing long-term political development.

17. In order to reduce pressure on inflation the IMF recently made the state budget deficit *before aid* into an obligatory benchmark. As observed by *The Economist* (28 June–4 July 1997, p. 51) this has led to Mozambique being unable to use the total amount of foreign aid pledged during donor meetings. According to Hanlon, 'By cutting this figure so much, the IMF is forcing donors to halve the money they give to the government for running social services, rebuilding schools and roads and so on' (Hanlon 1996, p. 31). Instead, the IMF suggested increased balance of payments support and simultaneously demanded that part of the support should be allocated to increasing the foreign exchange reserves. Such requirements are related to enabling Mozambique to service future credits from the IMF. Hence 'operational guidelines issued to the staff in 1988 emphasised the aim of limiting current account deficits to levels that could be financed by capital inflows which would not jeopardise the country's debt-servicing position, and the desirability of providing for an accumulation of international reserves to protect against adverse contingencies and to ensure the capacity to repay the Fund' (Killick 1995, p. 21 – confirmed during interviews in Washington conducted 1995–6. See, for example, interview no. 101, November 1995).

18. Estimates point to the destruction of some 50 per cent of the commercial and social infrastructure during the war of destabilisation. Some 75 per cent of all roads were frequently mined and inaccessible for maintenance.

19. This is especially so for rural areas, and has been reinforced by the process of privatising of the banking system. The transactions costs are high, and few commercial banks are motivated to enter areas where risks are also considered high. The problems of credits have been further aggravated due to difficulties in applying the Polak model in a Mozambican context. In essence, the model is based on a relationship between the velocity of money circulation (v), money supply (M) and Gross Domestic Production (GDP). As the model assumes the variable v to be constant, acceptable money supply depends on the size and growth of GDP. Increased productivity and national income permit corresponding increases in money supply. The problem occurs due to the underestimation of GDP. The income produced in the informal sector is not included, although much of the activity is based upon money transactions. Even more difficulties exist with the assumed constant velocity. The weight of this variable is based upon experiences from a post-World War II operational banking structure in Europe. In the rural areas in Mozambique, access to the banking system is difficult and there are a number of non-conventional means for securing money from theft, which in practice take money out of circulation for considerable periods. Accordingly, much common sense points to existing space for increased credit ceilings in the specific Mozambican context. The complications are increased by the fact that the effort towards transactions with a fast turnover at the expense of longer-term investments increases the velocity of money circulation, especially in urban areas. This does contribute to pressure on inflation. The general price index used when calculating national pressure on inflation for decision making on credit ceilings is based on the price trends of some urban consumer goods in Maputo, and though there may indeed be inflationist pressure in urban areas, the findings of the model are applied on a national level.

20. Although domestic trade has increased considerably, the lack of necessary credits and institutional support has not permitted the number of traders to increase and reinforce competition. A number of rural private traders lost their vehicles and cargoes, and are as a consequence still facing a residual debt which prevents them from participating in the marketing of agricultural surpluses. Accordingly, in rural areas a concentration of trade in the hands of some important wholesalers is giving rise to a kind of 'Godfather system', in which they benefit from the situation at the expense of the peasantry, who face deteriorating terms of trade.

21. As a consequence of the Fund's exclusive emphasis on the domestic failures, the programme was based on an overly optimistic prediction that exports would rise rapidly, following the necessary devaluations and liberalisations. The programme thus risks entering a number of possible intertwined vicious circles, interacting inward and outward where: devaluation $\rightarrow$ inflation $\rightarrow$ restrictive monetary policies $\rightarrow$ reduced supply response $\rightarrow$ increased import $\rightarrow$ increased prices $\rightarrow$ inflation $\rightarrow$ reduced money supply $\rightarrow$ reduced supply response $\rightarrow$ increased imports etc., and where increased imports (low degree of substitution) $\rightarrow$ widened trade deficit $\rightarrow$ depreciation $\rightarrow$ increased price for imports $\rightarrow$ small changes in expenditures from tradables to non-tradables $\rightarrow$ continued inflation $\rightarrow$ reinforced restrictive policies $\rightarrow$ reduced supply responses $\rightarrow$ small increases in output of tradables (low supply elasticities) $\rightarrow$ continued deficit in current account $\rightarrow$ etc.

22. This is a well-known phenomenon for the neo-classical growth models and has constituted a basic rationale for the theory of the big push in economic development (Branson 1972). In order to avoid such traps, the textbooks advocate that 'If savings rates could just be increased sufficiently, if the production function could be shifted up, or if a "windfall" of capital could be obtained, so that

k (capital–labour ratio) is increased above k* (the value of capital–labour ratio in equilibrium), the low-level trap could be bypassed and the economy would enter a phase of self-sustaining growth (Branson 1972, p. 397). However, underlining this possibility of low-level equilibrium does not mean failing to give due considerations to the importance of institutional capacity or social capital, which sometimes constrain economic growth more than lack of access to financial capital.

23. The 'petty corruption' considered as a necessity for survival has been spreading throughout the country fast over the last few years. Teachers increase their wages by forcing parents to pay coaching for their children, regardless of whether or not they need it, and nurses in X-ray departments demand extra payments to carry out their work. This 'petty corruption' has grown up alongside an increasingly large-scale corruption that has also been the subject of much debate. State officials whose employment is threatened, or political leaders with ambitions to launch commercial activities, organise different ways of enriching themselves to be able to invest and establish their private activities.

24. Chayanov shows how the 'subsistence law' complicated the introduction of an exchange economy when the main goal of production continued to be household consumption and not savings. The work done by each family member and the amount of total production were decided in the light of the number of people that had to be fed. This in turn varied over time according to the size of the household. The family cycle sometimes means that families have more land than they can cultivate. In some cases it is the daughters-in-law/children who help to cultivate. In other cases the land is lent to third parties. Such a loan is rarely remunerated, but almost always recompensed by gifts. Research carried out in southern Africa shows that should less work be required to sustain the family (for example, due to cheaper consumer goods, a change in family members or the entry into the family of daughters-in-law/children) this does not mean that production for sale necessarily increases. When the risks are reduced to the minimum and medium term food security is consolidated, then existing possibilities for increasing productivity may be maximised (Low 1986). On the other hand, Chayanov's law does not tell us anything about peasant behaviour with regard to savings when the risks are at the mimimum and food security is achieved. Research done in Mozambique shows that the portion of the income from migrant labour that can be saved, after the family has received the necessary support in both food and the consumer goods that are connoted with migrant work in South Africa (social status), is invested to improve production or housing or to buy cattle (Manghezi 1983).The need for a social protection network can be seen when the market economy makes its appearance and offers work opportunities, even though temporary ones. Such opportunities may be taken up, but the family land is never abandoned. However, relations between the sexes will be affected. It is the man who sells his labour power while the woman continues to be responsible for feeding the family. Thus there is a division of labour within the family, instead of among various families.

25. Monopolisation in the restricted sense means a situation in which there is one seller on the supply side with a large number of small buyers. In the broad sense it refers to a regime of making, buying or selling products or providing services to the public characterised by lack or the extreme limitation of competition. Oligopolisation is understood to mean domination of the market or a large part of the market by a small number of companies in which each one has major economic power that it exercises independently, with a large number of small buyers.

26. The lack of understanding of the rural realities, in combination with a certain
ethnocentricity meant that the World Bank approach of 'getting the prices right'
faced severe difficulties in coping with the low responsiveness of the peasantry,
not to mention frequent negative price elasticities. Low responsiveness can be due
to lack of land or labour in order to increase production. Furthermore, peasant
responses to increased producer prices may imply decreased production. This can
be the case when money transactions are used mainly in order to get access to some
specific services or goods, and if the subsistence needs of the peasantry are met. In
other words the peasants are concerned to minimise the labour in meeting their
different consumption needs, so that they maximise the utility of consumption.
Research carried out by Allan Low in southern Africa points to the male propensity to leave for urban areas as soon as increased productivity guarantees that the
household's supply needs will continue to be met (Low 1986).

Furthermore, the World Bank model assumes private savings to be a fixed
proportion of private disposable income, but in the rural areas of Mozambique
increased income does not necessarily imply increased saving. Investments can
equally be made in social relations, implying increased collective consumption,
and in any case increased savings do not necessarily mean monetarisation. Savings are frequently kept in cattle. The reason for this conceptual gap is to be found
in the basic assumption of predominant Westernised development thinking that
peasants all over the world are rational in the sense of being profit maximisers.
I'm aware that this neoclassical notion on rationality has been challenged by various scholars. Herbert Simon launched the concept 'bounded rationality' for those
cases in which individuals are restrained due to lack of information or intellec-
tually uncapable of processing it all (Herbert A. Simon 1982, *Models of Bounded
Rationality*, 2 vols, Cambridge: MIT Press, quoted in Keohane 1984). Although the
concept of bounded rationality sets a limit on the actual maximisation process,
it recognises the attempt of the individual to be rational. However, the rationality of the individual depends on his socio-political context, how he conceives his
situation and choices, as well as his need to pay respect to social and collective
obligations, something influenced by the framework of existing belief system, values and political configurations in force. In a Mozambican rural context, however,
the rationality of a peasant is different, and in fact the rationality of the peasantry
varies depending on circumstances and contexts. In Mozambique, the reciprocity
that characterised the economy of affection in Tanzania (Hydén 1980) seems to
be based upon a lower degree of equality and mutuality. The fieldwork carried
out points to the Mozambican peasantry, due to the colonial heritage and prevailing pattern of migrant labour, being more interdependent within a framework
of social inequality (Abrahamsson and Nilsson 1995b). The exercise of power is
based on different socially legitimate forms of behaviour born out of custom, kin-
ship and relations of production. As in all hierarchical societies, the exercise of
power means that all unequal relations are legitimated. Authority is preserved and
spread through forms of social communication and magic (rituals, ceremonies,
myths, etc.). The groups with a lower position learn to accept their social subordination, which becomes permanent over the generations. They are dependent
on the dominant clan in order to obtain a minimum of social security. This need
has obviously been reinforced by the war and subsequent social turmoil (Åkesson,
1996). For Hydén, the problem was the 'uncaptured' peasantry with the ability to
withdraw from the market and the state (Hydén 1980). Such capability is rare in
most parts of Mozambique. During the colonial period the peasantry became more

dependent on cash incomes, albeit minimal ones, for improving family consumption or its social status within the economy of affection. Hence the peasantry in Mozambique is moving in a grey area which makes the dichotomy between risk minimising or maximising the benefits less appropriate. Despite quite individualistic behaviour when permitted, individualism has seldom threatened the survival of the community for the simple reason that the community constituted the only source of protection and social safety. Nonetheless, as a consequence of the troubled transitions described, the community is becoming less and less able to provide such protection.

## 5   Theoretical Guidance

1.  As Björn Hettne points out, 'We are now "post"-something, whether "post-Keynesian", "post-Fordist, "post-modern", "post-hegemonic", "post-Westphalian" … and we need a "neo"-something, whether "neo-realism", "neo-liberal institutionalism", "neo-Marxism", "neo-mercantilism", neo-structuralism" or "neo-idealism", in order to understand what is going on and where we are heading' (Hettne 1995, p. 12).
2.  The debate is accounted for by Fred Halliday (1994) and Mark Neufeld (1995).
3.  During his studies of the economic realities of the Mediterranean 1400–1700, Braudel found it relevant to divide economic activities into three different spheres or different kinds of economies. Besides the market he identified a more worldwide developed capitalism at a level above it and a more rudimentary material life (or material civilisation) at a level below it (Braudel 1979, Vol. I, pp. 13ff, Swedish edition). The multilevel analysis provided by Braudel permitted an understanding of the local forces of change constituted by the dynamics between the three levels of the economic system he identified and based on what he called 'the limits of the possible of the material life' (or 'material civilisation' as Braudel called the 'traditional' society analysed). In this connection, it is important to remember that the term 'traditional society' does not mean a static society. Any society changes over time. By 'traditional' society is understood a society that is predominantly characterised by subsistence, where reciprocity and redistribution constitute the social order of production and distribution and where the law of the market and economics has not as yet become dominant (Polanyi 1957, p. 59).
4.  Inspiration for this endeavour can also be found in the Frankfurt School of thought and especially in the works of Jürgen Habermas, which over time implied rigorous rethinking within the discipline. Habermas distinguishes between three kinds of knowledge – positivist, hermeneutic and critical, of which only the last, according to him, constituted any contribution at all to the emancipatory project of humanity (Wiggershaus 1994). Of importance in this context is that the distinction provoked the emergence of a critical theory aiming at contributing to change, albeit primarily on the national level. The task for the discipline of International Relations became to 'extend the trajectory of the Frankfurt School critical theory beyond the domestic realm to the international, or more accurately, global realm' (Devetak 1996). Such a broad definition of the critical approach may be troublesome for researchers identifying themselves with a specific critical theory school. In the following text I will, nevertheless, basically refer to the Coxian conceptualisation of critical theory and place the notion on equal footing with how I conceive critical IPE.

5.  Cox points out that Gramsci enlarged the definition of the state in his search for consensual hegemony on the national level: 'When the administrative, executive and coercive apparatus of government was in effect constrained by the hegemony of the leading class of a whole social formation, it became meaningless to limit the definition of the state to those elements of government. To be meaningful, the notion of the state would also have to include the underpinnings of the political structure in civil society. Gramsci thought of this in concrete historical terms – the church, the educational system, the press, all the institutions which helped to create in people certain modes of behaviour and expectations consistent with the hegemonic social order' (Cox and Sinclair 1996, p. 124). Hence, for Gramsci, the general notion of 'state' 'includes elements which need to be referred back to the notion of civil society in the sense that one might say that State = political society + civil society, in other words hegemony protected by the armour of coercion' (Gramsci 1971, p. 263).

6.  This interpretation differs from conventional traditions within international relations theory. According to the realistic (or even neo-realistic) approach, with its focus primarily on the state as an actor, any rational actor has to comply with the anarchical structures prevailing, i.e. the structure of the system limits the possible. The neo-Marxist approach is even more deterministic, especially on the highest and horizontal level of the system. On this level, change of the structures is only possible through exogenous shocks. The liberal tradition on the other hand is more actor-oriented. The actors create and change structures without inherent constraints. For change to occur on the international level a multilateral effort is required. Accordingly, the concept of interdependence is an important driving force for structural adaptation.

7.  In his historical studies, Braudel divides time into different cycles where he distinguish between the more frequently observed short-term, relatively fast-moving events affecting every day life (*histoire événementielle*), somewhat more long-term conjunctural cycles (*temps conjunturelle*) and the much slower moving time of change, the so-called secular trends (*longue durée*) (Braudel 1979, Vol. 3, p. 60ff, Swedish edition). The rise and maturity of the capitalist system as such constitutes a slow-moving wave of longue durée. The Bretton Woods system, as well as the rise and fall of the Soviet empire, constitutes examples of long-term but conjunctural structures. Hence, the more slow-moving wave of secular trends (*longue durée*) is constituted by the sum of the very number of the long-term conjunctural cycles that the wave of secular trends carry, so to say, on its back. With structural change (or transformation) we refer to change or transformation of this kind of conjunctural cycle.

# 6   An Analytical Model for Action

1.  The term the French Regulation School refers to the research carried out in Grenoble by the Groupe de Recherche sur la Régulation de l'Economie Capitaliste (GRREC) under the leadership of Professor Destanne de Bernis.

2.  In one of the publications of the Trilateral Commission 'We have argued that industrial policies are needed to deal with structural problems in the modern economies. Thus, international action should not aim to dismantle these policies. The pressure should, rather, be toward positive and adaptive industrial policies, whether on the

part of single countries or groups of countries combined' (Pinder, Hosomi and Diebold 1979, p. 50).

3. This balance of power soon shifted to the advantage of the transnational corporations. The 'code of conduct' was gradually transformed into another 'code of conduct', which restrained the influence of host governments. This change was considered necessary in order to increase the flow of private investments to the Third World. An international multilateral fund was raised, the Multilateral Investment Guarantee Agency (MIGA) under the auspices of the World Bank based on the following argument: 'recognising that the flow of foreign investment to developing countries would be facilitated and further encouraged by alleviating concerns related to non-commercial risks; ... and under conditions consistent with their development needs, policies and objectives, on the basis of fair and stable standards of the treatment of foreign investments' (World Bank 1985, p. 1). By non-commercial risks and fair and stable standards for the treatment of foreign investments, reference was made to restrictions on currency transfer, expropriation and similar measures (World Bank 1985, Article 11, p. 5).

4. Despite attempts to save the system, e.g. the Smithsonian agreement, it finally broke down in 1973.

5. The Trilateral Commission, somewhat more reluctant about a more inwardly-oriented strategy, agreed on the condition that such self-reliance should not be allowed to 'degenerate into a rejection of an integrated world economy' (Triangle, paper 14, p. 17). During a follow-up interview in New York twenty years later, the Trilateral Commission maintained this understanding: 'a development strategy does not have an end in itself. If, in the case of Mozambique, it does not provide the required result, then the orientation of the strategy must change' (interview no. 149, New York, 5 September 1996).

## 7   A Globality with Contradictory Circumstances

1. The increased relevance of the contradictory circumstances is also reflected in various recent studies. The work carried out by the World Bank during the 1990s (World Bank 1996b; 1997) deals with the role of the state and market, the independent international commissions formed by an international political elite deals with the question of global governance (Brundtland 1987; Carlsson and Ramphal 1995) and the work carried out by UNDP during the 1990s deals with the increased gaps of inequalities (UNDP 1997). The agendas of the summit meetings of the decade have emanated out of this fear, last noted in the Denver Summit meeting June 1997 (see *News from the USIA*, Washington File, 22 June 1997).

2. This compromise has led most theorists within the field of International Political Economy to search for the dynamics of the interaction of state and market in a larger historical setting. As shown by Polanyi, any shift in the balance between state and market has a fundamental impact on the state–society complex, by redefining the legitimate social purposes in pursuit of which state power is exercised in the domestic economy.

3. Private foreign capital-flows to developing countries increased rapidly during the 1990s, reaching some US$250 billion in 1996. This partly compensated for decreased official flows. More than 80 per cent of the flow continued, however, to be channelled to the top 12 recipients in East Asia and Latin America. Sub-Saharan Africa received only 1 per cent when South Africa (which received 4 per cent) is excluded. At the same time, the debt burden became acute. Debt servicing from

developing countries amounted to $1.6 trillion for the years between 1980 and 1992, a figure three times the original amount owed in 1980. Developing countries still owe $2.2 trillion and payment of debt service takes most of the foreign exchange from exports, grants, and loans.

4.    The rise in real interest rates from an average 1.3 per cent in 1973–80 to 5.9 per cent in 1980–86 was the direct result of the economic policies followed by the new conservative governments installed in the major industrial countries after 1979 (Toye 1994, p. 20). In this regard, Tarp provides some tentative calculations showing the estimated losses from the relatively high rate of interest and the falling terms of trade faced by sub-Saharan Africa during the period 1980–87 and concludes that: 'had the terms of trade not changed and had the level of interest remained at previous levels Sub-Saharan Africa would *ceteris paribus* have had a considerable current account surplus from 1984 onwards' (Tarp 1993, p. 23).

## 8    Towards a Structural Opportunity for Change

1.    The neoclassical factor endowment theory stating that free flows of trade finance and information will produce the best outcome for growth and human welfare continues to constitute the conventional wisdom, though strong and legitimate criticisms are articulated in many of the textbooks, some of them arguing that 'the conclusion of traditional trade theory that free trade will tend to equalise income is no more than a theoretical construct' and that trade tends to 'reinforce inequalities between rich and poor nations and within nations between foreign residents, wealthy nationals and the majority of the population' (e.g. Todaro 1997, pp. 436–48). The same kind of argument is forcefully presented by UNDP (1997, p. 82).

2.    Michael Clough analysing the subordination of Africa to the US policy of containment entitled his book *Free at Last* (Clough 1992).

3.    *A Comprehensive Trade and Development Policy for the Countries of Africa*, report submitted by the President of the United States to the Congress on 5 February 1996, p. 6.

4.    It is important to understand the reasons behind present efforts by the US administration to use the Bretton Woods institutions as commercial tools. During the Cold War, US companies participated in globalisation with certain privileges vis-à-vis US Cold War allies. Needing to be united in the face of a Soviet threat, internal commercial rivalry in the West was downplayed by the incentive for deferring to US leadership. This is no longer the case. Consequently, the present intensification of commercial rivalry on the world market also appears to revitalise the need for an intervening and supporting state. The same actors that worked for reduced state intervention are now in need of stronger, not weaker home governments, in order to face the increased international competition. Ironically, though, the capacity of the state to provide such support has simultaneously decreased. The states try to compensate for their individual weaknesses through increased utilisation of multinational institutions acting on their behalf. This is why the role that can be played by the multilateral institutions as commercial tools for the US administration is frequently used by the US administration as an argument when trying to motivate the US Congress to continue participation in the institutions. Strengthened state capacity in the host countries is needed as well. It is not only a question of providing security but primarily of creating a sufficient and appropriate 'business climate'

to attract financial flows for investments. Hence the reduced capacity of the state increases the need of the multilateral institutions both for increased leverage in negotiations between home governments and host governments and for financial legitimation of the host country (confirmation of credit-worthiness in order to obtain an acceptable credit rating). Accordingly, the process of globalisation is reinforcing the role of the Bretton Woods institutions, not as originally intended to maintain an open economy and to reduce the role of state intervention but on the contrary to increase the impact of state intervention.

5. The antecedents to this affirmation by the US government are as follows: in September 1995, the IMF review mission visiting Maputo indicated that the structural adjustment programme might be declared off-track. Some twenty points of discrepancy between achievements and targets were handed over to the presidency. The main problem for the International Monetary Fund, however, did not lie in this study's area of concern. Despite improvements, the main problem was said to be that inflation exceeded its targets because the state banking sector did not respect credit ceilings. Inadequate measures had furthermore been taken in order to speed up the privatisation, not only of the banking sector but also of state-owned communication companies (telecommunications and airline), the custom authorities and possible the main ports in Maputo and Beira (IMF 1996a). The attitude of the IMF mission caused great concern within the donor community in Maputo. Declaring a programme off-track would in practice not only postpone rescheduling of the debt by the Paris Club, but would make it impossible for aid donors to provide continued balance of payments support, thus aggravating the situation of the country even further. Following an initiative taken by the US embassy in Maputo, several donor representatives therefore decided to act promptly and wrote a common statement to the General Director of the IMF explaining their concern, dated 6 October 1995. The 'donor statement' was unprecedented in the IMF's history as shareholders' points of view on IMF missions normally reach the directorate and the board from their respective Ministries of Finance or Central Banks. The statement therefore provoked strong reactions from various board members claiming irregularities, although its content was considered 'harmless'. In December the same year, a new IMF mission visited Mozambique. Based on the same figures the mission found enough reasons not to declare the programme off-track, serious concern regarding the performance notwithstanding. Consequently a new three-year ESAF arrangement was agreed in June 1996, enabling the Paris Club to consider a request by the government of Mozambique for a debt rescheduling agreement in November 1966. Various conversations held with the donor community in Maputo, November 1995 (especially interviews nos 105 and 106, October 1995) in Washington (no. 107, October 1995) and in New York, as well as follow-up interviews in Washington (no. 122, July 1996, nos 131, 132 and 134, August 1996, New York, no. 148, August 1996) and Maputo (nos 153 and 154, October 1996) in order to find the reason for the changed attitude of the IMF mission and the background to the initiative taken by the US embassy found evidence of an intricate utilisation by the USA of the IMF as a commercial tool. Wanting to increase pressure on the Mozambican government to reach an important commercial agreement with a US multinational (Enron), in summer 1995 the Clinton administration threatened to withdraw bilateral and multilateral aid from Mozambique (AC No. 24, December 1995). The threat was made explicit by National Security Adviser Anthony Lake in a letter to President Chissano, read by the author. It is said to have been frequently repeated by the US

ambassador in Maputo, Mr Denis Jett, and his DCO, Mr Michael McKinley. When the agreement was reached and the gas contract was signed on 13 November 1995, the IMF immediately sent a new mission referring to the 'donor statement' as a justification for its concern (December 1995). And as described above, based on the same figures as the previous IMF mission, the second IMF mission did not find reasons for declaring the programme off-track. Though contested by IMF officials, these events have been confirmed in various interviews, cited above, with high officials, from both the USA and the Mozambican governments.

6.  As becomes clear when going through declassified documents and various files in Washington, the fast spread of Islamic fundamentalism on the African continent is currently perceived as the main factor challenging Western values and ideas in the wake of the Cold War. The establishment's attempt to draw attention to the consequences of decreased US international commitment in fact resembles the Cold War debate. In an article, published in the periodical *Foreign Affairs*, Samuel Huntington (1996b) initiated a discussion on possible future clashes between civilisations. He wanted, in the post-Cold War era, to reintroduce the *real* East–West dimension as a way of finding new national security interests justifying a continuation of US international commitment. This new threat in Africa perceived by the Western countries, created by the fact that continued racial inequality could be exploited by the Islamic factor, logically brings one's mind back to the reasons behind the abolishing of apartheid in South Africa. At that time, the danger to the Western economic elite was not only economic in the sense that apartheid blocked the possibility for the market economy to expand. The problem became political with the danger of apartheid radicalising the black movement and taking it out of the control of the Western countries.

7.  During the interviews with representatives of the World Bank leadership in Washington DC in 1995–6, the importance of such 'soft mastery' was frequently emphasised in order to increase efficiency of implementation.

8.  The recent experience from Mozambique is illustrative in this regard. After several years of structural adjustment, in 1993 Mozambique was declared by the UN to be the most indebted and poorest country in the world. In 1995, the country was declared by the UN to be one of the principal transit areas for international drug trafficking. Later on the same year the IMF informed the donor community that it was considering declaring the country 'off track'. Then, suddenly, Mozambique was considered by the Bretton Woods institutions to be a success story. Not only because peace was kept but first and foremost for its macro-economic achievements. The official statements provided by the main shareholder began to give a different picture as regards development in Mozambique to that provided by this study: 'We had an opportunity to visit Mozambique where standards of living are increasing at a rate where, if it was sustained, you would see living standards almost double within a decade. And you saw that in new schools, in villages that had access to better water than they had had before' (Press briefing by Deputy Secretary of the Treasury, Larry Summers, 17 June 1997, The White House, Office of the Press Secretary, Washington DC). In the UN Human Development Report 2002, however, Mozambique is still described as one of eight countries in the world with a human poverty index showing 50 per cent of its population living under the poverty line.

9.  Strong resistance from the board of the World Bank notwithstanding, the NGO network behind the campaign was subsequently invited by the World Bank leadership in early 1996 to participate actively in future reviews of the impact of the structural

adjustment programmes and to assist the World Bank with the implementation of agreed measures. An extended network for this undertaking was created under the heading 'Citizen's structural adjustment participatory review network' (SAPRIN). The network presented its findings at the beginning of 2002 and pointed to several shortcomings in project design. The heavy criticism provided made the World Bank scale down the cooperation and the dialogue was abandoned.

10. The infighting between different positions is also notable within the US Treasury. Contrary to the more security interest-inspired approach articulated in the earlier quote from Secretary of Treasury Rubin, his deputy Lawrence Summers looks upon the US–Africa relationship more as a question of how to create an opportunity for US business to assist in tapping African resources. Delivering a speech to a symposium dedicated to private sector development in Abidjan, Côte d'Ivoire, on 27 May 1997 Mr Summers emphasised the importance of the fact that

> Old leaders and old ideas are giving way to new leaders with the new idea that the nations of Africa can best tap the energies of their people by relying on markets, integrating with the global economy, and running hard in the global race to attract capital' and regretted that 'African economic performance over the last 25 or 30 years has been profoundly disappointing... today, on the brink of a new millennium, in large parts of Sub-Saharan Africa a child is more likely to be malnourished than to learn to read, and more likely to die before the age of 5 than to go to secondary school. ... Growth performance has been so poor that standards of living in sub-Saharan Africa as measured by consumption per capita have declined by almost one-fourth since 1960. ... While there are differences between different analyses, a striking degree of consensus has emerged. It points to three primary factors in explaining Africa's disappointing performance: First, basic political stability is a prerequisite for growth. ... Second, the lack of macro-economic stability is inimical to growth. Third, policies that grossly distort the allocation of resources make growth impossible ... when conditions are right African countries can grow rapidly. The difficulty of tropical agriculture, closed world markets, and high debt burdens are not adequate excuses for slow growth. ... Whatever the problems of growth in Africa, they cannot be traced to lack of official external support. ... Where Africa has fallen down is in the worldwide race to attract private capital. In 1996, Sub-Saharan Africa received US$15 billion in official development assistance but only US$12 billion in private capital flows.

11. An important difference is that the process of 'delinking' (irrespective of its realism) was conceived as voluntary, whereas the present process of marginalisation is externally imposed.


# 9  Out of the Trap

1. By referring to 'Speenhamland' and the 'old' society's last attempt to defend itself, Polanyi described how the rules over time caused a 'popular demoralisation' (Polanyi 1957).
2. Hans Singer's summary of the various kinds of problems that structural adjustment programmes generally seem to confront points to the fact that it is not only Mozambique that suffers from incorrect diagnoses of the roots of the problems – and therefore from the wrong remedies. Mozambique's well-known problems of

neglected external factors, underfinancing, poor timing and sequencing, and over-emphasised importance of the financial sphere at the expense of the 'real economy' seem to be present in most countries undergoing structural adjustment (Singer 1995).

3. The Soviet debate in the 1920s is illuminating in this regard. As suggested by Preobrazjenskij (1972), the burden of surplus creation was placed upon the shoulders of the peasantry through a biased price system that favoured the industrial sector.

4. The local development concept also provides a space for multi-sectoral measures. Local development requires not only rural extension services but also, perhaps even more crucially, a physical, commercial and social infrastructure that can motivate the peasants to establish exchange relations. While these actions need to be implemented through existing institutions, the different ministries often lack the technical and administrative capacity to do so efficiently. This increases the importance of coordination and local participation, especially at the current time when the legitimacy of the state and social trust are being progressively whittled away. Measures to reactivate socio-economic development must be combined with democratic forms of political decision-taking which will guarantee human rights and permit increased local influence over political decisions on the use of common resources. Feelings of suspicion and fear must be overcome in order for economic relations to emerge and grow.

5. Similar understanding of the content of the development process can be found in the UN declaration on the right to development earlier referred to (Res.41/128, 4 December 1986 quoted in Hettne 1995a, p. 161), and is frequently reaffirmed (cf. *Rethinking Bretton Woods: Conference Report and Recommendations*, Washington, DC: Center of Concern, 1994).

6. Neither do I share the position commonly heard in the 1990s which argues that Africa should refrain from modernisation because of the ecological constraints and the North's continued consumerist expansion. However, the possibilities of transferring Western development theory and its concomitant accelerated modernisation to the African context must be questioned for other reasons. Cultural habits, economic and political disturbances brought about by colonialism and the current globalisation process all hamper both the consolidation in Africa of the nation-state on the European model and implementation of the adjustment programmes.

## 10　The Role of International Development Cooperation

1. Following the some logic as Galtung's notions of positive and negative peace (1969), John Burton pointed to the need in combining efforts to *prevent* conflict with efforts to *promote* development and invented in this regard the concept '*provention*' (Burton 1990).

## 11　Conclusion

1. This fact was discussed during the conference held in Madrid, 29–30 September 1994, on the future of the IMF and the World Bank. See Boughton, James and Sarwar, Lateef (1995), *Fifty Years after Bretton Woods* (Washington, DC: IMF/World Bank Group): statement by Layeshi Yaker on p. 165.

2. See Stephen Gill (1992) *Historical Materialism, Gramsci and IPE* and Robert, Gilpin (1987), *The Political Economy of International Relations* (Princeton University Press).
3. See, for example, Paul Kennedy (1987), *The Rise and Fall of the Great Powers*, and H.R. Nau (1990), *The Myth of America's Decline: Leading the World Economy into the 1990s.*
4. Such arguments were frequently presented during the 1980s. The need for an international regime capable of dealing with future economic and financial challenges becomes even more acute when we add global ecological stress to the problem.
5. An important contribution to our understanding of the logics of the embedded liberalism applied to the Third World, is provided in Thomas Callaghy (1989), 'Toward State Capability and Embedded Liberalism in the Third World: Lessons for Adjustment', in Joan Nelson (ed.) (1989), *Fragile Coalitions: The Politics of Economic Adjustment* (Washington, DC: Overseas Development Council). However, in this essay the author does not fully take into account the structural limits to achieve embedded liberalism on the national level in a globalised world.

# Main Sources and References

## Interviews

During the period of 1994–9, around 100 leading decision-makers as regards Sub-Saharan Africa, representing the Reagan, Bush and Clinton administrations, the Bretton Woods institutions as well as the US private non-governmental sector, were interviewed by the author. The most involved (marked by an *) were interviewed two to three times. The average length of interview was one to two hours. During 1996–2001, some 75 follow-up interviews were carried out with relevant decision-makers and senior scholars in the UK, South Africa, Mozambique and Angola. Notes from the interviews are in the possession of the author.

## US goverment officials

Susan E. Rice – Special Assistant to the President and Senior Director for African Affairs, NSC, The White House
Donald Steinberg – Senior Director for Africa, NSC, The White House
Shawn H. McCormick – Director for Africa, NSC, The White House*
Donald McHenry – Ambassador, Georgetown University
David F. Gordon – Professional staff member, US House of Representatives, Committee on Foreign Affairs*
Ernest Wilson, Dr – US Information Agency*
Christopher R. Riche – Country Desk Officer, US Department of State
Barry M. Schutz – Foreign Affairs specialist, Office of the Secretary of Defence*
Jean-Michel A. Beraud – Assistant Secretary of Defence, Pentagon
William J. Foltz – National Intelligence Officer, National Intelligence Council*
Charles R. Snyder – Director Bureau of African Affairs, Department of State
Vincent D. Kern II – Deputy Assistant Secretary, African Affairs, The Pentagon*
Theresa M. Whelan – Policy Analyst, African Affairs, The Pentagon*
Beryl B. Anderson, Bureau of International Narcotics Matters, Department of State*
Julius Schlotthauer – Advisor, US AID, US Department of State*
Stephen Donovan – Office of International Debt Policy, Treasury Department*
Edwin L. Barber III – Director, Office of African Nations, Department of Treasury*
Karen Lissakers – US Executive Director, IMF
Townsend Friedman – Former US Ambassador to Mozambique, Department of State
Michael Mc Kinley – Deputy Chief of Mission in Mozambique, Department of State*

## United States Senate and House of Representatives

Paul Simon, Senator
Lisa Alfred – Professional staff member, US Senate
Anne-Marea Griffin – Professional staff member, US House of Representatives

## Lobbyists

Anthony J. Carroll
Bruce P. Cameron
Jim Cason
George Dalley

## Think tank officers

Cathrine Gwin – Vice President, Overseas Development Council*
Wolfgang Reinicke – Research Associate, Brookings Institution
Nicole Ball – Research Fellow, Overseas Development Council*
Nicolas van der Walle – Research Fellow, Overseas Development Council*
Kathi Austin – Research Fellow, Institute for Policy Studies*
Carol Lancaster – Research Fellow, Institute for International Economics*
Francis M. Deng – Senior Fellow, Brookings Institution
Jakkie Potgieter, Institute for Security Studies, Johannesburg
Richard Cornwall, Institute for Security Studies, Johannesburg

## Bretton Woods institutions

Sergio Pereira Leite – Division Chief, Southern Africa Division, IMF*
Zuzana Murgasova – Economist, African Department, IMF*
Anupam Basu – Deputy Director, African Department, IMF
João do Carmo Oliveira – Senior Economist, IMF
Stephen Denning – Director, Africa Regional Office, The World Bank*
Dunstan M. Wai – Senior Adviser to the Vice-President, The World Bank
Mamadou Dia – Division Chief, Capacity Building, The World Bank
Patrick Low – Senior Economist, The World Bank
Phyllis Pomerantz – Country Manager for Mozambique, The World Bank*
Nils O. Tcheyan, Division Chief, The World Bank*
Kees Kastermas – The World Bank
René Bonnel – Senior Economist, The World Bank
Rocio Castro – Economist, The World Bank
Eliezer Orbach – Education and Training specialist, The World Bank
Roberto Chaves – The World Bank's representative, Maputo

## UN officials

José M. da Silva Campino – UN, New York Political Affairs Officer
Kamran Niaz – Minister, Permanent Mission of Pakistan to the United Nations
Ngoni Francis Sengwe – Minister, Permanent Mission of the Republic of Zimbabwe to
   United Nations
Dirk Salomons – Principal Officer, UNDP, New York
Aranda da Silva, Director, UN*, New York
Magid Osman – Director, UNDP* Maputo
Nora Niland – Director, UN, Maputo
Gil Fernandes, Political adviser, UN Luanda
Agnes Asekenye-Oonyu – UN, New York
Nicholas Howen – MONUA, Luanda

Francesco Strippoli – UN, New York
Carlos Veloso – UN, Luanda

## International diplomats

Hipólito Patrício – Ambassador, Republic of Mozambique*
Pedro Commissário – Ambassador at the UN, Republic of Mozambique*
Paulo Vireu Pinheiro – First Secretary, Embassy of Portugal*
Anli E von Maltitz – Political counsellor, Embassy of South Africa
Boniface G. Chidyausiku – Ambassador, Republic of Zimbabwe, Luanda
Tamar Golan – Ambassador of Israel, Luanda
Bjørg Leite – Ambassador of Norway, Luanda
Lena Sundh – Ambassador of Sweden, Luanda
Alex Laskaris – Political officer, US Embassy, Luanda
John Sunde – Ministry of Foreign Affairs, Pretoria
Josefina Pitra – Ambassador of Angola, Stockholm

## Non-government organisations

Peter J. Johnson – Rockefeller Plaza
John D. Sullivan – Executive Director, Center for International Private Enterprise
Antonio Pedro Rafael – Investimentos, Comercio e Turismo de Portugal
Michael P. Peters – Senior Vice President, Council on Foreign Relations*
Lilita Gusts – Director of Library Services, Council on Foreign Relations
Charles B. Heck – North American Director, Trilateral Commission*
Herman Cohen – Executive Director, Global Coalition for Africa*
Aileen Marshall – Assistant Director, Global Coalition for Africa*
Salih Booker – Senior Advisor to the Vice-President for Diversity in International Affairs, Council on Foreign Relations
Peggy Dulany – President, The Synergos Institute*
S. Bruce Schearer – Executive Director, The Synergos Institute
Jennifer Davis – Executive Director, American Committee on Africa*
William Minter – Associate Director, Washington Office on Africa*
Kevin G. Lowther – Project Director, Africare
Douglas Hellinger – Executive Director, Development gap*
Harry Magdoff – *Monthly Review Press*, New York*
Fernando Pacheco – adra, Luanda
Benjamin A. Castello – Acção das Igrejas en Angola, Luanda
Mary Daly – Development Workshop, Luanda
Alain Cain – Development Workshop, Luanda
Kato Lambrecht – Foundation for Global Dialogue, Johannesburg
Anthoni van Nieuwkerk – Foundation for Global Dialogue, Johannesburg
Marcus Reichardt – AngloAmerican Corporation, Johannesburg
Benjamin A. Castello – Church Action Angola
Idalinda Rodrigues – OMA
Ilda Carreira – OMA
Vicente Pinto de Andrade – Consultant
Mário Adauto – Consultant
Carlos Maria Feijó – Advocate
Jose Severino – Industrial Association of Angola

Maria do Carmo Nascimento – Entrepreneur
Lucas Benghy Ngonda – FNLA
Abel Chivukuvuku – UNITA
Valter Viegas – Oikos, Luanda
Elídigo da Silva – Oikos, Malanje
Fátima Fernando – Oikos, Malanje
Senhor Roque – ADRA, Malanje
Padre Manuel Viana – Malanje
Maria Fernandes – Caritas, Malanje
Reverend Chipenda – Congregational Church of Angola
Don Aldo Coralli – Núncio, Catholic Church

## Research fellows and scholars

Noam Chomsky – Professor, MIT, USA
Milton Leitenberg – Senior Research Fellow, Maryland University, Maryland*
Michael Clough – Senior Research Fellow, Council on Foreign Relations*
Chester A. Crocker – Professor of Diplomacy, Georgetown University*
Lynn Turgeon – Professor Emeritus of Economics, Hofstra University*
James Mittelman – Professor of International Relations, The American University
N'gugi Wa Thiongo – Professor, New York University*
Antonio Gaspar – ISRI, Maputo
Sergio Mathe – ISRI, Maputo
José Patricio – ISRI, Maputo
Augosto Kambwa – Universidade Agostino Neto
Victor Kajibanga – Universidade Agostino Neto
Daniel Mingas – Casimiro Universidade Agostino Neto
Gavin Cawthra – Witwatersrand University, Johannesburg
Patrick Bond – Witwatersrand University, Johannesburg
Thomas Ohlsson – Department of Peace and Conflict Studies, Uppsala
Tor Sellström – Scandinavian Africa Institute, Uppsala

## Follow-up interviews

Conducted follow-up interviews in Maputo, Luanda, Pretoria, London and Stockholm
to crosscheck and complement the US research findings:

Joaquim Chissano – President of Mozambique
Pascoal Mocumbi – Prime Minister of Mozambique*
Eneas Comiche – Minister at the Presidency, Mozambique
Oldemiro Baloi – Minister of Trade and Commerce*, Mozambique
Aguiar Mazula – Minister of Defence, Mozambique*
Henrique Banze – Deputy Minister of Defence, Mozambique
Arnaldo Nhavoto – Minister of Education, Mozambique*
Tomas Salomão – Minister of Finance, Mozambique*
John Kachamila – Minister of Natural Resources, Mozambique
Paulino Macaringue, General, Mozambique
Luisa Diogo – Vice-Minister of Finance, Mozambique
Castigo Langa – Vice-Minister of Natural Resources, Mozambique
Hipolito Patricio – Vice-Minister of Foreign Affairs, Mozambique

Brazao Mazula – Vice-Chancellor, University of Eduardo Mondlane, Mozambique
Jamisse Taimo – Vice-Chancellor, ISRI, Mozambique
Agostinho Zacarias – former Vice-Chancellor, ISRI, Mozambique
José Trindade – former Executive Director, Agricom, Mozambique
Joaquim de Carvalho – Alternate Executive Director, the World Bank* Mozambique
Pedro Couto – Ministry of Finance* Mozambique
Rui Baltazar – Ambassador of Mozambique in Sweden
Pedro Commissário – Ambassador of Mozambique in Portugal
Fransisco Masquil – former Governor, Beira, Mozambique
Texeira Manjama – former Mayor, Beira, Mozambique
Carlos Cardoso – Independent writer, Mozambique*
Raúl Domingos – Head of Renamo in Parliament, Mozambique
Esmeralda Fernandes – Banco de Moçambique, Mozambique*
Sra Graça Machel – Fundacão de Desenvolvimento da Comunidade* Mozambique
Mário Machungo – former Prime Minister of Moçambique, Mozambique*
Magid Osman – former Minister of Finance, Mozambique*
Prakash Ratilal – former Governor of Central Bank, Mozambique*
Yasmin Patel – Alternate Executive Director, IMF, Washington* Mozambique
Jorge Rebelo – former member of Frelimo Political Bureau, Mozambique*
Aranda da Silva – former Minister of Trade, Mozambique*
Dinis S. Sengulane – Bishop of Mozambique
Virgina Videira – Head of Division, CNP, Mozambique *

Pedro Sebastião – Minister of Defence, Angola
Kundi Payama – Minister of Defence, Angola
Albino Malungo – Minister of Social Assistance and Reintegration, Angola
Demóstenes Amos Chilingutila – Deputy Minister of Defence, Angola
Roberto Monteiro 'Ngongo' – Deputy Minister of Defence, Angola
George Chicoti – Deputy Minister of Foreign Affairs, Angola
Miguel Zau Puna – Deputy Minister of Territorial Administrration, Angola
José Van-Dunem – Deputy Minister of Health, Angola
Carlos Sumbula – Deputy Minister of Geology and Mines, Angola
André de Carvalho – Rear Admiral, Ministry of Defence, Angola
Colonel Domingos – Ministry of Defence staff, Angola
Eduardo Ferreira Martins – Institute of National Defence, Angola
Captain Lima – Institute of National Defence, Angola
Joao Ferreira – National Coordinator, Ministry of Planning, Angola
Luis Adriano Bagorro – General Secretary, Ministry of Geology and Mines, Angola
Miguel Bondo – Ministry of Geology and Mines, Angola
Laurinda Hoygaard – Vice-Chancellor, Universidade Agostino Neto, Angola
Eleutério Freire – Director, Ministry of Planning, Angola
Lúcio Lara – MPLA, Angola
Paulo Jorge – MPLA, Angola
Lopo do Nascimento – ex-Secretary General of MPLA, Angola
Eugénio Manuvakola – Member of Parliament, UNITA, Angola
Almerindo Jaka Jamba – Member of Parliament, UNITA, Angola
Idalina Valente – Member of Parliament, MPLA, Angola
Cândida Narciso – Member of Parliament, MPLA, Angola

Dennis Jett – Ambassador of the United States in Mozambique
Todd Greentree – Political officer, American Embassay in Angola

Birgitta Johansson – Ambassador of Sweden in Mozambique*
Manuel Lopes da Costa – Ambassador of Portugal in Mozambique
John Sunde – Ambassador of South Africa in Mozambique*
Richard Edis – Ambassador of United Kingdom in Mozambique
Manfredo di Camerana – Ambassador of Italy in Mozambique
Aldo Ajello – UN General Secretary representative in Mozambique
Wolfgang Schultes – UN, in Mozambique
Eric de Mul – Head of UNDP, in Mozambique*
Carlos Horta – Chief Economist, UNDP, Mozambique*
Ana Maria Rebeiro – Economist, European Union delegation in Mozambique*
Charles Namoloh – Ambassador of Namibia in Angola
Joao Armando Duarte – Ambassador of Cape Verde in Angola

Mr Pik Botha – Minister of Foreign Affairs during the P.W. Botha government, Republic of South Africa*
Lord (Geoffrey) Howe – Minister of Foreign Affairs during the Thatcher government, United Kingdom
Richard Dales – Assistant Under Secretary of State for Africa, Foreign and Commonwealth Office, London, United Kingdom
Mr Joseph Hanlon – independent writer, United Kingdom*

Ruth Jacoby – former Nordic Executive Director, The World Bank, Washington*
Asbjoern Loevbraeck – former Assistant to the Nordic Executive Director, The World Bank, Washington*
Arne Disch – The World Bank, Harare*

Jan Cedergren – Ministry for Foreign Affairs, Sweden
Sven-Olof Pettersson – Ministry for Foreign Affairs, Sweden
Carl Tham – Sida, Sweden
Annika Magnusson – Sida, Sweden
Ulla Andren – Sida, Sweden
Sten Rylander – Sida, Sweden

## Declassified documentation

Various declassified US governmental and non-governmental documentation obtained at the Council on Foreign Relations, National Archives and National Security Archive. Quoted reference numbers are catalogue numbers used by the respective archives. Copies of the quoted documents are in the possession of the author. Some of the documents have been partly or entirely published in Kenneth, Mokoena (ed.) *South Africa and the United States: The Declassified History* (New York: The New Press, 1993) and in Christopher, Simpson, *National Security Directives of the Reagan and Bush Administrations: The Declassified History of US Political and Military Policy, 1981–1991*, San Francisco: Westview Press, 1995).

## National Archives at College Park

NSC 68 April 14 1950, United States Objectives and Programs for National Security (00176).
NSC 68/1 United States Objectives and Programs for National Security (00177).

NSC 68/1 Annexes: United States Objectives and Programs for National Security (00178).
NSDM 10 April 11 1969, Aid and PL 480 Commitments,
NSDD 32, May 20 1982, US National Security Strategy
NSSD 3–83, March 14 1983, The US Approach to The International Debt Problem
NSDD 1–84, February 27 1984, US Third World Hunger Relief
NSDD 143, July 9 1984, US Third World Hunger Relief. Emergency Assistance
NSDD 156, January 3 1985, US Third World Food Aid: A 'Food for Progress' Program
NSDD 167, April 29 1985, Food for Progress Program Implementation
NSDD 235, August 18 1986, Strengthening US Policy Toward Cuba
NSSD 3–86, September 19 1986, US Support for Economic Growth in Sub-Saharan Africa
NSD 34, January 1990, Partnership with Panama: Action Plan to Foster Economic Recovery (U)
NSSD 2–85, November 15 1991, Economic Development for Central America, *National Security Review* 29
NSD 75, December 23 1992, American Policy Toward Sub-Saharan Africa in the 1990s Presidential Directive/NSC-5 Southern Africa

## National Security Archive

1957/04/03 (00507) NSC 5707/5 Review of Basic National Security Policy: Foreign Economic Issues Relating to National Security
1958/08/26 (00569) NSC 5818 US Policy Toward Africa South of the Sahara Prior to Calender Year 1960
1964/04/24 (01057) NSAM 295 US Policy Toward South Africa
1969/12/09 (01355) NSSM 39 Study in Response to National Security Memorandum 39: Southern Africa
1976/04/21 (01490) NSM 241 United States Policy in Southern Africa
1976/04/23 (00575) Secretary's Trip to Africa: Speech on Southern African Issues
1976/04/27 (00577) Address by the Honorable Henry A. Kissinger, Secretary of State, at a luncheon in the Secretary's honor, hosted by His Excellency Kenneth Kaunda, President of Zambia, The State House, Lusaka, Zambia April 27 1976
1978/05/23 (01572) PRM/NSC 36 Soviet/Cuban Presence in Africa
1979/02/07 (00896) Namibia: The Politics of Diamonds and Uranium. US Consulate General, Cape Town, informs State Dept and US mission to the United Nations
1981/01/21 (01110) *Current Foreign Relations*, No. 3, January 21 1981 (Section Entitled 'No Progress at Geneva')
1981/03/31 (01163) Consultations on Southern Africa (Regarding Chester Crocker's trip to consult with Frontline States, South Africa, Kenya and Zaire, on Southern Africa Issues)
1981/04/14 (01193) Department of State Press Briefing, April 14 1981: Regarding the Failure of the Pre-Implementation Meeting at Geneva to Give Effect to the UN Plan for Namibia
1981/04/15 (01196) News articles, April 15, on Mr Crocker's Africa Trip
1981/06/00 (01291) Bilateral – Philippine Foreign Minister Romulo: Regarding Carlos P. Romolu's Concern on the Apparent Shift in US Policy Toward South Africa
1981/08/29 (01315) Regional Security for Southern Africa – Address by Chester Crocker before the Foreign Relations and National Security Committe of the American Legion
1981/06/16 (01298) Department of State Press Briefing
1982/10/21 (01441) The UN General Assembly Requests IMF Not to Issue Credits to South Africa

1982/10/21 (01442) Explanation of the US Vote on Draft Resolution A/37/15
1982/11/03 (01443) *Current Foreign Relations*, No.44, November 3 1982
1982/11/03 (01444) IMF Loan for South Africa
1982/12/02 (01452) Export Controls and Constructive Engagement in Southern Africa
1982/12/22 (01459) *Current Foreign Relations*, No. 51, December 22 1982
1983/02/15 (01480) The Search for Regional Security in Southern Africa, Prepared Statement and Testimony by the Assistant Secretary of State for African Affairs (Crocker). Before a Subcommittee of the House Foreign Affairs Committee
1983/10/28 (01540) UN Secretary Council Condemnation of Linkage between Namibian Independence and Withdrawal of Cuban Troops from Angola, Resolution 539 (1983)
1983/10/28 (01541) Explanation of the US Vote on UN Security Council Resolution 539 (1983)
1985/01/03 (01829) NSDD 156 US Third World Food Aid: A Food for Progress Program
1985/04/29 (01846) NSDD 167 Food for Progress Program Implementation
1985/09/07 (01877) NSDD 187 United States Policy Toward South Africa
1986/02/10 (01945) NSDD 212 United States Policy Toward Angola
1987/05/07 (02017) NSDD 272 United States Objectives in Southern Africa
1987/05/07 (02019) NSDD 274 United States Policy Toward Angola


## Africa Confidential

*AC* Vol. 21, No. 2, Jan. 16 1980: 'Mozambique: Soviet relations'
*AC* Vol. 21, No. 22, Oct. 29 1980: 'US: Resource War?'
*AC* Vol. 22, No. 5, Feb. 25 1981: 'Mozambique: Wary of the West'
*AC* Vol. 22, No.17, August 19 1981: 'USA: Africa by trial and error'
*AC* Vol. 22, No. 24, Oct. 15 1981: 'Southern Africa: Socialist International'
*AC* Vol. 23, No. 1, Jan. 6 1982: 'USA: Africa policy reflections'
*AC* Vol. 23, No. 15, July 21 1982: 'Mozambique: Havoc in the bush'
*AC* Vol. 23, No. 16, August 4 1982: 'Mozambique II: Havoc in the bush'
*AC* Vol. 23, No. 25, Dec. 15 1982: 'US: Reflections'
*AC* Vol. 24, No. 1, Jan. 5 1983: 'US: Plenty of arms, no money'
*AC* Vol. 24, No. 7, March 30 1983: 'Southern Africa: The oil weapon'
*AC* Vol. 24, No. 7, March 30 1983: 'Mozambique: A waning MNR?'
*AC* Vol. 24, No. 11, May 25 1983: 'IMF: Calling the tune'
*AC* Vol. 24, No. 25, Dec 15 1983: 'The United States: Log-jams'
*AC* Vol. 25, No. 2, Jan. 18 1984: 'South Africa: Carrots?'
*AC* Vol. 25, No. 4, Feb. 15 1984: 'Mozambique: Politicising the ranks'
*AC* Vol. 25, No. 16, August 1 1984: 'Mozambique: A parting of the ranks'
*AC* Vol. 25, No. 17, August 15 1984: 'Mozambique: Aid from East and West'
*AC* Vol. 25, No. 19, Sept. 19 1984: 'Mozambique: Machel's dilemmas'
*AC* Vol. 25, No. 24, Nov. 28 1984: 'Mozambique: An infamous accord'
*AC* Vol. 26, No. 3, Jan. 30 1995: 'Mozambique: South Africa's nightmare'
*AC* Vol. 26, No. 5, Feb. 27 1985: 'South Africa: Military Embarrassment'
*AC* Vol. 27, No. 15, July 16 1986: 'USA: Constructive Engagement'
*AC* Vol. 27, No. 23, Nov. 12 1986: Mozambique: Pandora's boxes
*AC* Vol. 27, No. 10, May 7 1986: Mozambique: In desperation
*AC* Vol. 27, No. 22, Oct 18 1986: Mozambique: Soviet signal
*AC* Vol. 28, No. 1, Jan. 7 1987: USA: Schulz in charge
*AC* Vol. 28, No. 6, March 18 1987: Mozambique: What is the MNR?
*AC* Vol. 28, No. 8, April 15 1987: 'Soviet Union: African affairs'

*AC* Vol. 28, No. 24, Dec. 2 1987: 'Mozambique/South Africa: The Special Forces behind RENAMO'
*AC* Vol. 28, No. 25, Dec. 16 1987: 'Mozambique: The food factor'


## Published US Congressional documents

*Foreign Assistance and Related Programs Appropriations for fiscal year 1962: Hearings before a subcommittee of the Committee on Appropriations, United States Senate, Ninety-First Congress* (Washington, DC: US Govt. Printing Office, 1961)
*Foreign Assistance and Related Programs Appropriations for fiscal year 1982: Hearings before a subcommittee of the Committee on Appropriations, United States Senate, Ninety-Seventh Congress* (Washington, DC: US Govt. Printing Office, 1981)
*Foreign Assistance and Related Programs Appropriations for fiscal year 1984: Hearings before a subcommittee of the Committee on Appropriations, United States Senate, Ninety-Eighth Congress* (Washington, DC: US Govt. Printing Office, 1983)
*Foreign Assistance and Related Programs Appropriations for fiscal year 1985: Hearings before a subcommittee of the Committee on Appropriations, United States Senate, Ninety-Eighth Congress* (Washington, DC: US Govt. Printing Office, 1984)
*Foreign Assistance and Related Programs Appropriations for fiscal year 1986: Hearings before a subcommittee of the Committee on Appropriations, United States Senate, Ninety-Eighth Congress* (Washington, DC: US Govt. Printing Office, 1985)
*Foreign Assistance and Related Programs Appropriations for 1987: Hearings before a subcommittee of the Committee on Appropriations, House of Representatives, Ninety-Ninth Congress* (Washington, DC: US Govt. Printing Office, 1986)
*Food Production in Africa: The International Challenge: Hearing before the Subcommittee on African Affairs of the Committee on Foreign Relations, United States Senate, Ninety-Eighth Congress, March 1984* (Washington, DC: US Govt. Printing Office, 1982)
*Hunger in Africa: Hearing before the Subcommittee on African Affairs of the Committee on Foreign Relations, United States Senate, Ninety-Eighth Congress, March 1984* (Washington, DC: US Govt. Printing Office, 1984)
*US Policy on South Africa: Hearing before the Subcommittee on African Affairs of the Committee on Foreign Relations, United States Senate, Ninety-Eighth Congress, September 1984* (Washington, DC: US Govt. Printing Office, 1985)
*US Policy Toward Mozambique: Hearings before a Africa Subcommittee of the Senate Foreign Relations Committee, United States Senate, Ninety-Ninth Congress, June 1987* (Washington, DC: US Govt. Printing Office, 1987)


## Unpublished documents on Mozambique

International Monetary Fund (1987, May 12) *Report EBS/87/101: People's Republic of Mozambique – Request for Arrangements under the Structural Adjustment Facility* (Washington, DC).
—— (1991, August 19) *Report EBS/91/136: Republic of Mozambique – Request for Second Annual Arrangement,* (Washington, DC)
—— (1993, July 22) *Mozambique: Recent Economic Development* (Washington, DC)
—— (1996a, May 28) *Request for Arrangements under the Enhanced Structural Adjustment Facility* (Washington, DC)
International Monetary Fund (1996b) *Republic of Mozambique: Recent Economic Developments* IMF Staff Country Report No. 96/142 (Washington, DC)

People's Republic of Mozambique (1987, May 8) *Economic Policy Framework, 1987–89* (Maputo)
—— (1988, March 2) *Economic Policy Framework, 1988–90* (Maputo)
—— (1990, May) *Economic Policy Framework, 1990–92* (Maputo)
—— (1990, October 31) *Poverty Reduction Framework Paper* (Maputo)
—— (1991, August 8) *Policy Framework Paper, 1991–93* (Maputo)
—— (1991, October) *Strategy and Program for Economic and Social Development 1992–94* (Maputo)
—— (1993, December 1) *Policy Framework Paper, 1994–96* (Maputo)
—— (1995, October 30) *Situação da dívida externa Moçambicana* (Maputo)
Republic of Mozambique (1995, March) *The Poverty Reduction Strategy for Mozambique* (Paris)
Republic of Mozambique (1996, September) *Strategy for Reducing the External Debt in Mozambique* (Maputo)
Republic of Mozambique (1997, May) *Debt Strategy for Mozambique* (Maputo)
Republic of Mozambique (1996, April 11) *Policy Framework Paper for 1996–98* (Maputo)
—— (1966, April 2) *Steps Towards Economic and Social Development* (Maputo)
—— (1966, April) *Mozambique: Rural Poverty Profile* (Maputo)
World Bank (1985, May 30) *Report No. P-4100-Moz to the Executive Directors on a proposed credit* (Washington, DC)
—— (1987a, July 16) *Report No. P-4608-Moz to the Executive Directors on a proposed IDA credit* (Washington, DC)
—— (1987b, April 24) *Report No. P-5035-Moz to the Executive Directors on a proposed IDA credit* (Washinghton, DC)
—— (1988) *Report No. P-7094-Moz: Agricultural Sector Survey* (Washington, DC)
—— (1990a) *Report P-8370-Moz: Restoring Rural Production and Trade*, Vols I & II, (Washington, DC)
—— (1992, April 27) *Report No. P-5775-Moz to the Executive Directors on a proposed development credit* (Washington, DC).
—— (1993a, December) *From emergency to sustainable development in Mozambique* (Washington, DC)
—— (1993b, November) *Mozambique: 'Vision document'* (Washington, DC)
—— (1994, May 24) *Mozambique: Second Economic Recovery Program* (Washington, DC)

## Bibliography

Abrahamsson, Hans (1997) *Seizing the Opportunity: Power and Powerlessness in a Changing World Order* (University of Göteborg: Padrigu).
—— (1989) *Transport Structures and Dependency Relations in Southern Africa*, in Bertil Odén and Haroub Othman, *Regional Cooperation in Southern Africa* (Uppsala: Scandinavian Institute of African Studies).
—— and Susanne Hedman (1981) *Den Algeriska Utmaningen: En väg mot en oberoende, socialistisk utveckling* (Lund: Studentlitteratur).
—— and Anders Nilsson (1994) *Moçambique em Transição: Um estudo da história de desenvolvimento durante o período 1974–92* (Maputo: CEEI–ISRI).
—— and Anders Nilsson (1995a) *Future World Order: and National Governance* in Mozambique (University of Göteborg: Padrigu).
—— and Anders Nilsson (1995b) *Mozambique: The Troubled Transition* (London: Zed Books).

Abrahamsson, Hans and Anders Nilsson (1996) *The Washington Consensus and Mozambique* (University of Göteborg: Padrigu).
—— *et al.* (2001) *Poverty, Conflict and Development*, (University of Göteborg: Padrigu).
Abreude, Antonio and Ruy Baltazar (1992) 'Fiscal and Monetary Policy: The Impact of the Economic Recovery Program (PRE)', paper presented to the seminar on Mozambique: Post-War Challenges and Realities, Maputo, December.
Adedeji, Adebayo (ed.) (1993) *Africa within the World* (London: Zed Books).
—— (ed.) (1996) *South Africa and Africa: Within or Apart* (London: Zed Books).
Aglietta, Michel (1976) *Régulation et Crises du Capitalisme* (Paris: Calmann-Lévy).
Åkesson, Gunilla (1992) *School-Books and Buying Power* Education Division mimeo no. 59 (Sida, Stockholm).
—— (1994) *Sistemas de produção agrária e realidade sócio-económica em três aldeias*, mimeo, Direcção Provincial de Agricultura e Pescas (Tete-DANIDA, mimeo, Copenhagen)
—— (1996) *A participação nas actividades de extensão agrária*, mimeo, Direcção Provincial de Agricultura e Pescas (Tete-DANIDA Mimeo, Copenhagen).
Akinrinade, Olusola (1992) 'Mozambique and the Commonwealth: The Anatomy of a relationship', *Australian Journal of Politics and History*, Vol. 38, no. 1.
Amin, Samir (ed.) (1987) *SADCC: Prospects for Disengagement and Development in Southern Africa* (London: Zed Books).
—— (1990) *Delinking: Towards a Polycentric World* (London: Zed Books).
Ashenden, Samantha and Owen, David (1999) *Foucault contra Habermas* (London: Sage).
Austin, Kathi (1994) *Invisible Crimes* (Washington: Africa Policy Information Center).
Balaam, David and Veseth, Michael (1996) Introduction to International Political Economy (New York: Simon & Schuster).
Bates, Robert H. (1981) *Markets and States in Tropical Africa: The Political Basis of Agricultural Policies* (Berkeley: University of California Press).
Bayart, Jean-François (1993) *The State in Africa: The Politics of the Belly* (London: Longman).
Beckman, Björn (1988) 'Comments on *State and Nation under Stress* by Goran Hydén', in P. Frühling (ed.), *Recovery in Africa: Challenge for Development Cooperation in the '90s* (Stockholm: Almqvist & Wiksell).
Bernis, Gerard de Destanne and Maurice Bye (1977) *Relations économiques internationales* (Paris: Dalloz).
—— (1987) *Relations économiques internationales* (Paris: Dalloz).
Bissell, Richard E. and Chester A. Crocker (eds) (1979) *South Africa into the 1980s* (Boulder, CO: Westview Press).
Blechman, Barry M. *et al.* (1997) *The Partnership Imperative: Maintaining American Leadership in a New Era* (Washington, DC: Overseas Development Council).
Blumenfeld, Jesmond (1991) *Economic Interdependence in southern africa – from conflict to cooperation* (London: Pinter Publishers).
Booker, Salih (1996) *Thinking Regionally: Priorities for US Policy toward Africa* (Washington, DC: Council of Foreign Relations).
Boughton, James M. and Sarwar K. Lateef (eds) (1995) *Fifty Years after Bretton Woods: The Future of the IMF and the World Bank* (Washington, DC: International Monetary Fund and the World Bank Group).
Bower, Tom (1993) *Tiny Rowland: A Rebel Tycoon* (London: Mandarin).
Brandt Commission (1980) *North–South: A Programme for Survival, the Report of the Independent Commission on International Development Issues under the Chairmanship of Willy Brandt* (London: Pan Books).

Branson, William H. (1972) *Macroeconomic Theory and Policy* (New York: Harper & Row).

Braudel, Fernand (1977) *Afterthoughts on Material Civilization and Capitalism* (Baltimore: Johns Hopkins University Press).

—— (1979) *Civilisation materielle et capitalisme* (Paris: Armand Colin).

Bretton Woods Commission (1994) *Bretton Woods: Looking to the Future* (Washington, DC: Bretton Woods committee).

Brown, Michael Barratt and Pauline Tiffen (1992) *Short Changed: Africa and World Trade* (London: Pluto Press).

Brundtland, Gro Harlem (1987) *Our Common Future: The World Commission on Environment and Development* (New York: Oxford University Press).

Brzezinski, Zbigniew (1963) *Africa and the Communist World* (Palo Alto, California: Stanford University Press).

—— (1983) *Power and Principle* (London: Weidenfeld & Nicolson).

—— (1993) *Out of Control: Global Turmoil on the Eve of the 21st Century* (New York: Macmillan).

Brynes, Asher (1966) *We Give to Conquer* (New York: W.W. Norton).

Burton, John (1972) *World Society* (Cambridge: Cambridge University Press).

—— (1990) *Conflict: Resolution and Prevention* (Houndmills, Basingstoke: Macmillan).

Bushin, Vladimir (1989) *Social Democracy and Southern Africa* (Moscow: Progress Publishers).

Buzan, Barry (1991) *People, States and Fear* (New York: Harvester Wheatsheaf).

Callaghy, Thomas (1989) 'Toward State Capability and Embedded Liberalism in the Third World: Lessons for Adjustment', in Joan Nelson (ed.), *Fragile Coalitions: The Politics of Economic Adjustment* (Washington, DC: Overseas Development Council).

Callaghy, Thomas M. and John Ravenhill (eds) (1993) *Hemmed in: Responses to Africa's Economic Decline* (New York: Columbia University Press).

Calleo, David (1987) *Beyond American Hegemony: The Future of the Western Alliance* (Brighton: Wheatsheaf).

Campbell, Kurt M. (1986) *Soviet Policy towards South Africa* (London: Macmillan).

Cardoso, Carlos (1996) 'A solidão do Presidente', *Mediafax, No. 1122, 18.10.96.*

Carlsson, Ingvar and Shridath Ramphal (1995) *Our Global Neighbourhood: The Report of the Commission on Global Governance* (New York: Oxford University Press).

Carr, E.H. (1939) *The Twenty Years' Crisis, 1919–1939* (London: Macmillan).

Cassen, Robert (ed.) (1985) *Soviet Interests in the Third World* (London: Sage).

Castel Branco, Carlos (1995) Opções Económicas de Moçambique, 1975–95, in Brazão Mazula, *Moçambique, Eleições, Democracia e Desenvolvimento* (Maputo).

Chambers, Robert (1983) *Rural Development: Putting the Last First* (New York: John Wiley).

Chayanov, A. (1966) *The Theory of Peasant Economy* (Homewood, IL: Richard D. Irwin).

Chazan, Naomi and Donald Rothchild (1993) 'The Political Repercussions of Economic Malaise', in Thomas M. Callaghy and John Ravenhill (eds), *Hemmed in: Responses to Africa's Economic Decline* (New York: Columbia University Press).

Cheru, Fantu (1996) 'Africa and the New World Order: Rethinking Development Planning in the Age of Globalization', in Adebayo Adedeji (ed.), *South Africa and Africa: Within or Apart* (London: Zed Books).

—— (1997a) 'The Silent Revolution and the Weapons of the Weak: Transformation and Innovation from Below', in Stephen Gill and James H. Mittelman (eds), *Innovation and Transformation in International Studies* (Cambridge: Cambridge University Press).

—— (1997b) 'Global Apartheid and the Challenge to Civil Society: Africa in the Transformation of World Order', in Robert Cox (ed.), *The New Realism* (London: Macmillan).

Chevalier, Jean-Marie (1973) *Le nouvel enjeu pétrolier* (Paris: Calmann-Lévy).

Christie, Ian (1988) *Machel of Mozambique* (Harare: Zimbabwe Publishing House).

Clough, Michael (1985) 'Beyond Constructive Engagement', *Foreign Policy*, no. 61, Winter 85/86.

—— (1988) 'Southern Africa: Challenges and Choices', *Foreign Affairs*, Vol. 66, no. 5.

—— (1992) *Free at Last US Policy toward Africa and the End of the Cold War* (New York: Council for Foreign Relations).

Coffin, Frank (1964) *Witness for Aid* (Boston: Houghton Mifflin).

Commission on America's National Interest (1996) *America's National Interest* (Washington, DC).

Cooper, Richard N. *et al.* (1977) 'Towards a Renovated International System', *Triangle Papers 14* (New York: Trilateral Commission).

Cornia, G.A., R. Jolly and F. Stewart (eds) (1987) *Adjustment with a Human Face: Protecting the Vulnerable and Promoting Growth* (Oxford: Clarendon Press).

Cox, Robert (1979) 'Ideologies and the New International Economic Order: Reflections on Some Recent Literature', *International Organization*, Vol. 33, no. 2.

—— (1981) 'Social Forces, States and World Orders', *Millennium, Journal of International Studies*, Vol. 10, no. 2: 126–55.

—— (1983) 'Gramsci, Hegemony and International Relations: An Essay in Method', *Millennium, Journal of International Studies*, Vol. 12, no. 2:162–75.

—— (1987) *Production, Power and World Order: Social Forces in the Making of History* (New York: Columbia University Press).

—— (1992) 'Towards a Post-hegemonic Conceptualization of World Order: Reflections on the Relevancy of Ibn Khaldun', in James N. Rosenau and Ernst-Otto Czempiel (eds), *Governance without Government; Order and Change in World Politics* (Cambridge: Cambridge University Press), pp. 132–59.

—— (1992a) 'Global Perestroika', *Socialist Register* (London: Merlin Press).

—— (1992b) 'Multilateralism and World Order', *Review of International Studies*, Vol.18, no. 2: 161–80.

—— (1993) 'Structural Issues of Global Governance: Implications for Europe', in Stephen Gill, *Gramsci, Historical Materialism and International Relations* (New York: Cambridge University Press).

—— (1995) 'Critical Political Economy', in B. Hettne (ed.), *International Political Economy: Understanding Global Disorder* (London: Zed Books).

—— and Timothy Sinclair (1996) *Approaches to World Order* (New York: Cambridge University Press).

—— (1997) (ed.), *The New Realism* (London: Macmillan).

Cowen, M.P. and R.W. Shenton (1996) *Doctrines of Development* (New York: Routledge).

Crocker, Chester A. (1981a) 'South Africa: Strategy for Change', *Foreign Affairs*, Vol. 59, no. 2 Winter 80/81.

—— (1981b) *South Africa's Defense Posture* (Washington, DC: Georgetown University).

—— (1992) *High Noon in Southern Africa: Making Peace in a Rough Neighborhood* (New York: W.W. Norton).

—— (1995) 'Why Africa Needs Our Attention', *Cosmos: A Journal of Emerging Issues*, Spring 1995 (Washington, DC).

—— *et al.* (eds) (1996) *Managing Global Chaos: Sources of and Responses to International Conflict* (Washington, DC: United States Institute of Peace).

Cronje, Suzanne *et al.* (1976) *Lonrho: Portrait of a Multinational* (New York: Penguin Books).

Daniels, Walter (ed.) (1951) *The Point Four Program* (New York: Wilson).

Denzin, Norman K. and Yvonna S. Lincoln (1994) *Handbook of Qualitative Research* (London: Sage).

Devetak, Richard (1996) 'Critical Theory', in Scott Burchill *et al.* (eds), *Theories of International Relations* (New York: St Martin's Press).

Dolan, Chris and Jessie Schafer (1997) *The Reintegration of Ex-combatants in Mozambique, Manica and Zambezia Provinces: Final Report to USAID, Mozambique.* Refugee Studies Programme, Queen Elizabeth House (Oxford: University of Oxford.)

Dolman, Antony J. (ed.) (1976) *Reshaping the International Order: A Report to the Club of Rome* (New York: E. P. Dutton).

Dréze, Jean, Amartya Sen and Athar Hussain (eds) (1995) *The Political Economy of Hunger: Selected Essays* (Oxford: Clarendon).

Driscoll, David D. (1994) *What is the International Monetary Fund?* (Washington, DC: External Relations Department, International Monetary Fund).

Duffield, Mark (2001) *Global Governance and the New Wars* (London: Zed Books).

Economic Commission for Africa (1989a) *South African Destabilisation: The Economic Costs of Frontline Resistance to Apartheid* (Addis Ababa: UN Department of Public Information).

Economic Commission for Africa (1989b) *African Alternative to Structural Adjustment Programmes (AA–SAP): A Framework for Transformation and Recovery* (Addis Ababa: UN Department of Public Information).

Engberg-Pedersen, Poul *et al.* (1996) *Limits of Adjustment in Africa* (London: James Currey).

European Union (1996) *Newsletter*, No. 3, November.

European Union (1997) *Identifying New Approaches to Partnership, in Beyond Lomé IV: Exploring Options for Future ACP–EU Cooperation*, Policy Management Report No. 6 (Maastricht: European Centre for Development Policy Management).

Falk, Richard (1999) *Predatory Globalization: A Critique* (Cambridge: Polity Press).

Flower, Ken (1987) *Serving Secretly: Rhodesia's CIO Chief On Record* (London: John Murray).

Fontana, Andrea and James H. Frey (1994) 'Interviewing – The Art of Science', in Norman K. Denzin and Yvonna S. Lincoln (eds), *Handbook of Qualitative Research* (London: Sage).

Food and Agriculture Organization (1996) *World Food Summit: Food Security Situation and Issues in the Africa Region*, Nineteenth FAO regional conference for Africa, Ouagadougou, Burkina Faso, 16–20 April 1996 (Rome: FAO).

Foucault, Michael (1980) *Power/Knowledge. Selected Interviews and Other Writings 1972–1977* (Hemel Hempsted: Harvester).

Friedman, Milton (1962) *Capitalism and Freedom* (Chicago: University of Chicago Press).

Fukuyama, Francis (1992) *The End of History and the Last Man* (New York: The Free Press).

—— (1999) *The Great Disruption* London: Profile Books.

Galtung, Johan (1969) 'Violence, Peace and Peace Research', *Journal of Peace Research*, Vol. 6, no. 3.

—— (1996) *Peace by Peaceful Means: Peace and Conflict, Development and Civilization* (London: Sage).

Gardner, Richard N. (1969) *Sterling Diplomacy: The Origins and the Prospects of Our International Economic Order* (New York: McGraw-Hill).

Gastrow, Peter and Marcello Mosse (2002) *Mozambique: Threats Posed by the Penetration of Criminal Networks* (Cape Town: Institute of Security Studies).

Geest, Willem van der (ed.) (1994) *Negotiating Structural Adjustment in Africa* (London: James Currey).

Geldenhuys, Deon (1982) *What Do We Think? A Survey of White Opinion on Foreign Policy Issues*, Occasional Paper, Pretoria: South African Institute of International Affairs.

George, Susan and Fabrizio Sabelli (1994) *Faith and Credit: The World Bank's Secular Empire* (Boulder, CO: Westview Press).

Gibbon, Peter (1993) 'The World Bank and the New Politics of Aid', *European Journal of Development Research*, Vol. 5, no. 1.

Gill, Stephen (1990) *American Hegemony and the Trilateral Commission* (New York: Cambridge University Press).

—— (1993) *Gramsci, Historical Materialism and International Relations* (New York: Cambridge University Press).

Gills, Barry K. (ed.) (2000) *Globalization and the Politics of Resistance* (London: Macmillan).

Gilpin, Robert (1987) *The Political Economy of International Relations* (Princeton, NJ: Princeton University Press).

Gramsci, Antonio (1971) *Selections from Prison Notebooks* (London: Lawrence & Wishart).

Griesgraber, Jo Marie and Bernard C. Gunter (1995) *Promoting Development: Effective Global Institutions for the Twenty-first Century* (London: Pluto Press).

Gwin, Catherine (1994) *US Relations with the World Bank 1945–92* (Washington: Brookings Institution).

Halliday, Fred (1983) *The Making of the Second Cold War* (London: Verso).

Halliday, Fred (1994) *Rethinking International Relations* (Houndmills, Basingstoke: Macmillan).

Hanlon, Joseph (1986) *Beggar Your Neighbours* (London: James Currey).

—— (1991) *Who Calls the Shots?* (London: James Currey).

—— (1996) *Peace without Profit* (Oxford: James Currey).

—— (2002) 'Are Donors to Mozambique Promoting Corruption?' Paper submitted to the conference 'Towards a New Political Economy of Development', Sheffield, July 2002.

Haynes, Jeff (1997) *Democracy and Civil Society in the Third World: Politics and New Political Movements* (Cambridge: Polity Press).

Haq, Mahbub ul (1976) *The Poverty Curtain: Choices for the Third World* (Columbia University Press).

Harlov, Jens (1997) *Regional Cooperation and Integration within Industry and Trade in Southern Africa* (Aldershot: Avebury).

Hettne, Björn (1984) *Approaches to the Study of Peace and Development* (Tilburg: EADI).

—— (1988) 'Comments on *State and Nation under Stress* by Göran Hydén', in P. Frühling (ed.), *Recovery in Africa: Challenge for Development Cooperation in the '90s* (Stockholm: Almqvist & Wiksell).

—— (1995) 'The International Political Economy of Development', *European Journal of Development Research*, Vol. 7, no. 2.

—— (1995a) *Development Theory and the Three Worlds* (Harlow: Longman).

—— (ed.) (1995b) *International Political Economy: Understanding Global Disorder* (London: Zed Books).

—— (1997) 'Development, Security and World Order: A Regionalist Approach', *European Journal of Development Research*, Vol. 9, no. 1.

—— et al. (1999) *Globalism and the New Regionalism* (London: Macmillan).

Hirst, Paul and Grahame Thompson (1995) *Globalization in Question* (Cambridge: Polity Press).

Hobsbawm, Eric (1959) *Primitive Rebels* (London: Manchester University Press).

Howe, Geoffrey (1994) *Conflict of Loyalty* (London: Pan Books).

Hodgson, Godfrey (1973) 'The Establishment', *Foreign Policy*, Vol. 10.

Hoeven, Rolph van der and Fred van der Kraaij (1994) *Structural Adjustment and Beyond in Sub-Saharan Africa* (London: James Currey).

Holmberg, Johan (1995) 'Future Food Needs, International Agricultural Research and the Role of SAREC', in Karin von Schlebrügge (1997) *Research for Development: SAREC 20 Years* (Kristianstad: Sarec).

Huntington, Samuel, P. (1988) 'The US – Decline or Renewal?' *Foreign Affairs*, Vol. 67, no. 2.

—— (1996a) *The Clash of Civilizations and the Remaking of World Order* (New York: Simon & Schuster).

—— (1996b) 'The West and the World', *Foreign Affairs*, Vol. 76, no. 6.

Hydén, Göran (1980) *Beyond Ujamaa in Tanzania: Underdevelopment and an Uncaptured Peasantry* (Los Angeles: University of California Press).

—— (1983) *No Shortcuts to Progress* (Los Angeles: University of California Press).

—— (1988) 'State and Nation Under Stress', in P. Frühling, (ed.) *Recovery in Africa: Challenge for Development Cooperation in the '90s* (Stockholm: Almqvist & Wiksell).

—— and Bo Karlström (1991) 'Understanding Structural Adjustment: Tanzania in Comparative Perspective', in Magnus Blomström and Mats Lundahl (eds) (1993), *Economic Crisis in Africa: Perspectives on Policy Responses* (New York: Routledge).

International Monetary Fund (1996) *World Economic Outlook* (Washington, DC: IMF).

Johnson, Phyllis and David Martin (1986) *Destructive Engagement* (Harare: Zimbabwe Publishing House).

Kanet, Roger E. (1982) *Soviet Foreign Policy in the 1980s* (New York: Praeger).

Kaldor, Mary (1999) *New and Old Wars* (Cambridge: Polity Press).

Kaplan, Robert D. (1994) 'The Coming Anarchy', *Atlantic Monthly*, Vol. 273, no. 2:44–75.

Karlsson, Mats (1997) Opening Statement by Mats Karlsson, State Secretary, Ministry for Foreign Affairs, Sweden, in Henock Kifle *et al.*, *A New Partnership for African Development* (Uppsala: Nordiska Afrikainstitutet).

Karlsson, Svante (1986) *Oil and the World Order: American Foreign Oil Policy* (Leamington Spa: Berg).

Kay, Geoffrey (1975) *Development and Underdevelopment: A Marxist Analysis* (New York: Macmillan).

Kennan, George F. (1967) *Memoirs 1925–1950* (New York: Pantheon Books).

Kennedy, Paul *et al.* (1996) 'Pivotal States and US Strategy', *Foreign Affairs*, Vol. 75, no. 1.

Kennedy, Paul (1987) *The Rise and Fall of the Great Powers* (New York: Random House).

Keohane, Robert O. (1980) 'The Theory of Hegemonic Stability and Changes in International Economic Regimes, 1967–1977', in Ole Holsti *et al.*, *Change in the International System* (Boulder, CO: Westview Press).

—— (1984) *After Hegemony: Cooperation and Discord in the World Political Economy* (Princeton, NJ: Princeton University Press).

—— (ed.) (1986) *Neorealism and its Critics* (New York: Columbia University Press).

—— (1995) 'Hobbes's Dilemma and Institutional Change in World Politics: Sovereignty in International Society', in Hans Holm and Georg Sørensen, (eds) *Whose World*

*Order? Uneven Globalization and the End of the Cold War* (Boulder, CO: Westview Press).

—— and Joseph S. Nye, Jr. (1975) 'International Interdependence and Integration', in Paul Viotti and Mark Kauppi (1993; 2nd edn.) *International Relations Theory* (New York: Macmillan).

—— and Joseph S. Nye, Jr (1977) 'Realism and Complex Interdependence', *Power and Interdependence: World Politics in Transition* (Boston: Little Brown; reprinted in Paul Viotti and Mark Kauppi (1993, 2nd edn.) *International Relations Theory* (New York: Macmillan).

Keynes, John Maynard (1936) 'The General Theory of Employment, Interest and Money', in the *Collected Writings of John Maynard Keynes*, Vol. VII (London: Macmillan, 1980).

Keynes, John Maynard (1941) 'Proposals to counter the German New Order', in the *Collected Writings of John Maynard Keynes*, Vol. XXV (London: Macmillan, 1980).

Keynes, John Maynard (1944) 'Activities 1941–1946 Shaping the Post-War World', in the *Collected Writings of John Maynard Keynes*, Vol. XXVI (London: Macmillan).

Kifle, Henock *et al.* (1997) *A New Partnership for African Development* (Uppsala: Nordiska Afrikainstitutet).

Killick, Tony (1995) *IMF Programmes in Developing Countries* (New York: Routledge).

Kindleberger, Charles P. (1973) *The World In Depression 1929–39* (Berkeley: University of California Press).

—— (1981) Dominance and Leadership in the International Economy, *International Studies Quarterly*, Vol. 25, no. 3.

Kirshner, Orin (ed.) (1996) *The Bretton Woods–Gatt System: Retrospect and Prospect after Fifty Years* (New York: M.E. Sharpe).

Kissinger, Henry (1994) *Diplomacy* (New York: Simon & Schuster).

Klare, Michael T. (1981) *Beyond the Vietnam Syndrome. US Intervention in the 1980s* (Washington, DC: Institute for Policy Studies).

Kojo, Yoshiko (1992) 'Burden-sharing under US Leadership: The Case of Quota Increases of the IMF since the 1970s', in Henry Bienen (ed.), *Power, Economics, and Security: The United States and Japan in Focus* (Westview Press).

Krasner, Stephen D. (ed.) (1983) *International Regimes* (Ithaca, NY: Cornell University Press).

Krueger, Anne (1993) *Economic Policies at Cross Purposes: the United States and Developing Countries* (Washington, DC: Brookings Institution).

Kuttner, Robert (1991) *The End of Laissez-Faire* (New York: Alfred A. Knopf).

Kühne, Winrich (1987) 'What Does the Case of Mozambique Tell Us About Soviet Ambivalence Toward Africa?', in Helen Kitchen (ed.), *Angola, Mozambique and the West* The Washington Papers 130 (New York: Praeger).

Lappalainen, Tomas (1994) *Maffia* (Stockholm: Månpocket).

Leys, Colin (1996) *The Rise and Fall of Development Theory* (London: James Currey).

Lipumba, Ngoyuru H.I. (1994) *Africa Beyond Adjustment*, Policy Essay No. 15, (Washington, DC: Overseas Development Council).

Lipsey, Richard G. and Peter O. Steiner (1975) *Economics* (New York: Harper & Row).

Lipton, M. (1977) *Why Poor People Stay Poor: A Study of Urban Bias in World Development* (London: Temple Smith).

Lissaker, Karen (1977) *International Debt, the Banks, and US Foreign Policy* (Washington: Subcommittee on Foreign Economic Policy of the Committee on Foreign Relations, United States Senate).

Low, Allan (1986) *Agricultural Development in Southern Africa: Farm Household-Economics and the Food Crisis* (London: James Currey).

Lundqvist, Jan and Peter Gleick (1997) *Comprehensive Assessment of the Freshwater Resources of the World* (Stockholm: Stockholm Environment Institute).

Lundström, Hans (1988) 'Economic Adjustment and Swedish Assistance', in P. Frühling (ed.), *Recovery in Africa: Challenge for Development Cooperation in the '90s* (Stockholm: Almqvist & Wiksell).

Manghezi, Alpheus (1983) 'Ehu Thekela: Strategies for survival against Famine in Southern Mozambique', in *Estudos Maçambicanos*, no. 4, 1983, Maputo: Eduardo: Mondlone University.

Manley, Michael (1987) *Up the Down Escalator: Development and the International Economy – A Jamaican Case Study* (London: André Deutsch).

Marte, Fred (1994) *Political Cycles in International Relations: The Cold War and Africa 1945–1990* (Amsterdam: University Press).

Martin, David and Phyllis Johnson (1981) *The Struggle for Zimbabwe* (Harare: Zimbabwe Publishing House).

Martin, Ben L. (1989) 'American Policy Towards Southern Africa in the 1980s', *Journal of Modern African Studies*, Vol. 27, no. 1.

Mason, Edward and Robert Asher (1973) *The World Bank since Bretton Woods* (Washington, DC: Brookings Institution).

Max-Neef, Manfred *et al.* (1989) 'Human Scale Development: An Option for the Future', *Development Dialogue* 1 (Uppsala: Dag Hammarskiöld Foundation).

Melanson, Richard A. (1996) *American Foreign Policy since the Vietnam War: The Search for Consensus – from Nixon to Clinton* (New York: M.E. Sharpe).

Mill, John Stuart (1875) *Dissertations and Discussions – Political, Philosophical, and Historical*, Vol. III, 2nd edn (London: Longman, Green, Reader & Dyer).

Minter, William (1986) *King Solomon's Mines Revisited* (New York: Basic Books).

—— (1994) *Apartheid's Contras: An Inquiry into the Roots of War in Angola and Mozambique* (London: Zed Books).

Mokoena, Kenneth (ed.) (1993) *South Africa and the United States – the Declassified History* (New York: The New Press).

Morgenthau, Hans J. (1948) *Politics among Nations* (New York: Alfred Knopf).

Mugabe, Robert (1987) 'Struggle for Southern Africa', *Foreign Affairs*, Vol. 66, no. 2.

Munslow, Barry (ed.) (1985) *Samora Machel: An African Revolutionary* (London: Zed Books).

Murray, Martin (1987) *South Africa: Time of Agony, Time of Destiny* (London: Verso).

Nau, H.R. (1990) *The Myth of America's Decline: Leading the Word Economy into the 1990s* (New York: Oxford University Press).

Neufeld, Mark (1995) *The Restructuring of International Relations Theory* (Cambridge: Cambridge University Press).

Nilsson, Anders (1993) 'From Pseudoterrorism to Brigandage', *Review of African Political Economy*, Nos 57 and 58.

—— (1999) *Peace In Our Time* (Göteborg: PADRIGU)

Nixon, Richard (1980) *The Real War* (New York: Warner Books).

Nunn, Elizabeth (1996) 'The Rational Choice Approach to IPE', in David N. Balaam and Michael Veseth, *Introduction to International Political Economy* (New York: Simon & Schuster).

Odén, Bertil and Haroub Othman (eds) (1989) *Regional Cooperation in Southern Africa* (Uppsala: Nordiska Afrikainstitutet).

Ohlsson, Leif (1999) *Environment, Scarcity and Conflict* (Göteborg: PADRIGU).

Ohlson, Thomas and Stephen J. Stedman (1994) *The New Is Not Yet Born: Conflict Resolution in Southern Africa* (Washington, DC: Brookings Institution).

Östergaard, Tom (1989) 'Aiming Beyond Conventional Development Assistance: An Analysis of Nordic Aid to the SADCC Region', in, Bertil Odén and Haroub Othman (eds), *Regional Cooperation in Southern Africa* (Uppsala: Nordiska Afrikainstitutet).

Owen, Daniel (1997) *Rapid Rural Assessment of Cashew-growing Areas in Nampula and Gaza/Inhambane* (Maputo: Ministry of Tourism, Trade and Industry).

Oyejide, Ademola, T. (1997) 'Opening Up, Integrating Africa, and Linking it with the World'. Paper prepared for the Nordic Africa Institute Conference on Relinking Africa, Abidjan, Côte d'Ivoire, 20–21 January 1997.

Payer, Cheryl (1974) *The Dept Trap: The IMF and the Third World* (New York: Monthly Review Press).

—— (1982) *The World Bank* (New York: Monthly Review Press).

Pedersen, Poul, *et al.* (eds) (1996) *Limits of Adjustment in Africa* (Oxford: James Currey).

Pinder, John, Takashi Hosomi, and William Diebold (1979) *Industrial Policy and the International Economy* (New York: The Trilateral Commission).

Pires, Pena *et al.* (1984) *Os Retornados: Um Estudo Sociográfico* (Lisbon: Instituto de Estudos para o Desenvolvimento).

Polanyi, Karl (1957) *The Great Transformation* (Boston: Beacon Press).

Popkin, Samuel (1979) *The Rational Peasant: The Political Economy of Rural Society in Vietnam* (Berkeley: University of California Press).

Preobrazjenskij, E. (1972) 'Socialist Primitive Accumulation', in Nuti Nove, *Socialist Economics* (Harmondsworth: Penguin Books).

Putnam, Robert O. (1993) *Making Democracy Work: Civil Traditions in Modern Italy* (Princeton, NJ: Princeton University Press).

Ratilal, Prakash (2001) A proposito de desinvolvimento economico. Mimeo (Maputo).

Reason, Peter (1994) 'Three Approaches to Participative Inquiry', in Norman, K. Denzin and Yvonna S. Lincoln *Handbook of Qualitative Research* (London: Sage).

Reno, William (1998) *Warlord Politics and African States* (London, Lynne Rienner).

Riddell, Roger (1993) 'The future of the manufacturing sector in Sub-Saharan Africa', in Thomas M. Callaghy and John Ravenhill (eds), *Hemmed In: Responses to Africa's Economic Decline* (New York: Columbia University Press).

Rizopoulos, Nicholas X. (ed.) (1990) *Sea Changes: American Foreign Policy in a World Transformed* (New York: Council on Foreign Relations).

Rockfeller, Nelson (1951) *Partners in Progress, A Report to the President by the International Development Advisory Board,* quoted in Walter Daniels (ed.), *The Point Four Program* (New York: Wilson).

Rostow, Walter (1960) *The Stages of Economic Growth* (Cambridge: Cambridge University Press).

Rothchild, Donald (1993) 'Foreword' to Kenneth Mokoena (ed.), *South Africa and the United States: The Declassified History* (New York: The New Press).

Rubin, Robert (1997) 'A Dynamic Africa will Benefit both Africa and US', US Treasury Secretary Robert Rubin address to CCA summit, Washington, 21 April 1997.

Rubinstein, Alvin, Z. (1989) *Soviet Foreign Policy since World War II* (London: Scott, Foresman).

Ruggie, John (1983) 'International Regimes, Transactions and Change: Embedded Liberalism in the Postwar Economic Order', in Stephen, D. Krasner (ed.), *International Regimes* (New York: Cornell University Press).

Ruttan, Vernon W. (ed.) (1993) *Why Food Aid* (Baltimore: Johns Hopkins University Press).

Samuelson, Paul A. (1948) 'International trade and equalization of factor prices', *Economic Journal* (June 8): 163–184.

Sanford, Jonathan E. (1983) *US Foreign Policy and Multilateral Development Banks* (Boulder, CO: Westview Press).

Saul, John (1979) *The State and Revolution in Eastern Africa* (New York: Monthly Review Press).

—— (1991) 'The End of the Cold War in Southern Africa', in *Review of African Political Economy*, No. 50.

Schatzberg, Michael G. (1991) *Mobuto or Chaos? The United States and Zaire 1960–1990* (New York: University Press of America).

Schraeder, Peter J. (1994) *United States Foreign Policy toward Africa* (New York: Cambridge University Press).

Scott, James C. (1976) *The Moral Economy of the Peasant* (London: Yale University Press).

Shaw, Timothy M. (1992) 'Africa', in Mary Hawkesworth and Maurice Kogan (eds), *Encyclopedia of Government and Politics*, Vol. II, pp. 1178–200 (London: Routledge).

—— and John E. Inegbedion (1994) 'The Marginalization of Africa in the New World (Dis)Order', in Richard Stubbs and Geoffrey R.D. Underhill (eds), *Political Economy and the Changing Global Order* (Toronto: McClelland & Stewart).

—— (1995) 'Globalisation, Regionalism and the South in the 1990s: Towards a New Political Economy of Development', in Björn Hettne (ed.), *International Political Economy of Development*, EADI, Vol. 7, no. 2.

Shoup, Lawrence H. and William Minter (1977) *Imperial Brain Trust: The Council on Foreign Relations and United States Foreign Policy* (New York: Monthly Review Press).

Shultz, P. George (1993) *Turmoil and Triumph* (New York: Macmillan).

Simpson, Christopher (1995) *National Security Directives of the Reagan and Bush administrations, 1981–1991* (San Fransisco: Westview Press).

Simpson, Mark (1993) 'Foreign and Domestic Factors in the Transformation of Frelimo', *Journal of Modern African Studies*, Vol. 31, no. 2:309–37.

Singer, Hans W. (1995) 'Rethinking Bretton Woods: From a Historical Perspective', in Jo Marie Griesgraber and Bernard C. Gunter *Promoting Development: Effective Global Institutions for the Twenty-first Century* (London: Pluto Press).

Singham, A.W. and Shirley Hune (1986) *Non-Alignment in an Age of Alignments* (London: Zed Books).

Sklar, Holly (ed.) (1980) *Trilateralism – the Trilateral Commission and Elite Planning for World Management* (Quebec: Black Rose).

Smith, Adam (1776) *An Inquiry into the Causes and Nature of the Wealth of Nations* edn (Oxford: Clarendon, 1976).

Sørensen, Georg (1996) 'Development as a Hobbesian dilemma', *Third World Quarterly*, Vol. 17, no. 5:903–16.

Soros, George (1997) 'The Capitalist Threat', *The Atlantic Monthly*, Vol. 279, no. 2: 45–58.

—— (1998) *The Crisis of Global Capitalism* (New York: Public Affairs).

Spero, Joan Edelman (1990) *The Politics of International Economic Relations* (New York: St Martin's Press).

Stavrianos, L.C. (1981) *Global Rift: The Third World Comes of Age* (New York: William Morrow).

Sterling, Clare (1994) *Thieves' World* (New York: Simon & Schuster).

Stockwell, John (1978) *In Search of Enemies: A CIA Story* (New York: W.W. Norton).

Strange, Susan (1988) *States and Markets* (London: Pinter).

—— (1990) 'The Name of the Game', in Nicholas X. Rizopoulos (ed.), *Sea Changes: American Foreign Policy in a World Transformed* (New York: Council on Foreign Relations).

—— (1996) *The Retreat of the State* (New York: Cambridge University Press).

Stubbs, Richard and Geoffrey R.D. Underhill (1994) *Political Economy and the Changing Global Order* (Toronto: McClelland & Stewart).

Summers, Lawrence (1997) 'US Economic Policy in Africa', speech delivered to a symposium on private sector development in Abidjan, Côte d'Ivoire, 27 May 1997.

Svendsen, Knud Erik (1996) 'Overview of the Debate on Structural Adjustment in Africa', in Paul Pedersen *et al.* (eds), *Limits of Adjustment in Africa* (London: James Currey).

Tarp, Finn (1993) *Stabilization and Structural Adjustment* (New York: Routledge).

Taylor, Lance (1993) *The Rocky Road to Reform* (Helsinki: WIDER).

Teunissen, Jan Joest (ed.) (1996) *Regionalism and the Global Economy* (The Hague: FONDAD).

Thatcher, Margaret (1993) *The Downing Street Years* (London: HarperCollins).

Tickner, Vincent (1992) 'Structural adjustment and agricultural pricing in Mozambique', *Review of African Political Economy*, no. 53.

Todaro, Michael, P. (1997) *Economic Development*, 6th edn (New York: Longman).

Toye, John (1994) 'Structural Adjustment: Context, Assumptions, Origin and Diversity', in Rolph van der Hoeven and Fred van der Kraaij (eds), *Structural Adjustment and Beyond in Sub-Saharan Africa* (London: James Currey).

Triffin, Robert (1967) *Gold and the Dollar Crisis* (New Haven: Yale University Press).

Truman, Harry, S. (1949) *A New Era in World Affairs: Selected Speeches and Statements*, General Foreign Policy Series 18 (Washington, DC: Department of State).

Turgeon, Lynn (1996) *Bastard Keynesianism: The Evolution of Economic Thinking and Policymaking since World War II* (London: Greenwood Press).

United Nations Development Programme (1992) *Human Development Report* (New York: Oxford University Press).

—— (1994) *Human Development Report* (New York: Oxford University Press).

—— (1996) *Human Development Report* (New York: Oxford University Press).

—— (1997) *Human Development Report* (New York: Oxford University Press).

—— (2002) *Human Development Report* (New York: Oxford University Press).

United Nations Research Institute for Social Development (1995) *States of Disarray: The Social Effects of Globalisation* (Geneva: UNRISD).

US Department of State (1948) *Proceedings and Documents of the United Nations Monetary and Financial Conference, Bretton Woods, New Hampshire, July 1–22 1944* (Washington, DC: US Government Printing Office).

US Department of State (1982) 'A New Partnership with Africa', speech by Vice-President Bush, Kenya Chamber of Commerce, Nairobi, 19 November 1982, printed in *Realism, Strength, Negotiation: Key Foreign Policy Statements of the Reagan Administration* (Washington, DC: United States Department of State, Bureau of Public Affairs).

—— (1983) 'Foreign Aid and US National Interests': speech by Secretary Shultz, Southern Center for International Studies, Atlanta, 24 February 1983 printed in *Realism, Strength, Negotiation: Key Foreign Policy Statements of the Reagan Administration* (Washington, DC: United States Department of State, Bureau of Public Affairs).

—— (1984) *Realism, Strength, Negotiation: Key Foreign Policy Statements of the Reagan Administration* (Washington, DC: United States Department of State, Bureau of Public Affairs).

US Department of Treasury (1982) *United States Participation in the Multilateral Development Banks in the 1980s* (Washington, DC: US Government Printing Office).

—— (1994) *Replenishment of the IDA Credits for Fiscal Year 1995* (Washington, DC: US Government Printing Office).

US General Accounting Office (1996) *World Bank: US Interests Supported, but Oversight Needed to Help Ensure Improved Performance* (Washington, DC).

US Information Agency (1997) *The Final Communique of the Denver Summit of the Eight* (Washington, DC: USIA).

Vaksberg, A (1991) *The Soviet Mafia* (New York: St Martin's Press).

Valkenier, Elisabeth (1986) 'Revolutionary Change in the Third World: Recent Soviet Reassessments', *World Politics*, Vol. 38, no. 3.

Vernon, Raymond (1996) 'The US Government at Bretton Woods and After', in Orin Kirshner (ed.), *The Bretton Woods–Gatt System: Retrospect and Prospect after Fifty Years* (New York: M.E. Sharpe).

Vinthagen, Stellan (2002) *Motståndets globalisering*, in Mikael Löfgren (ed.), (Stockholm: Ordfront).

Viotti, Paul and Mark Kauppi (1993) *International Relations Theory*, 2nd edn (New York: Macmillan).

Volcker, Paul and Toyoo Gyohten (1992) *Changing Fortunes: The World's Money and the Threat to American Leadership* (New York: Times Books).

Wallerstein, Immanuel (1974) *The Modern World System: Capitalist Agriculture and the Origins of the European World Economy in the Sixteenth Century* (New York: Academic Press).

Waltz, Kenneth, N. (1979) *Theory of International Politics* (Reading, MA.: Addison-Wesley).

Waltz, Kenneth, N. (1986) 'Political Structures', in Robert, O. Keohane (ed.), *Neorealism and its Critics* (New York: Columbia University Press).

Wapenhaus, Willi (1994) 'The Political Economy of Structural Adjustment: An External Perspective', in Rolph van der Hoeven and Fred van derKraaij (eds), *Structural Adjustment and Beyond in Sub-Saharan Africa* (London: James Currey).

Weber, Max (1964) *Theory of Social and Economic Organization* (New York: Free Press).

Wiggershaus, Rolf (1994) *The Frankfurt School: Its History, Theories and Political Significance* (Cambridge, MA: MIT Press).

Williams, Appleman William (1962) *The Tragedy of American Diplomacy* (New York: Dell).

Williamson, John (1989) *What Washington Means by Policy Reform*, mimeo (Washington, DC: Institute for International Economics).

—— (1996) *The Washington Consensus Revisited*, mimeo (Washington, DC: Institute for International Economics).

Wolfensohn, James D. (1995) 'New Directions and New Partnership', address to the Board of Governors, the World Bank (Washington, DC. 10 October).

World Bank (1981) *Accelerated Development in Sub-Saharan Africa: An Agenda for Action* (Washington, DC: World Bank).

World Bank (1985) *Convention Establishing the Multilateral Investment Guarantee Agency* (Washington, DC: World Bank).

—— (1993a) *The East Asian Miracle: Economic Growth and Public Policy* (New York: Oxford University Press).

—— (1993b) *Country Assistance Strategy for Mozambique* (Washington, DC: World Bank).

—— (1994) *Adjustment in Africa: Reforms, Results, and the Road Ahead* (New York: Oxford University Press).

—— (1995) *Staff Appraisal Report, Republic of Mozambique, Health Sector Recovery Program* (Washington, DC: World Bank).

—— (1996a) *Global Economic Prospect and the Developing Countries* (Washington, DC: World Bank).

—— (1996b) *From Plan to Market: World Development Report* (New York: Oxford University Press).

—— (1997) *The State in a Changing World: World Development Report* (New York: Oxford University Press).

Yanov, Alexander (1977) *Détente after Brezhnev* (Berkeley: University of California Press).

Young, Oran R. (1969) 'Interdependencies in World Politics', *International Journal*, Vol. 24: 726–50, quoted in Robert, O. Keohane and Joseph S. Nye, Jr (1975) 'International Interdependence and Integration', in Paul Viotti and Mark Kauppi (1993), *International Relations Theory*, 2nd edn (New York: Macmillan).

Zacarias, Agostinho (1991) *Repensando Estratégias sobre Moçambique e África Austral* (Maputo: ISRI).

Zartman, I. William (1989) *Ripe for Resolution: Conflict and Intervention in Africa* (New York: Oxford University Press).

—— et al. (1991) *Conflict Resolution in Africa* (Washington, DC: Brookings Institution).

—— (ed.) (1995) *Elusive Peace: Negotiating an End to Civil Wars* (Washington, DC: Brookings Institution).

Zimmerman, Robert F. (1993) *Dollars, Diplomacy, and Dependency: Dilemmas of US Economic Aid* (London: Lynne Rienner).

# Index